The Futures of
School Reform

The Futures of School Reform

Edited by Jal Mehta,
Robert B. Schwartz, and
Frederick M. Hess

Harvard Education Press
Cambridge, Massachusetts

Library of Congress Control Number 2012937486

Paperback ISBN 978-1-61250-471-1
Library Edition ISBN 978-1-61250-472-8

Published by Harvard Education Press,
an imprint of the Harvard Education Publishing Group

Harvard Education Press
8 Story Street
Cambridge, MA 02138

Cover Design: Deborah Hodgdon
Cover Photo: beyond/Corbis
The typefaces used in this book are Adobe Garamond Pro and Scala Sans.

CONTENTS

1   INTRODUCTION

The Futures of School Reform

If We Keep Doing What We're Doing, We're Never Going to Get There

Jal Mehta, Robert B. Schwartz, and Frederick M. Hess

13   ONE

Learning from Abroad

Rapid Improvement Is Possible, Even in a System Like Ours

Ben Levin, Robert B. Schwartz, and Adam Gamoran

35   TWO

Building on Practical Knowledge

The Key to a Stronger Profession Is Learning from the Field

Jal Mehta, Louis M. Gomez, and Anthony S. Bryk

65   THREE

Moving to a Mixed Model

Without an Appropriate Role for the Market, the Education Sector Will Stagnate

Terry M. Moe and Paul T. Hill

95   FOUR

"Unbundling" Schools and Schooling

Let's Think More Flexibly About How to Structure Institutions and Jobs

Frederick M. Hess and Olivia Meeks

CONTENTS

119 FIVE

Addressing the Disadvantages of Poverty
Why Ignore the Most Important Challenge of the Post-Standards Era?
Jeffrey Henig, Helen Janc Malone, and Paul Reville

151 SIX

Redefining Education
The Future of Learning Is Not the Future of Schooling
Elizabeth A. City, Richard F. Elmore, and Doug Lynch

SEVEN
177 **The Courage to Achieve Our Ambitions**
Five Pathways for the Future
Jal Mehta

211 APPENDIX

The Futures of School Reform Participants

213 *Notes*
231 *Acknowledgments*
235 *About the Editors*
237 *About the Contributors*
245 *Index*

Introduction

THE FUTURES OF
SCHOOL REFORM

If We Keep Doing What We're Doing,
We're Never Going to Get There

**Jal Mehta, Robert B. Schwartz,
and Frederick M. Hess**

If we keep doing what we're doing, we're never going to get there.

For almost thirty years, since the publication of *A Nation at Risk* in 1983, the United States has been seized by a blizzard of school reform strategies.[1] Standards. Vouchers. Charters. Merit pay. Alternative teacher certification. More money. More data. More accountability. These strategies have been embraced by districts, states, and eventually even the federal government with great gusto, but, if we were to honestly appraise all of this activity, we would have to conclude that the results have not been what we hoped.

Here are a few facts, likely numbingly familiar, but no less important for being so. In a post-industrial economy, good schooling is the ticket to middle-class life, but huge swaths of students continue to drop out of school—as many as 40–50 percent in many urban districts—and most students do not graduate from high school ready for a four-year college. Large gaps in student skills persist by race and class: National Assessment of Educational Progress (NAEP) results suggest that the average black twelfth-grader has a reading level lower than that of the average white eighth-grader. Even among more advantaged schools, recent studies continue to suggest low levels of cognitive challenge in classrooms: the most recent Program for International Student Assessment (PISA) results show that the United States is seventeenth in reading, twenty-seventh in science, and thirty-third in math, trailing such countries as Estonia and the Slovak Republic. Schools serve not only economic but also civic and other functions; the failings of our schools will, over time, become the failings of our democracy.

While the challenge is clear, what to do about it is not. Four years ago, the Harvard Graduate School of Education put together a national working group on the "Futures of School Reform" to try to think about what was wrong and what could be done. The group included well-known academics (e.g., Richard Elmore, Jeffrey Henig, Paul Hill, Frederick Hess, Susanna Loeb, Terry Moe, James Spillane), governmental officials at the federal, state, and district levels (e.g., Mike Smith, Brad Jupp, Paul Reville, John King, Kaya Henderson), charter operators and folks strongly associated with the "reform" community (Michael Goldstein, Dacia Toll), foundation representatives (e.g., Anthony Bryk, Stacey Childress, Paul Goren), a policy wonk (Andrew Rotherham), an elected representative (Colorado state senator Michael Johnston), entrepreneurs (e.g., Wireless Generation cofounders Larry Berger and Greg Gunn), and one member with an international perspective (former Ontario deputy minister of education Ben Levin). (A full list of participants can be found in Appendix A at the end of this volume.) We intentionally picked a group that was ideologically diverse in its views, and people who could see the sector from a variety of vantage points.

The charge of the group was to think anew about why our current strategies are insufficient to reach our goals and to lay out some possibilities for what might be next. The project was modeled in part after a similar initiative, the Pew Forum on Education Reform, which one of us

(Robert Schwartz) helped to launch in 1990. That group, which similarly brought together about thirty leading researchers, policy makers, and practitioners, coalesced around the promotion of standards-based reform. Looking back twenty years later, two things are clear. One, ideas have consequences. That effort spurred standards-driven reform in the states and helped create the basis for a federal standards-based reform strategy that culminated in the No Child Left Behind Act in 2001 (NCLB). Two, whatever the merits of those developments, even their staunchest advocates concede that they have not been sufficient to deliver the transformational improvement we believe American schooling requires.

From Best Practices to System Transformation

As one of us (Frederick Hess) has argued in *Education Unbound: The Promise and Practice of Greenfield Schooling*, much of what passes as today's "reform" can be loosely termed the "best practices" approach.[2] Advocates champion laws and instructional standards that promote familiar themes like curricular alignment, formative assessment, and professional development. Schools and systems come home from site visits to heralded schools or districts, hoping to emulate the practices they've seen over the course of a few hours. Underlying this approach is the presumption that improving schools and systems is primarily a matter of learning from "what works"; that the right mix of remedies is already known—or will soon be identified—and that the challenge is primarily a technical one of growing and transferring it.

At one level, this all makes good sense. More telling, though, is that these well-intentioned efforts have consistently disappointed, and the hoped-for outcomes never seem to materialize at scale. In what Revolutionary Schools founder Heather Driscoll has referred to as education's "silver bullet culture," disappointing results are inevitably chalked up to flawed implementation or a lack of buy-in. School and district leaders, as a result, are left looking for the next solution they can "photocopy and cheer on."

The sad truth is that, while individual schools have successfully produced superior results (at least for a while), best practice reform rarely if ever delivers examples of successfully transforming a mediocre school system into a high performing one. There are a number of highly respected suburban districts we can point to—such as Montgomery County, Maryland, or Fairfax County, Virginia—but these systems inevitably start with the advantages conferred by educated, relatively affluent, and education-conscious parents and community members. Meanwhile, touted examples of urban reform such as those in Charlotte, Boston, and Austin deserve their due, but the reality is that these acclaimed districts are impressive only relative to their peers. In terms of student learning, achievement, or attainment, even proponents concede that these districts have a long way to go.

Sensible best practices should and do have a worthy place in the future of education reform. But to truly maximize educational improvement efforts, we must recognize that the "best practices" approach only addresses the tip of the iceberg, and that the failure of most such efforts is due to the six-sevenths of the iceberg that lurks below the surface, encumbering today's school systems. If we are to deliver transformative improvement, it is not enough to wedge new practices into familiar schools and districts; we must reimagine the system itself.

Inside the Futures of School Reform

With that as backdrop, the futures group had four meetings between 2009 and 2011, three in Cambridge, and one in New Orleans. The meetings were not always easy and were sometimes downright heated—not surprisingly, there were wide differences of opinion on what should be done and even what the core nature of the problem is. You will see those differences reflected in this volume; our goal from the start was not to produce banal consensus, but rather to lay out provocatively different (if sometimes overlapping) ideas of what's not working and what a better future might look like.

4

Group members did all agree on one thing: we are thinking too small. That is, the current debate over school reform—stretching from Michelle Rhee to Diane Ravitch, from merit pay to the common core—is just not commensurate to the scale of the challenge we face. *Almost all of the ideas currently on the mainstream table leave the basic structure of American schooling fundamentally unchanged: the same teachers, in the same schools, teaching the same subjects, with the same stock of knowledge, trained in the same places, working toward many of the same ends.* Given the scope of the problem—large gaps in performance, by race and class within the United States, as well as between the United States and leaders in the rest of the world—these incremental reforms will not bring about the better schools that we want. *If we keep doing what we're doing, we're never going to get there.*

The group reached this sobering conclusion not from theory but from experience. Not far under the surface, you will find considerable frustration among this book's authors with the failings of the current system. Many of them have spent their careers, in one role or another, trying to work within the constraints of the system to deliver higher-level instruction more consistently for all students. In the pages that follow, you will see that even the least radical among them are no longer convinced that such outcomes can be realized within the existing system.

The upcoming essays seek to begin to break that logjam. In essence, each of them strikes at one of the major pillars of the current system, one of the things that we leave unchanged when we say that we are "reforming" schooling. To pursue any of these visions seriously would be to significantly change a core aspect of the American school system, and in so doing, might create the kind of substantial improvement that we seek.

The essays also challenge some assumptions that are rarely surfaced in most school reform discussions. One essay suggests that the problem is that we assume teachers all have to do the same jobs; the authors propose instead a much more differentiated profession, with some specialists and others serving in support roles. Another confronts the split between how knowledge is produced and how it is used; rather than delegating production to university researchers and implementation to teachers, the authors advocate creating new structures in which knowledge developed in practice would be shared, refined, and vetted. A third essay challenges the focus of the American system on producing individual accountability, suggesting that, from an international perspective, building systems of trust and mutual respect is more important than assigning individual responsibility.

For those of you who think you know the work of the authors, there will be some surprises in the pages to come. Richard Elmore and Elizabeth City, best known for their advocacy of careful attention to improvements in the "instructional core," propose here a much more open system in which schools fade in their importance and students are more directly linked to available knowledge. Robert Schwartz and Paul Reville, two longtime champions of the standards movement, acknowledge in the following pages that standards are not sufficient for the improvement they seek, and each suggests a new path—Schwartz gleaning lessons from the international leaders, and Reville seeking to link school and social reform. In our discussions, we found more overlap in what people thought than their previous writings would lead you to expect; we hope that as you read you will similarly find overlaps and complementarities, as well as tensions, among the different essays.

To that end, we ask that you read these essays not as a menu of options, but more like a cubist painting that offers a variety of lenses on American schooling. Taken together, their critiques form a damning picture of the ways in which the current system does not live up to our ideals; their prescriptions provide a range of ideas about how to improve different aspects of the system. It seems highly likely that the actual future will not be any one of these visions but rather some combination thereof, and we invite you to think about how they might fit together to create a better world.

At the same time, we do not want to underplay the real differences that exist between the visions. Very real debates about what education should be for, whether its governance should shift more toward individual choice or collective decision making, what role technology should play, and whether it should be more driven by student interests or adult choices are just a few of the many differences that you will see in the pages to come. We invite you to think about these essays in light of what you would want for your own child as well as for society as a whole, assessing the different possibilities against your core values, hopes, and dreams.

Not all of the proposals will be politically feasible or practical in the short term. That's okay. The goal here is to open up possibilities for the long run. Some readers will doubtless deem one or another piece downright objectionable. That's okay too. Schools are critically important and highly valued social institutions, so proposals to change them will be met fairly with some skepticism. We ask only that you remember the many children being shortchanged by the current arrangements, and read with an open mind.

There is also no presumption that these visions are the only or the best paths forward. Rather, they reflect the passion and expertise of the contributing authors. Our hope is that they may spark fertile discussions about policy, institutions, pedagogy, technology, and the rich opportunities to rethink American schooling in the light of a new century.

What's to Come

In chapter 1, Ben Levin, Robert Schwartz, and Adam Gamoran draw on evidence from a range of nations that are outperforming the United States on common assessments to argue that there is an emerging consensus on the needed steps for educational improvement. Among the elements they emphasize are attracting, retaining, and developing strong teachers and school leaders; high expectations, coupled with efforts to keep all students on track from the beginning of their schooling; extra support for high-poverty students and schools; strong efforts to connect schooling to a range of viable employment paths; and a culture of trust rather than punitive accountability pervading the system. While they acknowledge that these steps seem prosaic, they argue that in important ways the United States has not attended to them (particularly in its emphasis on high-stakes accountability), and that it is consistent and sustained attention to these core elements that will gradually lead to significant improvements in performance. In the latter part of their essay, they consider what steps the United States could feasibly take to move in this direction.

In chapter 2, Jal Mehta, Louis Gomez, and Anthony Bryk argue that the primary challenge is to transform the system from its antecedents as a bureaucratic, Industrial Age structure into a modern professional organization. They argue that with respect to simple work, top-down, compliance-oriented structures may suffice, but in the case of complex work, structures need to allow practitioners to develop and share expertise as they grow across the course of their careers. They suggest a new mode of creating and sharing knowledge, a "networked improvement community," that would allow practitioners across sites to work together in developing knowledge that is relevant for practice. They argue that this more inclusive and practice-centered approach to knowledge production has the potential to reshape the ethos and identity of the field—from a highly atomized one into one in which teachers would see themselves as part of a common profession that draws on a shared stock of knowledge to consistently help students learn. In the last part of the essay, the authors imagine how an array of actors in the system—districts, states, foundations, and teacher training institutions—might shift if they took seriously the need to transform from an industrial structure into a professional one.

In chapter 3, Terry Moe and Paul Hill argue that the problem lies in what they see as an extreme emphasis on government-run schools, and suggest that a "mixed model" that draws on the strengths of both markets and the state would be preferable. They envision a world in which the money follows the students, in which online offerings proliferate, and in which districts lose their geographic monopoly as students' primary providers. This world would be much more varied in the kinds of schools that students choose to attend—traditional, online, or a hybrid of both—with student choice and markets determining which models flourish and which die out. To achieve this world, they suggest, would require relaxing a wide number of regulations, rethinking assumptions about how to do schooling, and creating more space for new alternatives to emerge. Moving toward this vision would not require instituting a new "one best system" to replace the old, they argue, but rather developing the right kind of architecture and ecosystem in which different possibilities would have the opportunity to thrive.

In chapter 4, Frederick Hess and Olivia Meeks argue that the future lies in "unbundling" the school system. Rather than keeping the structure of schooling roughly the same and seeking to "scale up" good programs or find many more "superpeople" to do the teaching, they argue that we should break down schooling into its core elements and reorganize those elements for the twenty-first century. In this vision, schools might look more like hospitals, with a corps of highly skilled teachers directing instruction while aided by a variety of support staff fulfilling the other functions that students need. Such a system would also unleash much higher levels of choice and customization: students would choose from a wide range of providers in different content areas as they put together a menu of offerings well suited to their interests. Governance would evolve from the conventional bureaucratic mechanisms used for holding schools accountable toward a more flexible system in which an array of different providers could be assessed and held accountable. Such a system would also be well adapted to the fast-growing online schooling sector, as it would welcome the vast selection of online offerings into a newly configured school system.

In chapter 5, Jeffrey Henig, Helen Janc Malone, and Paul Reville argue that the problem is limiting educational reform to school reform, and propose instead an approach that would aggressively link school and nonschool approaches to improve outcomes. Drawing on decades of research on the importance of nonschool factors in affecting academic outcomes, the authors argue that the current educational moment is fundamentally misguided in limiting itself to reforming only schools. Citing examples of cross-sectoral collaborations that have proven effective, they suggest concrete ways in which such school-nonschool partnerships might be structured to avoid the common barriers that plague efforts at integration across agencies or sectors. They also point to new developments, including the increasing use of data and the growth of general-purpose government (as opposed to domain-specific government), that they think might facilitate a joint effort. They conclude by outlining three different paths by which such an all-encompassing effort might be mounted, suggesting ways to counter skeptics and build these kinds of collaborations.

In chapter 6, Elizabeth City, Richard Elmore, and Doug Lynch argue that the structure of schooling is obsolete. In a world in which knowledge is expanding faster than we can keep up, the idea that committees of adults at the state, district, and school levels should vet and define what students learn is fundamentally mistaken. The narrow "portal" into this larger world of knowledge that a school represents fundamentally limits student learning; schools, or whatever replaces them in the future, will seek to directly connect students to the world of available learning. In this essay, the authors provide a number of examples drawn from various sectors where this transformation has already happened, and envision what it might look like in the K–12 sector. They suggest that governance and assessment functions will also need to be rethought, and assert that student mastery over domains that they care about is the right standard for evaluating learning in the future.

In chapter 7, Jal Mehta seeks to draw together, compare, and synthesize the visions laid out across the previous chapters. He argues that, as a whole, the essays in the volume make the case that American education is unlikely to significantly improve without a change to at least one major dimension of its structure. The chapter lays out five pathways for the future, arguing that we can: 1) *transform* the system by changing who is doing the teaching and what they know; 2) *replace* the institutions that currently compose the system with new institutions filling the same functions but performing them better: 3) *reassemble* the system by changing its roles, structures, elements, and incentives; 4) *expand* the system by integrating school and nonschool factors; or 5) *dissolve* the system by providing students with more direct access to the ever-growing universe of knowledge. The essay identifies the likely strengths and weaknesses of each pathway from the perspective of both the system as a whole and that of a parent with a real child who might be enrolled in it. Mehta concludes with a brief discussion of ways to create political support for the kind of sustained and long-term changes that would be needed to achieve any of these visions.

This is not a book for the faint of heart. It imagines fundamental changes to our school system and tries to tell us why such changes are necessary, what they might look like, and how we might get there. We are under no illusions that these changes will come tomorrow, but we hope to invigorate the debate about how to create a school system that is worthy of the considerable ambitions we have for it.

1

LEARNING FROM ABROAD

Rapid Improvement Is Possible, Even in a System Like Ours

Ben Levin, Robert B. Schwartz, and Adam Gamoran

A S THE CHAPTERS IN THIS BOOK ILLUSTRATE, ideas abound for the best ways to improve the U.S. public education system. In this chapter, we propose an approach that builds on strategies that have been successful in other parts of the world but are not yet central in the U.S. education debate. Although our proposal is more complicated than some of the other positions in this book because it does not rest on a single driver of improvement, such as competition or accountability, we believe its success in other countries signifies substantial promise for the United States.

Our starting point is this: for the past two decades, the U.S. has been engaged in a sustained effort to improve academic achievement and to reduce persistent racial and socioeconomic gaps in achievement in its schools. While some states and large urban districts have made significant progress during this period, overall improvement in performance has been disappointingly modest.[1]

Meanwhile, international assessments such as the Trends in International Mathematics and Science Study (TIMSS) and Program for International Student Assessment (PISA) allow U.S. policy makers to compare the performance of our schools and students with those in other countries.[2] These assessments leave no doubt that there are nations (or in some cases, states or provinces) whose education systems achieve both higher overall performance and more equitable outcomes than the United States. The studies also highlight the fact that some countries have shown dramatic improvement in educational outcomes over relatively short periods; for example, Korea and Singapore have gone from having very low levels of education to very high levels for large numbers of people in only two or three decades.[3]

But while these international rankings tend to get most of the media attention, they are only a small part of the TIMSS and PISA findings, and in many ways the least interesting element. If one digs deeper, one finds sophisticated studies that look behind the achievement levels to understand the dynamics driving them. The tests themselves are carefully designed to ensure that they are not culturally biased, and they factor in data on related matters such as students' motivation and sense of belonging as well as teachers' and principals' ideas about good policy and practice.[4] Moreover, the consistency in results across multiple administrations, especially in PISA, suggests that these studies are indeed capturing important dynamics of the various systems.

Of course, countries cannot simply imitate one another's policies, whether in education or in other fields. Each context is different, which means that policies have to be adapted to fit local conditions. Education policy does not travel easily from Alaska to Alabama or Massachusetts to Montana, so one cannot simply copy what's been done elsewhere and expect it to work. Teaching Finnish to all U.S. children, for example, would likely not reproduce Finland's high levels of literacy. However, it is possible to understand this need for adaptation of policy and still believe that one can gain important ideas from systems in other places. Understanding the policy framework that is successful in one place does not mean adopting it entirely in another, but equally, differences in context should not mean that there is nothing to learn.

In fact, the United States itself has been a major exporter of ideas and policies around the world, and has advocated their adoption in places with different cultures and histories. Moreover, the education policy lessons from other countries that we emphasize in this chapter are not just those of one place, but those that appear to be effective in a number of diverse settings. Just as we should not blindly accept the results of one research study but look for similar results across a number of studies, we should also ensure that potential policy approaches have proven effective in several places, not just one, before they are the subject of serious interest.

Our approach is to look at some of the common elements in countries that have yielded very high levels of education performance or have made large improvements in recent years, or both. The countries that fit this definition include some that are quite different from the U.S., such as Finland, Singapore, Japan, and Korea, and others that are much more similar, such as Canada and Australia. Those six systems differ in many ways—in basic structural features, size, homogeneity, culture, and so on. Some have unitary systems, while others, such as Australia and Canada, are federal states like the United States. Canada and Australia also have high levels of population diversity like the U.S. The fact that all these jurisdictions share some common features lends weight to the contention that it is these features, more than the peculiarities of each country, that have produced improvement.

And, again, in a few cases this improvement has taken place in a relatively short time. Some of these jurisdictions have shown very substantial improvement in educational outcomes—catching up to or surpassing those in the United States—over only the last twenty or thirty years. Finland, for example, saw a very large upturn in performance when it changed its approach twenty or so years ago.[5] And as we noted earlier, some countries, like Korea and Singapore, have gone in less than fifty years from being very poorly educated countries to being among the best educated in the world. Several studies have also cited the province of Ontario in Canada for its significantly improved outcomes in the last few years, while Quebec and Alberta have been high performing in all rounds of PISA and in TIMMS.[6]

These countries do not employ a common recipe. They embody many differences that reflect their varied histories, values, and institutional structures. However, there are some core features that distinguish them, that are closely connected to their excellent results, and that could richly inform U.S. education policy.

International Leaders' Common Elements

Let's start with what these jurisdictions do *not* do. Several of the most significant features of recent education policy debate in the U.S. are simply not found in any of these countries—for example, charter schools, pathways into teaching that allow candidates with only several weeks of training to assume full responsibility for a classroom, teacher evaluation systems based on student test scores, and school accountability systems based on the premise that schools with low average test scores are failures, irrespective of the compositions of their student populations. Nor is choice or competition a main driver in any of these countries, though several have some degree of parent choice.

Instead, these countries share seven common elements:

1. A focus on attracting, retaining, and developing talented people as educators.
2. Priority attention to requiring—and helping—all schools and educators improve their work, not through the imposition of practice but through the development of common approaches based on research and evidence.
3. Careful attention to developing leaders.
4. High expectations for all students coupled with real efforts to keep students on track for success from the very beginning of their schooling.

5. Strong efforts to connect secondary education to the economy and employment as well as to post-secondary education.
6. National policies and resources that focus on minimizing disparities in outcomes and on helping most those schools that face the greatest challenges in terms of student demographics.
7. A positive approach that builds trust and commitment while engaging all partners in efforts toward further improvement.

This list may seem rather prosaic. There are no dramatic steps here, no measures that will single-handedly produce transformation. Indeed, we take the view that it is precisely the steady pursuit of improvement, rather than the desire for the single dramatic change, that is key to better education, just as it has been in many other fields of human activity. In developing this list, we are drawing on several sources of knowledge about high performing education systems.[7]

In the following pages, we'll say a little more about each element, noting that space permits only a very brief discussion of these complex issues.

1. A focus on attracting, retaining, and developing talented people as educators

Successful education systems focus intensively on what happens in schools and classrooms between students and teachers. These systems understand that teachers need to be well prepared, and consequently, that the programs that prepare educators need to be rigorous. In Finland, for example, all prospective teachers must go through a five-year, university-based program that culminates in a master's degree. Finland, like most high performing countries, recruits aspiring teachers from the top third of the talent pool, and its university training programs now have ten applicants for every available position. In Canada, there are typically three or four applicants for every teacher training place, while teacher education programs in Singapore and Korea are also highly selective.

Legislators and policy makers in high performing countries understand that to attract top talent into teaching, the work must be seen as professional, and schools must be organized to support the continuous

17

learning and development of teachers. In Japan, this takes the form of setting aside substantial time during the school day for teachers to have collaborative planning opportunities and lesson study. Strong education systems give their highest priority to helping their teachers and principals get better at their work. This means more than professional development workshops; it involves creating a school culture where the adults, just like the students, are encouraged and expected to think about their work and to continue improving their skills. Recent studies in the U.S. suggest that these supports are no less important in our context.[8]

Some high performing systems also provide career opportunities for teachers so they can advance in the profession without having to leave the classroom entirely, unless they choose to. In Singapore, for example, teachers can choose among three pathways once they have established themselves as highly effective teachers. They can move onto an administrative track, heading toward the principalship. They can become specialists in areas like research, assessment, or technology. But they can also choose a pathway leading them to successive levels of responsibility as teachers. The pay scales in each pathway are comparable, so a master teacher can make as much as a senior administrator.

2. Priority attention to requiring—and helping—all schools and educators improve their work, not through the imposition of practice but through the development of common approaches based on research and evidence

Most high performing countries begin with some form of national curriculum that provides overall coherence and direction to students' studies across the entire system. However, their curriculum documents are often thinner and less structured than those in the United States. They highlight a few key topics in each subject and grade level that are essential for students to master, and provide guidance to teachers on how these topics might be approached, but they leave a substantial amount of discretion for teachers—at the local level—to account for local preferences and students' needs. Again, unlike most of the U.S., assessments are closely linked to the curriculum, including attention to higher-order skills. Where assessments reflect the breadth of curriculum goals, teaching to the test is also teaching to the curriculum, so the whole emphasis on test preparation is much diminished. In many successful systems, the assessments are also designed to provide diagnostic and instructional, in addition to—or even instead of—student or school accountability information.

A common curriculum allows for both initial teacher preparation and ongoing professional development programs to focus on helping teachers develop the capacity to teach the curriculum. In Japan, for example, lesson study enables teachers to share best practices for teaching key topics or lessons in the national curriculum. Primary reading instruction in Ontario, to take another example, is much more consistent across classrooms and schools, a major factor in improved results there. In the U.S., by contrast, one can never be entirely sure that two teachers in the same subject area in the same school are working on the same assignments and lessons, so this form of professional development rarely occurs.

High performing countries typically put into place thoughtful processes for the periodic revision of their curriculum, systematically collecting evidence from the analysis of student performance data and the testimony of teachers about areas for improvement. In Finland, for example, the only national assessments that are administered before the end of secondary school are designed to produce system-level data at two grade levels to inform policy makers about the strengths and weaknesses of the system as a whole, not for school or student accountability. Australia uses state and national data to identify schools that need additional support, as well as areas that require more attention across the system. A key aspect of this approach to improvement is the expectation that all schools are involved in improvement, not just a small proportion seen as struggling or failing.

3. Careful attention to developing leaders

School systems also require high-quality leadership from people who understand the core business of teaching and learning, and who focus their attention on teachers and classrooms.

Singapore provides perhaps the best international example of a system that gives substantial attention to the identification and development of school leaders. Singapore explicitly models its leadership development strategy on the best practices of large private corporations. Vivien Stewart, an experienced observer of Asian educational systems, recently described this strategy in an Organisation for Economic Co-operation and Development (OECD) report as follows:

> In Singapore young teachers are continuously assessed for their leadership potential and given opportunities to demonstrate and learn, for example, by serving on committees and then being promoted to head of department at a very young age. Some are transferred to the Ministry of Education for a time. After these experiences are monitored, potential principals are selected for interviews and go through leadership situational exercises. If they pass these, then they are eligible to go to the National Institute of Education for six months of executive leadership training, with their salaries paid. The process is comprehensive and intensive and includes a study trip and a project on school innovation in another country.[9]

Contrast this talent identification and development approach with U.S. practice, where any teacher can enroll in an administrative certification program and then seek a position as principal. While districts may be supporting leadership development, as with curriculum and teaching, a more systematic approach will yield greater consistency and better results.

Other countries are also investing in leadership development as a system activity, including leadership institutes in several Australian states and a national organization, and a leadership framework and strategy in several Canadian provinces. Moreover, in these systems leadership development is closely linked to better instruction and school improvement, and highly connected to system goals and strategies.

4. High expectations for all students coupled with real efforts to keep students on track for success from the very beginning of their schooling

What we know from much research is that virtually all students have the potential to perform at higher levels given enough motivation and support. Systems that give students additional supports as needed and offer many routes for them to return to standard or better levels of progress are more likely to generate success for more students.

High expectations for all students is a mantra in the U.S., but the rhetoric is not matched by the reality. There are still many situations in which the responsibility for poor performance is seen to lie with students or their families, and schools feel unable to change that. The reality is that high expectations are of no use unless they are matched by the necessary skills.

Here, too, there is much we can learn from the Finns. After a long public debate, Finland abolished its two-tiered middle school system in the mid-1960s and moved to a single comprehensive education system for all students from grades one through nine. Two decades later, the country abolished within-school tracking. In doing this, it understood that its teachers would require a different level of training to serve all students effectively, regardless of family background or perceived academic ability. Consequently, Finland placed much greater emphasis on its upgraded teacher preparation programs in equipping teachers to recognize and respond to learning difficulties, and it decided to create a new position in each school, called the "special teacher," for someone with an additional year of training. While Finland does have separate special education programs for severely handicapped children, the special teacher's job is to work closely with the regular class teachers to provide individual or small-group support to students who may at any given point be struggling to keep up with the rest of the class. Because most students at some point in their schooling careers will receive help from the special teacher—perhaps because they were ill and missed a few days of school, or because they just need some extra tutoring to understand a particular mathematics concept—there is no stigma attached to receiving such help. The goal is to ensure that no student falls between the cracks, and that virtually all students are able to stay in the mainstream program and keep up with their peers. This focus on providing early intervention and support helps explain why Finland, in addition to its consistent high performance, is the country with the least variation in within-school and between-school performance. This pattern stands in stark contrast to the U.S., where a student's socioeconomic background is highly predictive of academic achievement.

There is a lively debate about how much difference schools can make in the areas of inequality and achievement in a society.[10] Clearly, schools are not solely responsible for inequality, but that does not mean they are powerless to respond to the challenges of diverse student populations. We have evidence that schools with very similar demographics vary greatly in outcomes, and also lots of evidence that individual schools or groups of schools can generate significant improvement given the right supports. We do not, therefore, accept the view that schools will inevitably mirror or necessarily exacerbate inequalities in the larger society.

At the same time, there is no reason to think that schools are immune from larger social forces, or that they can, no matter how heroic the efforts, compensate for vast inequalities in society. Children who start school— or life—with few or no positive factors face a much harder struggle than do the more fortunate. Children with health problems, poor nutrition, unstable housing, fetal alcohol syndrome, or other such issues are not playing on level ground with children who don't have these challenges. Education policy cannot be divorced from social policy more broadly.

The United States is one of the richest countries in the world, and among the most unequal of all wealthy countries.[11] There is clearly a link between high levels of child poverty, huge inequalities in wealth, poor health care for millions, lack of any system of child care, and the gaps in achievement in American schools. Indeed, the entire gap between the U.S. and other countries is accounted for by poor performance at the bottom of the achievement distribution, and these are overwhelmingly young people growing up in poverty. In our view, the United States cannot solve its educational challenge by focusing only on schools. Schools should not be let off the hook for doing their share, of course, but if the rest of the nation is unwilling to do its part, we cannot expect them to remedy all the problems created outside their walls. (For more on the impact of poverty on education in the United States, see chapter 5.)

5. Strong efforts to connect secondary education to the economy and employment as well as to post-secondary education

At the end of lower secondary school (grade nine or ten), most high performing systems, especially those in northern Europe, provide students with a choice between a pathway leading to university and one leading more directly to a career.[12] The career-oriented pathways are well developed, cover a broad range of occupations (high-tech, low-tech; white-collar, blue-collar), and have strong employer involvement in shaping curriculum and qualifications. These programs typically provide a mix of work-based and classroom-based learning, extend over three or four years, and culminate in a certificate with real currency in the labor market. These are mainstream systems, serving between 40 and 70 percent of young people in countries like Denmark, Finland, Germany, the Netherlands, and Switzerland.

If one converses with young people in these European apprenticeship systems, it is easy to understand the appeal. After nine or ten years of sitting in classrooms, many (perhaps most) young people are eager for an opportunity to learn by doing, to be learning and working alongside adults who are skilled and knowledgeable, and to earn while they are learning so they can begin to establish their independence. Because these countries have built pathways that enable young people to continue on to some form of advanced education after they have completed their upper secondary vocational program, students are not closing off options by entering the vocational pathway. These systems recognize that skilled occupations are increasingly integrated with various aspects of post-secondary education.

Despite the checkered past of vocational education in the U.S., recent advances in career and technical education suggest that the groundwork is being laid for a more robust articulation between the education system and the work force. The 2006 reauthorization of the Perkins Act, the primary federal funding program for career and technical education at both the secondary and post-secondary levels, required each district to develop at least one program of study aimed at work force preparation through a coherent sequence of courses across levels.[13] At the secondary level, curricular innovations demonstrate the feasibility of integrating academic content with technical studies in a manner that elevates academic performance without detracting from the growth of students' technical knowledge.[14] Numerous examples of sophisticated technical education programs are now available that, if implemented widely, would mirror their productive European counterparts.[15]

6. National policies and resources that focus on minimizing disparities in outcomes and on helping most those schools that face the greatest challenges in terms of student demographics

High performing systems invest significant attention and resources in prevention and early intervention rather than remediation. The goal is to keep all students on track with their peers, not to build separate treatment systems for students who are behind (and from which students rarely escape). In Finland, as indicated previously, teachers are well trained to diagnose learning difficulties, and every school has a special teacher whose job it is to work closely with regular classroom teachers.

Successful systems quickly mobilize support from all available sources for students and families in need of specialized help, and generally work hard to make sure that no student falls through the cracks. The special education system is less formal: providing the right supports for learning is more important than giving students a label. There is little or no emphasis on "diagnosis." In Finland, as in other Scandinavian countries, all students are in a common, untracked curriculum through lower secondary school (the U.S. equivalent of ninth or tenth grade), and there is a strong preference for inclusion rather than separate special education classes. In Ontario, all high schools have systems to identify students who are in danger of failing courses, leading to early intervention to prevent that failure.

24

Similarly, high performing systems respond to struggling schools early with intervention and support, not punishment. Ontario and other high performing states and nations do not close low performing schools. Instead, the ministry of education in Ontario works closely with school district leaders to ensure that low performing schools receive intensive technical assistance and support. The process is collaborative and based on support rather than blame. As a result, the number of struggling schools in the province has dropped from 110 to 18 in two years, and high school graduation rates rose by nearly 20 percent.[16]

While these steps are important, the ability of the schools to keep students on track is also closely related to the overall state of the society; a country with greater economic and social inequality is likely to have those challenges in the schools as well. We return to that issue at the end of this chapter.

7. A positive approach that builds trust and commitment while engaging all partners in efforts toward further improvement

This point is stated last but is perhaps most important. Indeed, if we could identify only one change for the U.S., it would be to move away from a culture of blame to one of mutual support and effort.

Successful systems and countries build a positive approach to education improvement. They are not engaged in bashing teachers, attacking teacher unions, denigrating parents, or blaming problems on someone else. In fact, blame is not important at all in these settings; instead, these systems make an effort to have all partners work together in support of better outcomes for all students. They do this through a good balance of clear overall goals and standards coupled with significant school and district autonomy, and by directing resources to supporting better teaching and learning rather than to administrative processes. In successful systems, individual schools or districts do not have independent goals, but they do have considerable scope as to how they pursue various communal goals. Progress is based on strong partnerships in which every level of the system has a genuine sense of respect and engagement.

This work is accomplished through "large and small p" political processes. In many European countries, there are regular mechanisms for educators, employers, students, and education authorities to discuss key education issues. Ontario created a "partnership table" that brings all the stakeholders together to review major policy initiatives before they are finalized and implemented. Finland uses a highly consensual process to develop education policy, and the same approach is characteristic of Asian countries. Also, these education systems have high alignment at the school, district, regional, and national levels, unlike the fractured system in the U.S., with its many small but independent districts and weak states. It is not a question of centralization (though Canada has many fewer districts relative to size than does the U.S.), but a matter of bringing people together to agree on courses of action and approaches to implementation.

As a consequence of these features, high performing systems generally have a more collaborative and trust-based school culture than what typically characterizes the U.S. system. Their administrative leaders are relentlessly positive and optimistic in their communications, stressing capabilities and contributions, not deficiencies. They focus on improvement, not blame. They try not to divide people or to declare winners and losers, but to keep everyone—students, parents, teachers, and others—engaged in a positive way. This kind of cooperation is characteristic of all high performing systems. U.S. research on trust in schools—among educators, as well as between educators and parents and community members—suggests that the same benefits could accrue here if such cooperation were more widespread.[17]

Getting There: Feasible First Steps for the United States

Americans who sympathize with the argument so far may be asking how this can happen in the U.S. given our current governance and politics. This is certainly a vexing question. The United States is a big and unruly country, with a high degree of decentralization, little appetite for central direction, and large regional variations in practice and culture.

It is not likely ever to have a national education system in the way that most countries do. There is the challenge of how to make things happen in a system with fifty states, fifteen thousand districts, several hundred colleges of education, and millions of educators. American education will remain variable by state and locality. This variation can be a good thing if it supports the values of local communities, while at the same time drawing on the many groups and organizations that might assist and support learning across diverse programs and systems. Diversity in approach can be a strength if it is harnessed to respectful dialogue and collective learning. But at the time we write this, national politics is in a gridlock, and many states are also caught in vicious political struggles.

At the same time, there is strong interest in the United States in looking at new approaches to improving education, including the recognition that past strategies have not yielded the desired results. The strong response to international studies and increasing attention to the examples of other countries are hopeful signs, as are many of the local, regional, and national efforts to create more consensus on effective strategies for change and improvement. While there are real obstacles, the United States still benefits from a strong sense of social purpose, excellent research institutions, and a growing understanding of the importance of strong education for all.

What kind of steps might be feasible in this institutional and political environment? We suggest three areas in which we think there could be progress even within these constraints. They have to do with the research and innovation process, the recruitment and development of teachers, and the relationship between schools and the workplace.

Research and Innovation

First, we suggest taking more advantage of the existence in the United States of a well-developed network of organizations interested in making better use of research and other forms of evidence. These range from lobby groups and think tanks to foundations, university research centers, and nonprofit organizations. Almost all of these groups are engaged in trying to influence public opinion and policy through using evidence of various kinds. Of course, some of these efforts are quite partisan and begin with a position rather than with the evidence. But even if we accept that this political give and take is a central feature of democracy, more could be done to seek informed consensus on current knowledge in education. Other sectors, such as medicine, have built mechanisms to do this work. There *are* some examples in education, such as the reports issued by the National Academies on important areas such as motivation and testing. However, in general, insufficient efforts are being made in education to assess current knowledge and to share it in a nonpartisan manner with the education sector and the public. Using principles of "knowledge mobilization," the U.S. could do much to bring together leading scholars, policy makers, and activists to identify areas where there is enough evidence and consensus to guide policy and practice.[18] The goal would be to produce the same kinds of guidelines in schools as are characteristic of the health sector, providing a firm grounding for everyday work in important areas. Many of the topics identified earlier in this chapter would fit this definition.

This kind of connection between research and practice is also characteristic of high performing systems, which want to base their work on knowledge rather than ideology. In Singapore and Korea, there are very close connections between the research centers—mainly in universities in those countries—and the policy-making apparatus in ministries of education. Singapore also has a strong connection between its teacher education and its research enterprise, reinforcing the professional nature of teaching as a research-based activity, like other professions. In Ontario, the major efforts at improvement in the last few years were deeply grounded in and closely connected with a research strategy to increase the amount, quality, and especially the dissemination of research knowledge.

The research enterprise also needs a much stronger connection to the way that innovation occurs and is evaluated in the U.S. education system. There are two sides to the discussion of innovation in schools— one arguing that more innovation is the lifeblood of improvement, and the other asserting that education is too much influenced by fads and that few innovations last or have reached sufficient scale to make a difference. Our view, borrowing from James March, is that some innovation is essential to improvement, but only if (a) innovations are well grounded in current knowledge and have a reasonable theory of action; (b) there is careful assessment of impact; and (c) even more importantly, real efforts are made to scale up innovations that are found to be effective.[19] In the U.S. education system, none of these features is in place. A much more organized approach to learning from thoughtful innovation is needed and entirely consistent with the approach to research we advocate here.

Of course, research does not answer all questions about education, and skilled professionals will always be needed to interpret and apply general findings to specific situations. However, a stronger base of evidence could help the U.S. make better use of its resources and also help curb some of the political polemic in the field. Moreover, this would be a relatively inexpensive activity given the scale and scope of the education system—and it would support the other initiatives discussed next.

Teacher Recruitment and Development

A second area we see as ripe for action is teaching policy. Since the Carnegie Forum's *A Nation Prepared* report in 1986, and supported by the ongoing work of the National Commission on Teaching and America's Future and other policy organizations, there has been a growing recognition of the importance of a highly professional teaching corps for U.S. education.[20] The policy argument has been strongly buttressed in recent years by a growing body of research confirming what most suburban parents have long believed: that the teacher your child has can matter even more than the school your child attends.[21] For low-income and minority children, having three great teachers in a row in the primary grades can enable them to function on a par with their more advantaged classmates, while having three weak teachers can place them so far behind that they may never catch up.

29

Over the past two decades, two major organizations have emerged that represent radically different responses to the challenge of raising the status of teaching in the United States. An idea originally proposed by the late Albert Shanker and then incorporated into the recommendations of the commission that issued *A Nation Prepared*, the professionally led National Board for Professional Teaching Standards (NBPTS) was designed to align the professional status of teaching more closely with better established professions (such as medicine and law) by developing rigorous standards for accomplished teaching, designing rich assessments to measure the attainment of such standards, and awarding nationally recognized certificates to those meeting the standards. The NBPTS deliberately chose at the outset to avoid the challenge of convincing fifty states to adopt common standards for entering teachers by requiring candidates for board certification to have already taught for at least three years. By operating in a space where there was no competition, the NBPTS radically reduced the resistance it might have encountered from states and was able to able to generate enough political and financial support in the early years to do its work slowly and carefully. Consequently, it is now a well-established fixture in the teacher policy landscape, with a solid research base confirming the validity of its assessment system and nearly one hundred thousand teachers who have attained its certificates.

The second extraordinary organization created during this period is Teach for America (TFA), which has been equally impressive and successful in accomplishing its mission: to furnish underresourced urban and rural schools with highly motivated, well-educated students from America's most selective colleges willing to commit two years of service to schools with acute staffing challenges. TFA also has a second important goal—to develop a set of future leaders who are passionate advocates for educational equity and excellence in their professional and civic lives after their period of service in the schools. Early evidence suggests that this goal is being met as well.

If the U.S. were serious about wanting to align its teacher policies with those of higher performing nations, one way to start would be to bring together the leaders of NBPTS, TFA, the American Association of Colleges of Teacher Education (AACTE), and the organizations that have led the development of the Common Core State Standards for students (the National Governors Association, the Council of Chief State School Officers, and Achieve) to develop a new national strategy to upgrade the teaching profession. The first step would be for the U.S. Department of Education and the states to agree to work together to eliminate the teacher shortages in urban and rural districts that prompted TFA's creation twenty years ago. The second step would be for the states to agree to work together to develop a system for certifying beginning teachers, and to agree that after an appropriate phase-in period, no new entrants would be allowed who had not met the new standards, regardless of method of preparation. The NBPTS standards are a crucial resource for this process and could be adapted for beginning teachers. Another resource is the Teacher Performance Assessment, developed by AACTE and currently being piloted in 140 teacher preparation programs in twenty-five states.[22] TFA could potentially become the national recruiting arm for this new system, using its reputation and expertise to try to make teaching a career of choice for hundreds of thousands of talented young (and not so young) Americans each year. Over time, the goal should be to draw U.S. teachers from the top third of the talent pool—as Finland, Singapore, Japan, and Canada routinely do—and also to improve their initial preparation and ongoing development. While this would be an ambitious achievement, it is certainly not an impossible one. And again, it has relatively low costs, political or financial.

The Relationship Between Schools and the Workplace

The third area where U.S. policy makers could begin to adapt lessons from higher performing nations into our system is education for employment. While the PISA results have focused the attention of U.S. policy makers on the relatively weak academic performance of our fifteen-year-olds, a more important question we should be asking is, *how do we compare with other countries in equipping our young people by the age of twenty-five with the skills and credentials to function effectively in an increasingly challenging global economy?* Recently, President Obama and other leaders have sounded the alarm about our college completion rate, which has remained flat while other countries have zoomed past us. Less than one young American in three has a bachelor's degree by twenty-five; that number rises to 40 percent when combined with those with associate's degrees. In the absence of a well-developed vocational system, this means more than half our young adults lack credentials with currency in the labor market. In an economy in which even those with bachelor's degrees are struggling, it is no surprise that youth unemployment rates in the U.S. are about 20 percent. By contrast, in Switzerland, which leads Europe in the percentage of its young people in the vocational system, youth unemployment has consistently remained in single digits.

Early in 2011, the Harvard Graduate School of Education released a report called *Pathways to Prosperity: Meeting the Challenge of Preparing Young Americans for the 21st Century.*[23] Coauthored by one of us (Robert Schwartz), the report has touched off a national conversation about whether the U.S. needs an additional set of pathways alongside the dominant four-year college pathway, especially since only 30 percent of young Americans successfully complete that one. In nearly half the states, governmental, education, and/or business organizations have convened large meetings to discuss the implications of the report and to request advice from the *Pathways* authors in moving these ideas forward. Unlike the teacher policy area, this issue seems likeliest to take root at the state and regional labor market level. Thus, the strategy we would advocate is a more decentralized one, with a handful of states with strong, committed governmental and corporate leadership forming the equivalent of European "social partnerships" to fashion strategies that over time can better align integrated academic and technical education programs, spanning the last years of high school and at least one year of post-secondary education, with the current and emerging needs of regional labor markets. This is complicated, long-term, system-building work, but for a variety of reasons—continuing concern about the dropout crisis, middle-class anxiety about the costs of college, the rising number of college graduates working in jobs that do not require a college education—the time seems right to take a closer look at those European systems that equip a much larger fraction of their young people with skills and credentials with currency in the labor market.

This is an ambitious strategy, but a number of conditions are converging that make it seem feasible. First, the Obama administration has called for massive new investments in community colleges, with an eye toward better work force preparation.[24] While this initiative has yet to be fully funded, it signals federal recognition of the scope of the challenge and the resources needed to address it. Second, innovations in career and technical education provide new opportunities to integrate academic and technical preparation and to strengthen ties between the educational institutions and the labor market. Third, as noted in the *Pathways* report, exemplars of work force development demonstrate that the benefits of strong linkages between education and the workplace extend not only to potential workers but also to employers, who would thus have strong incentives to support this strategy.

Conclusion

In a chapter this brief, we can sketch only the main lines of the kind of policy approach we advocate. While the U.S. education system has many strengths, we do not believe that the current policy direction can or will yield the desired results. More choice, more accountability, and more innovation may be needed, but they are not enough. There must be a focus on systematic improvement in every school in the whole country, and this must be tackled in a systematic way. A few good schools here and there is simply not good enough.

The obstacles to moving in this direction are, as we noted earlier, substantial. We do not have some naïve view that they can be swept away and that education policy in the United States will start to re-semble Finland or Korea. However, we do see room to maneuver, and in the three suggestions posed here, think there is the impetus to the kind of thoughtful, coherent, and consistent approach to U.S. educa-tion policy that is necessary for progress.

2

BUILDING ON PRACTICAL
KNOWLEDGE

The Key to a Stronger Profession
Is Learning from the Field

Jal Mehta, Louis M. Gomez,
and Anthony S. Bryk

O UR THESIS IN THIS CHAPTER is straightforward: to significantly improve education in the United States, schools need to transform themselves from the bureaucratic Industrial Age structures in which they originated into modern learning and improvement organizations. Such a transformation will require the educational system to change its approach to the teaching profession and organize its work in a very different way. For simple work, complying with specified processes to achieve uniformity is viable; for complex work, developing the knowledge, skill, and opportunities for systemwide learning among practitioners is paramount. Teaching is complex work. Only an approach that recognizes this reality has the potential, over time, to ensure consistent, quality instruction and learning across fourteen thousand districts and one hundred thousand schools. To implement this vision will be extremely difficult: it will require a new mind-set, the creation of a new infrastructure, and new patterns of authority and power. But this transformation is necessary to achieve our goal of educating all students to high levels.

The Nature of the Problem: From Bureaucratic Hierarchies to Professional Organizations

Teaching in the United States institutionalized into its modern form in the Progressive Era. One-room schoolhouses were transformed into the "one best system," wherein city superintendents were empowered to act like CEOs to direct the improvement of school systems from above. Trained by leading universities in the latest business management techniques, these administrators sought to remove schools from politics and rationally administer the school system. As is still true today, the form of the system was hierarchical and bureaucratic: the superintendent would set the direction, choose the programs, and assess the results; the teachers and the schools would implement the policies specified from above. Over time, states and the federal government built upon this foundation but left its essential form unchanged: higher powers create standardization by selecting policies and requiring schools and teachers to implement them.[1]

While rational on its face, this model has not worked well, for reasons that have been detailed at length by scholars of implementation. They have noted that schools are part of "loosely coupled systems": the actual work of classrooms is difficult to monitor from afar and is thus often decoupled from reforms mandated from above. Teaching is also complex work that is not easily amenable to external rationalization. If the goal is to help students think at more than the most basic levels, teachers will necessarily have to be empowered to do the same. In their efforts to create control, top-down reforms tend to distrust the knowledge that local practitioners possess and to disregard the need for local learning and adaptation, both of which characterize high performing professional organizations. The result has been what one scholar aptly describes as a "so much reform, so little change" pattern of school reform.[2]

Understandably frustrated with the slow pace of change and the very real failings of the school system, policy makers in recent years have sought to generate better results through external accountability systems, but in so doing have effectively doubled down on the flawed industrial model. External accountability turns out to be a relatively weak technology for significant improvement. The best studies of such reforms in the United States and elsewhere suggest that these strategies can generate more focus and effort around the measured indicators, but that they afford no mechanisms for generating the increased practitioner skill that is required for greatly improved performance.[3]

Conspicuously absent from these systems are an infrastructure and a consistent set of processes that would develop teachers' *expertise*— the ability to draw upon a knowledge base to recognize patterns of problems, develop repertoires of solutions, and make informed judgments about how to handle particular cases.[4] Professions systematize this process—they develop knowledge, train and license practitioners, and create ongoing standards of practice. As education developed with teachers at the bottom of a bureaucratic hierarchy rather than as a full-fledged profession, it did not create the core of practical knowledge, process of significant training, and apprenticeship to develop expertise that characterize other more fully developed professions. Thus, each teacher essentially has to figure out how to teach on her own, resulting in wide variation in teaching skill from school to school and even from classroom to classroom within a single school. Some teachers and schools do well, but the overall quality of the system's performance is highly variable. In comparison to more developed professions, education, especially teaching, lacks internal mechanisms to develop genuine knowledge about practice, to train novices in its use, to articulate the arc of development from novice to expert practice, and to continuously test all of these components against evidence of efficacy in action.

Consequently, the field is highly vulnerable to repeated movements for external control.[5]

A related problem is the divorce of research from practice. Again, beginning in the Progressive Era we have seen a split of research from practice, with the idea that university researchers would develop knowledge and pass it to administrators, who would then direct teachers to implement it. This structure is consistent with the hierarchical form and social control orientation of the school system, with our respect for science, and with the academic needs of university researchers, and thus has proven resilient. But, again, while rational on its face, it has also proven flawed at each link of the chain: university researchers develop knowledge that is more useful for advancing disciplinary understanding than it is for practice, administrators are too far from schools to know what they need, and teachers are resistant to top-down mandates. The divide between research and practice also tends to freeze knowledge in place: we learn a lot about interventions holding context constant, but little about what features of the context make it work in one place as opposed to another.[6] This system of knowledge is also rarely at the level of granularity that would be useful to teachers. Knowledge about how to produce better lesson plans, ask better discussion questions, and control disruptive students is highly relevant to teachers but less so to university researchers.

The traditional model also does little to develop, evaluate, and share practical knowledge generated in the field, what Lee Shulman calls the "wisdom of practice."[7] Given the various complexities of teaching—potentially unwilling clientele, uncertain chemistry across groups of students, and the need to make decisions in real time—teachers need a deep, multidimensional knowledge that allows them both to assess situations quickly and to draw upon a variety of repertoires for intervention.[8] Individual teachers possess considerable such knowledge, but it is largely invisible to the field as a whole. There are few ways for it to be gathered, codified, and shared. Nor is there a way for it to be evaluated. Some practitioners know much while others only think they do, and there are few mechanisms to separate one from the other. Even in fields like medicine, where the underlying basic and applied science is extremely strong and often quite prescriptive, quality control advocates have observed that there is wide variation in doctors' actual practice and effectiveness. Consequently, there are a number of current efforts under way to complement the biomedical knowledge base with one centered on individual and organizational practice.[9] In education, where the underlying science is much less developed but the nature of the task requires a high degree of expertise, we are particularly disadvantaged if we do not find a way to capture, share, evaluate, grow, and improve knowledge about practice.

The result of these varied problems from above is that they have provoked a norm of defensive individualism from the teachers below. While "industrialists" have tried to press change from the top, this defensive local counternorm prompts teachers to argue, "every class is unique; each of us must figure it out on our own." In the absence of a codified knowledge base, working in a loosely coupled system— one that often has conflicting goals and ill-informed demands from above—it is not surprising that many teachers conclude that they are not actually part of a shared enterprise but rather just need to find something that works with their students.[10] The meeting of this defensive individualism from below with tone-deaf mandates from above has proven to be a bad combination, breeding rampant distrust between policy makers and practitioners, with policy makers seeking ever more intensive ways to compel practitioners to do their bidding, and practitioners equally determined to resist external intervention. We say, with tongue in cheek, "every classroom a Leonardo."[11] More aptly, we might say that what we really have in many classrooms is a struggling journeyman incapable of producing a masterpiece.

If we want a better future, we will need a different kind of system, one that moves away from the failed industrial model of hierarchy and control and instead seeks to create a professional style of work organization in which developing the knowledge and skill of frontline practitioners is the central concern. In truly professional organizations, across a variety of sectors, the emphasis is less on control and regulation and more on creating structures in which talented, frontline practitioners can learn from one another, develop new ideas, and spread them.[12]

The need for this shift is buttressed by international research on Program for International Student Assessment (PISA) leading nations. Unlike the United States, countries as varied as Singapore, Korea, Canada, and Finland all draw their teachers from the top third of their college test score distribution, train them extensively, and then enable them to work with one another on problems of practice within schools to develop better pedagogical practices and deeper content knowledge. The famed Japanese model of lesson study was an early example of how to promote such cultures of inquiry within schools. While this research is still in its early stages, the emerging conclusions are consistent with the idea that higher performing nations embrace this knowledge-intensive view of system improvement. As Marc Tucker and Organisation for Economic Cooperation and Development (OECD) PISA Director Andreas Schliecher say in their review of the practices of PISA leaders, "The common element is the degree to which they are all creating forms of work organization that are moving from Tayloristic, bureaucratic management to the kinds of professional forms of work organization more likely to be found in professional partnerships than in mass-production industrial operations."[13]

Such a system would need to remedy the various aforementioned problems. It would need a way to grow a knowledge base that is deeply rooted in and connected to practice. It would draw on the wisdom of practice, but it would also consistently evaluate different claims to practical knowledge. It would need a way to convey knowledge to new and ongoing practitioners, and it would need to create a day-to-day work environment in schools in which teachers could see themselves as members of a shared professional community. It would need an assessment and accountability structure consistent with a focus on improving ongoing processes. And it would need a political and organizational strategy to invent new kinds of institutions that can move a calcified industrial structure and all the people who work comfortably within it toward a professional organization for the future. In the pages to come, we will outline some of these elements, particularly those centered on developing shared practical knowledge. We hope that you will join our effort by thinking about how different parts of the system would need to be redesigned to transform an industrial structure into a professional one.

Generating Knowledge for a Knowledge Profession

What is useful knowledge depends on your vantage point and the goal you have in mind for knowledge. In education, we are fond of saying that we are conducting research to improve policy and practice. While there is surely overlap between the research needs of the policy community and those of the practice community, they are not one and the same. Researchers, policy makers, and practitioners have somewhat different knowledge needs because the demands each places on knowledge are different. Our goal here is to think about how to develop knowledge useful for practice, which is in our judgment the least developed of the three spheres, in large part because no one is directly responsible for producing it.

A new system of practical professional knowledge for teaching ought to have at least two important characteristics. First, such a system has to be energized by practical needs and built with significant contributions from the practitioners that the knowledge will serve. Second, the system must meld understanding from the learning, cognitive, and social sciences with clinical understanding from everyday settings of teaching. We posit that such a knowledge system has to be forged and purposely engineered so that it will guide the work of teachers in rigorous and disciplined ways.

Translational Research and Action Research

The centerpiece of a system that forms the foundation of a profession's knowledge base should be disciplined inquiry aimed at improving practice. As we have suggested elsewhere, two ideal types—*transla-tional research* and *action research*—lay claim to this space, but neither is up to the task of practice improvement at scale.[14]

Translational research has guided much of educational inquiry in the era of No Child Left Behind (NCLB). It has value because, among other things, it is organized to codify insights and make them easily shareable across a field. Translational research fits innovation neatly into the idea of stage-wise linear inquiry processes. In a recent paper, Donald Peurach and Joshua Glazer suggest that inquiry of this sort is typified by research, development, dissemination, and utilization (RDDU) sequences.[15] Linearized inquiry aimed at innovation is char-acterized by three inquiry phases that are arranged to bring important insights from the social and learning sciences to scale. In the first phase, research is organized to uncover promising ideas. The second phase is organized to craft promising innovations developed in phase one. In the third phase, assuming an innovation has been deemed promising, inquiry is organized to judge that innovation's effectiveness at scale—often via randomized field experiments. Undergirding this inquiry ma-chinery is a perspective that at this point practitioners can and should implement with fidelity the programs that have been proven effective.

A benefit of translational research is that it makes interventions trac-table because knowledge typically flows from social science theories—in fields like cognitive and behavioral science—to practice through its ap-plication in the design of particular educational programs and technol-ogies. This approach has sometimes shown success. Carefully designed writing interventions, based on several decades of social psychological research, for example, have recently been shown to have significant ef-fects on student achievement that persist for years.[16] A further strength of this kind of translational research is its explanatory power: when in-terventions demonstrate progress on important problems, their success can be explained by well-warranted theories. At the same time, to work at scale, these interventions typically are propagated with a core belief that a high degree of fidelity of implementation is required for success.

While generality is its strength, translational research often fails to capture and accommodate local insights and perspectives. Issues of context, integration into unique local settings, and adaptability and local ownership receive short shrift, often limiting the utility of this approach.

By contrast, action research flows from practice. It is highly contextualized and focuses on individual practice settings. Action research has great value in that it organizes on-the-ground practitioners around problems of practice that are, by definition, important to an institution or group. Cathy Caro-Bruce, Ryan Flessner, Mary Klehr, and Kenneth Zeichner describe these important problems of practice as "felt needs" of classrooms and schools.[17] Local practitioners, individual teachers, or small groups of teachers take up these problems of practice; action research aims to create localized learning for improvement. Unlike translational research, action research methods are nonlinear, characterized by cycles of planning, acting, observing, and reflecting on the changes in the social situations.[18] Inquiry that is guided in this way has attention to adaptability at its very core and allows for the feedback loops that are critical for improving practice. It also frequently links researchers and practitioners in an effort to address problems of practice, a collaboration that we see as a promising feature of this approach.

However, although action research has many demonstrated successes in addressing particular problems, it tends to place much lower priority on generalizable mappings of cause and effect. It is less concerned with explaining successes by means of basic theories. It also places less emphasis on the generalizability of innovations beyond the local context. The knowledge that is generated in action research is particularized, can be costly to codify, and is challenging to transfer beyond the individual settings in which it was created. In short, important insights often live and die with those who created them. Consequently, successful action research projects tend to remain locally bound cases of innovation with little access to, or means to inform, other contexts.

The kinds of problems that a professional practice of teaching must confront are causally diverse and require much more coordination and organizational learning than are typically produced by even the most thoughtful execution of translational or action research. Yet both forms of research lend value, conceptually, to addressing these problems. The professional practice of teaching needs to be undergirded by an infrastructure that recognizes "felt problems of practice" and provides a context that allows teachers, researchers, and designers to work together toward solutions in a coordinated fashion. It also requires the flexibility, adaptability, and ownership that are at the heart of action research. But addressing the problems of a professional practice of teaching at scale also requires rigor that can lead to the kind of broad-based, fieldwide sharing that is at the core of translational, RDDU approaches. There is, from our perspective, a missing piece in the current infrastructure of educational inquiry. If we are to enable a more rigorous professional practice of teaching, we need a set of inquiry tools that has the connection to practice that is the hallmark of action research, as well as the potential for generalizability that is the cornerstone of translational research.

Networked Improvement Communities: A Third Way

Recently, we have explored a new model of educational research and development that we call *educational improvement research*.[19] This model has two important dimensions that afford potential to create a more useful knowledge base for the professional practice of teaching. First, it builds on the practical intellectual heritage of W. Edwards Deming, Joseph Juran, Walter Shewhart, and others who pioneered principles of *continuous quality improvement*.[20] For example, it embraces *improvement science*, which—as we'll discuss shortly—seeks to bring the principles and practice of disciplined inquiry to bear on the continuous improvement of products, services, or processes.[21] The work of continuous quality improvement has proven to be valuable across a wide spectrum of domains.

Of particular import to the practice of education is the application of quality improvement techniques to health care. Don Berwick and his colleagues at the Institute for Healthcare Improvement (IHI) pioneered a set of inquiry practices and conceptual frameworks that are now broadly applied to improving health services worldwide.[22] Health care bears a strong resemblance to education and learning for many reasons—not the least of which is that both fields are populated by professionals who have a strong sense of individual and independent agency. However, the lives of users (students or patients) are more likely to be improved by purposeful, relentless attention to practice and its improvement in a coordinated fashion among diverse sets of professionals. IHI has been instrumental in reshaping how the health professions define the problems they work on and how they work together to make progress.[23]

The second cornerstone of the educational improvement research model is a new take on social infrastructures for continuous improvement across organizations. Here we are building on the insights of Douglas Engelbart about the value of *networked improvement communities* (NICs) to spur social learning and innovation. Engelbart defines an NIC as a distinct organizational form that arranges human and technical resources so that the community is capable of "getting better at getting better."[24] To understand the power of NICs, consider these three domains of organizational activity delineated by Engelbart:

- A-level activities are the day-to-day work of carrying out the organization's primary business. In the case of schools, this is the work of classroom teaching.
- B-level activities are those designed to improve the on-the-ground work, typically taking place within a single organization. In schooling, this is the work of districts that, for example, organize professional development for instructors or provide data intended to improve school management.
- C-level activity is much less common and typically involves cross-organizational coordination and learning aimed at helping organizations learn from one another. Here institutions engage in concurrent development, working on problems and proposed

solutions that have a strong resemblance. Concurrent activity across organizations places relevant aspects of the context in focus and can help each local setting see its efforts from new vantage points. In principle, this functions as an asset to local problem solving and cross-organizational generalization. Engelbart observes that C-level activity affords mechanisms for testing the validity of local knowledge, adjusting local understanding of the true nature of a problem, and advancing local support structures for improvement.[25]

Networked communities engaged in improvement research combine elements from both translational and action research in a way that facilitates cross-network learning and the improvement of practice. Like translational research, NICs try to integrate and build upon existing social science theories in ways that improve practice. Like action research, NICs also draw insight and innovations from the experiences of practitioners, whose practice is also transformed by participation in the network. The basic conjecture is that improvements at scale may best arise from fleets of small, ongoing studies, coordinated across many contexts, rather than from one, large field trial or discrete local efforts carried out in isolated practice settings. To achieve effective and reliable outcomes at scale requires diverse participants working in diverse organizational contexts, but within a common infrastructure that coordinates their inquiries.

We posit that educational improvement networks can generate a more productive knowledge base for teaching than either translational or action research alone because they combine infrastructure forms to integrate both local and more general knowledge. They may allow networks of schools to learn faster than individual teachers or schools can by themselves. Together, the features of these networks can create a social infrastructure that encourages incremental improvement: each member receives highly personal rewards that are aligned with a collective goal. We believe that such networks can seed a sustained professional practice to reshape education.

How Networked Improvement Communities Work

How do NICs accomplish this? Anthony Bryk and his colleagues analyzed the workings of successful organizations that appeared to have many of the fundamental characteristics of NICs, and found that they shared several important elements:[26]

- Common targets with measurable and ambitious (but feasible) goals
- A shared language community around an explicitly mapped, complex problem space
- A continuous improvement ethic undergirded by an agreed-upon and rigorous set of inquiry methods

Common targets. The semiconductor industry provides an illustrative example, albeit one taken from a very different context. Gordon Moore, cofounder of Intel, noted in 1965 that the number of transistors that could be cost-effectively placed on an integrated circuit had doubled every year since the invention of the transistor.[27] Moore conjectured that he saw no technical reason why this trend would not continue for at least the next twenty years. Moore's prediction turned out to be correct, and his observation was later named "Moore's Law." In the semiconductor industry, Moore's Law is a beacon. It guides work for a diverse collection of colleagues within and across firms in that industry. It shapes the activities of engineers who design and construct devices, and it influences how corporate leaders invest capital. Further, since Moore's Law is anchored in evidence about past performance and a perspective of feasible developments, it offers a reason to believe that targets are actually attainable. The combination of feasibility and the knowledge that everyone is working in a common direction provides a significant disciplining power in a community. In essence, the targets help to create cycles of joint accountability centered on building a shared and useful knowledge base.

The education sector is no stranger to the use of targets. NCLB goals have had the power to move people to collective action. But without a grounded sense of feasibility, those goals have also faced skepticism, disaffection, and ultimately suboptimal changes in practice. We posit that NIC-initiated targets, growing from bottom-up aspirations and experience, will be perceived differently and enjoy the motivating effects and focused, constructive collective action that targets have played in other intentionally designed networks. The fact that the targets come from professional experience and the felt needs of practitioners may energize the field, or significant parts of it, to engage in a sustained effort to build a common knowledge base.

Absent a predictive theory like Moore's Law, a networked improvement community in education might use the range and variance of its own prior performance as a way to estimate initial targets and to iterate toward a firmer one. As a simple example, consider a community that seeks to improve school attendance. The range of prior successes within the network can inform what is possible for the community going forward. The network might assume that the poorest or best records are not good initial targets for what is reliable, reachable, and desirable for everyone. Rather, it might set an initial goal using the average scores augmented by its reach aspirations. Later in this chapter, we will describe a networked community, created by the Carnegie Foundation for the Advancement of Teaching and its partners, that has initiated a similar strategy.

Shared language and commonly understood problem space. A significant challenge for network initiatives is organizing the problem space so that different efforts can be coordinated in a way that will speak to the larger whole. The semiconductor industry uses an artifact called a *roadmap* to specify how targets become realized in the work of design, development, and engineering in different contexts. Because the terrain for possible innovation is vast and complex, the roadmap organizes the challenges to be confronted in this space in agreed-upon ways. It establishes standards for how developments in different domains must fit together, and then sets microgoals, domain by domain. In these ways, the roadmap helps to coordinate the activity so that different innovations can be expected to inter-operate at designated times in the future. A good related example is the computer software community Linux, where a common open platform and operating system plays the coordinating function of the roadmap, allowing a diverse collection of programmers to work modularly to develop and refine different pieces of Linux.

How might this work in education? To return to our school attendance example, there are myriad reasons students do not come to school that are related to different "subsystems" of the schooling enterprise. For example, the "leadership subsystem" might be concerned with how students' disengagement from adults in the school is contributing to the dropout problem. The "instructional subsystem" might be concerned with how students feeling underprepared to do the classroom work could lead them to drop out. Finally, the "community outreach subsystem" might be concerned that students are finding greater economic opportunity and community in gangs and are thus not coming to school. In an NIC, different schools might each work on one aspect of this problem, with one group of schools seeking to foster better relationships with adults, another seeking to build students' academic skills, and a third working with community agencies to combat local gangs. Over time, what is learned on each of these fronts would be integrated into a more systemic approach.

In essence, the roadmap does two kinds of organizational heavy lifting. First, it provides a shared deconstruction of a complex problem space. In doing so, it gives diverse actors common referents for their talk and joint actions. The roadmap militates against the all-too-common trend we see in education where large numbers of people and institutions may work hard on a common problem, but their aggregated activity does not add up to broadscale improvement.

Roadmaps and other coordinating structures don't evolve on their own. They can be created by the participating actors, like a group of schools or districts that sets out to work on a problem, or they can be created by national standard-setting bodies, which is the approach in the semiconductor industry. In the early stages of the Linux community, it was the evangelizing leadership of Linus Torvalds and the small collection of Linux devotees that provided the coordinating energy. In a similar vein, the Carnegie Foundation for the Advancement of Teaching has created a central hub to provide coordination services to a collection of community colleges working together to build new educational pathways that will support students in and through developmental mathematics.

At the beginning, coordination among institutions not in the habit of working together requires special effort. As in the cases of the semiconductor industry and the now-mature Linux, coordination and governance within this collection of community colleges will, ultimately, move to the institutions and the networks they have created. In principle, the organizing and coordinating energy can come from multiple sources that range from formal organizations to, in the Linux case, highly committed and motivated individuals. In the case of education, this energy can be bottom up from teachers or top down from institutional actors.

Common protocols for inquiry. Following James Hiebert and his colleagues, effective network learning requires common protocols that allow participants to share, test, and generalize local observations across a professional community of practice.[28] These common inquiry protocols distinguish activity aimed at building professional knowledge from individual, clinical decision making. While such protocols may be specified in somewhat different ways, there are certain general features that characterize their use. They are iterative in execution—involving multiple, small, rapid tests of change. The goal is to learn fast and cheaply, revise and retry. Thus, the activity is more akin to the dynamics of action research than to the single definitive field test at the heart of translational research. They are also anchored in a field-generated, cause-effect model about the problem to be addressed, in which explicit hypotheses about change are set out and measures gathered to test whether the proposed changes are actually an improvement. In this regard, improvement research follows the rudiments of a scientific discipline and, as mentioned previously, is referred to as improvement science.[29] This approach is akin to Engelbart's B-level learning activity, described earlier.

Simultaneously, these protocols structure possibilities for accumulating evidence from diverse inquiries occurring across varied contexts and time. They provide data for examining the generalizability of results across different populations and context. In essence, this is a planned form of meta-analysis. The breadth of evidence generated, coupled with diversity among network contexts and participants, creates opportunities for new synthetic insights that are unlikely to occur within any one study. In short, these common protocols operate as structuring agents for the systematic, interorganizational learning that characterizes the C-level activity detailed by Engelbart. They are the organizational practices and norms of a deliberate effort to accelerate learning in and through practice to improve. In these C-level networks, several local organizations are carrying out the same intervention simultaneously.

Continuing with the example of schools facing an attendance problem, even schools that decide to take a similar approach (say, by implementing advisories to build connections between students and an adult) would implement them in slightly different ways. Under an arrangement whereby the schools have common data collection protocols and a commitment to shared data, they would have an opportunity for C-level, interorganizational learning, allowing them to investigate what works for which schools under what circumstances. Such learning is largely missing in today's educational R&D, in which inquiries are either largely idiosyncratic or more formalized but disconnected from practice.

Improvement Networks in Practice

To ground these ideas in the particular, we return to the community college network we mentioned earlier. Through the catalytic efforts of the Carnegie Foundation for the Advancement of Teaching (of which one of us, Anthony Bryk, is president), more than one hundred faculty members and others, including deans and college presidents from over thirty community colleges, have joined together to seed a networked educational improvement community. The topic is the alarmingly high failure rate of students in introductory mathematics courses in community colleges—courses that are gateways for many other courses that the colleges offer. The colleges, together with design partners and researchers, have organized themselves to advance on a measurable target: increasing, by 50 percent, the number of developmental (i.e., not college-ready) math students who achieve college credit in mathematics after one year of study.

The network is carrying out its work within a common improvement framework that has several important elements. The colleges have a shared hypothesis about improvement: math that matters can be the organizing content for ambitious learning opportunities. Additionally, they have an explicit focus on the social psychology of student engagement and perseverance as a way to help students understand effective habits of mind. Finally, they share a belief that rethinking the language of instructional materials can remove barriers that derail some students in developmental math classes. Each of these elements is aimed toward advancing teaching to redress the variability in outcomes that has plagued developmental math programs. The work is buttressed by common analytics to test and share results networkwide.

To further highlight the organizing power of networks of this sort, faculty from these colleges have agreed to engage in a common lesson study protocol.[30] This enables faculty to vet and share their progress in bringing to life the materials they have prototyped to teach developmental math through highly contextualized problems rather the standard context-free problem sets. The instructors are learning how to teach a common set of materials in new ways. Their lesson study groups are, in effect, multiple simultaneous trials of the materials across different contexts. The network becomes a coordinating venue through which members can compare experiences because lesson study provides a common disciplining protocol.

Three aspects of the network's work deserve to be highlighted. First, development encompasses efforts of intra- and inter-campus colleagues, designers, and researchers, who are cocreating shared routines to enable them to focus on a specific common target. Their work includes defining a shared practical theory of the problem, a common language to vet progress, and common protocols of inquiry and measurement. Second, each college in the network will do its work in a somewhat different way as it seeks to adaptively integrate change into the local context. In this regard, the college network's variability in practice is a natural experiment. By observing the variation, the colleges can learn from practice in order to improve practice. Third, new organizational and institutional challenges must be confronted for this social learning to unfold. It requires the emergence of new problem-centered hubs to detail an initial problem; recruit a cadre of leaders to the work; establish rules, roles, and responsibilities for participation; create an initial conceptual framework; and offer an analytic and technical infrastructure for the work of the community. It also entails establishing the initiating conditions for the subsequent growth of a self-generating learning community.

How Improvement Networks Could Contribute to Professionalizing Teaching

Education improvement networks can jointly lay the groundwork for a revitalized professional practice of teaching. First, through improvement networks, teaching can be essentially organized around a public theory, that, in the most general terms, constitutes a working framework of practice improvement. In our case, the working theory is a systems theory of practice. The theory is organized around core constructs like common targets and common measures. There are basic inquiry protocols to evaluate knowledge claims. Taken together, these components lay the groundwork for a social proof network among practitioners to adjudicate competing claims about both evidence and theory. These are the rudiments of a science of improvement with the power to reshape the identity of practitioners.

Second, as we envision it, the theory would engender sets of individual and collective routines, like constantly monitoring and sharing progress toward targets that enable inquiry to be executed. These routines will, we suspect, have the power to begin reshaping the practitioners' professional identities because they will be tightly coupled to teachers' day-to-day actions. The power to change identity is less about ostensive pronouncements and more about everyday actions. The routines will become the sorts of signature practices that can enable revitalized professionalism within school organizations. They can help to create a common identity across organizations and to bind professionals to a shared set of beliefs about the nature of the profession.

To say that teachers would be engaged in a common science of improvement is not to deny the more affective or imaginative elements of teaching. We do not want to downplay the degree to which teaching is built on relationships with students and teachers' capacity to inspire the imagination of their charges, nor are we denying the importance of creating the kind of social and moral communities that are at the heart of good classrooms and schools. But we are saying that if the goal is high-quality practice at scale, these elements need to be fused with a sense of being part of a broader profession, a profession committed to creating and using an accumulating knowledge base, which will in turn help all students, teachers, and schools succeed.

In the long run, our hope is that the kind of social learning arrangements we describe here will gradually reshape the ethos and identity of the educational field. While not everyone will participate in NICs all of the time, we hope that everyone will feel it is a professional right to participate and a professional responsibility to contribute some of the time. As in the practice of medicine, teachers would come to view themselves as part of a national profession, drawing on a well-developed knowledge base. In this world, being a teacher would not mean closing the door against misguided mandates from above, but rather participating in a common profession with a highly developed body of expertise, which one would both draw upon and contribute to.

Creating a System to Support a Knowledge Profession

To move from a bureaucratic structure to a more professional one would require not only new methods for developing knowledge and ongoing learning, but also changes across a number of other dimensions. We consider how things might change in three major arenas: the training of new teachers; the role of states, districts, and nonprofits; and the overall policy and regulatory environment.

Human Capital: Building a Pipeline for a Knowledge Profession

Central to a revamped knowledge profession is the training of new teachers. Most professions do much of their quality control work on the front end: by carefully choosing who can enter the field and what knowledge they must possess before beginning to practice, these professions assure the public of minimum standards of quality. The traditional problem in the educational domain is that teacher training has been minimal and (from teachers' reports) of limited utility, in part because it has emphasized theory over practical knowledge that is useful in the classroom. In recent years, there has been a shift toward more practice-relevant training: alternative certification providers essentially do almost all of their training in tandem with work in the classroom; residency models (like the Boston teacher residency) mix classroom teaching with instruction and coaching; new National Council for Accreditation of Teacher Education (NCATE) guidelines increasingly require traditional training institutions to do more clinical training; and, perhaps most intriguingly, schools themselves are beginning to get licensed to run their own training programs to credential teachers, such as High Tech High in San Diego, Teacher U in New York, and Match in Boston.

We think this shift toward more intentional training that is highly informed by the needs of practice is the right one. But for it to work, we need to greatly develop the stock of knowledge. Some of this knowledge will be fairly general and transferable (e.g., how to achieve baseline order in a class, how to ask a good question), and other parts of it will be content-specific (e.g., how to integrate phonetic and whole-language approaches to reading, how to teach fractions).[31] We can imagine that this knowledge, developed by both researchers and experienced practitioners through the aforementioned networked learning communities, would then feed back into training. New practitioners would need to study this knowledge, have opportunities to practice it, and be guided in such practice. These are the common threads in the development of expertise in any field.

Drawing on NIC-generated knowledge would have the ancillary effect of showing beginning teachers that the knowledge they are learning was created in part by more experienced teachers, a dimension that would help to instill the idea that teachers are expected to be knowledge generators as well as recipients. Not coincidentally, Finland, which is at the top of the PISA rankings, requires its teachers to complete a research thesis as part of their training, precisely because it embodies the notion that teachers should be researchers. What is important about this Finnish effort is that practice and research are joint components of preparation, a conjunction that signals to those entering the profession how these elements will be central to their work in the years to come. It follows that, as their careers unfold, these teachers will expect to find ways to deepen their expertise in both practice and research as part of their unified professional development work. Such a perspective is not unlike the national participation in lesson study in Japan, through which a broad swath of teachers has the right and feels the responsibility to participate. The goal here is that new teachers are socialized into a different kind of profession, one in which deliberate social learning is a central part of their professional identity and practice.

This is not the place to engage in a full-throated discussion of human capital. It suffices to say that we agree with the conclusions that have been voiced in a number of recent reports that our patchwork non-system of approaching human capital is not working, and that we need a more comprehensive approach that would rethink all aspects of the talent pipeline—initial recruitment, selection, training, evaluation, and tenure.[32] We are struck by the fact that top PISA nations draw their entering teachers from the top third of the test score distribution and train them extensively, while the United States draws students from the bottom two-thirds of the distribution and trains them minimally. We need both parts of the equation: if we don't attract the right people, the rest of what we propose will likely go for naught; conversely, choosing the right people won't help much if we don't put in place much improved methods of training and ongoing learning. Strong professions are good at both, and this is what American education needs to aspire to.

There is also the question of who might effectively carry out this kind of training. University-based teacher education programs have long been faulted for their emphasis on theory over practice; our analysis suggests that there may also be a problem in the decoupling of teacher preparation from their ongoing work in practice. We might be better off if organizations like New Visions for Education in New York, a high-quality operator of networked schools, took increasing responsibility for training, a step that would forcibly link the norms we seek to generate in the field with the kind of training we favor. To do this at the level of the sector is a huge challenge, as we will need either disruptive actors to reshape the norms of practice or existing actors to refashion themselves in the direction we suggest here.

States and Districts: Supporting the Growth of a Knowledge Profession

Moving from a bureaucratic to a professional orientation and organization would also require a sea change in the role of states and districts. Rather than seeing their role as ensuring that schools comply with mandates and regulations from above, states and districts would need to see a central part of their role as providing the infrastructure that would support the growth, learning, and improvement of schools and teachers. (They would presumably continue to play other roles, but we will focus here on the ways in which they can support the growth of professional practice.) Networked improvement communities require considerable infrastructure—to help create goals, loop schools together, organize meetings, and then facilitate the substance of the work through proto-cols. This is a function that some entity outside of schools should do. States and districts could play this role, perhaps initially by contracting with intermediaries who have experience with this type of work. States and districts could also create the technological platforms on which schools and teachers can share their practice.[33]

There is also a substantial role for foundations and nonprofits, which can take a longer view. These entities are perhaps best suited to take on the "problem of the hub" and its role in network initiation. Some en-tity must establish the initiating conditions—the initial resources, the invitations/recruitment to join, and the "good rules" for how the work together proceeds. Foundations and nonprofits may initially be "out-side of the field," but the goal over time is to invigorate the field to take on such functions as part of self-governance. Given the long time ho-rizon, the need to coordinate collective action, and the emphasis on professional control, foundations and well-funded nonprofits are well suited to this work. Even though public funds will clearly be required for initiatives to grow and be sustained, nongovernmental actors may need to be the initial catalyst for action.

Districts could also revamp their governance structures. In portfo-lio districts, which we see in New York, New Orleans, and to a lesser extent Chicago and Washington, DC, there has been an ideological shift from districts as "school systems," where the district's job is to create programs that will be implemented across schools, to "systems of schools," where the district's job is to manage, support, and hold accountable school leaders who are given expanded power to manage their schools. If a district moved fully to the portfolio strategy (rather than as a modest aside for a set of district-run schools), it could conceiv-ably function as a hub for network initiation and growth, as we have described here. Rather than individual schools being left simply to sink or swim on their own, schools in networks could learn from one an-other, mobilizing insights from schools that are succeeding with a par-ticular problem of practice to other schools that are not.

At the same time, we want to be clear that even districts that have embraced the portfolio strategy have taken only the first steps toward the model we envision. Most districts still operate primarily under political control with much weaker professional influence than is found in some high performing countries. Networked communities require strong professional control. Can states and districts give over genuine control to a professionalizing teaching force? Can teachers organize themselves into the kind of profession that demands the self-governing authority that we see in other sectors? While we are encouraged to see pockets of practice among teachers and schools that embrace these ideas and admire the effort of some districts to empower frontline practitioners, there is a long way to go toward the kind of transformed system we sketch here.

Policy: Creating a Greenfield for Social Learning

It would be nice to be able to say exactly what policy levers need to be pulled to create the vision we present here. But we think that to do so would be premature, given that the improvement networks we aspire to are currently only in their infancy. We need time and space for different approaches to improvement networks to be tried, and we should expect some to succeed and others to fail. IHI, for example, has only recently turned its attention to policy after ten years of working to achieve better results in practice. As these networks develop, there will surely be ways that policy can help them to grow, but it is too soon to know exactly what they might be.

What we *can* say is that it would be helpful if a variety of governmental actors created the kind of "greenfield" or healthy ecosystem in which different attempts to create social learning can grow and thrive. This ecosystem might include government money for the creation of improvement networks, as well as freedom from the usual regulations for sets of schools seeking to work together to grow their learning. It also could include authorization of new human capital providers to credential or train teachers, creating more space for different approaches to practice-based learning to flourish. Again, this would require a significant cultural shift—away from compliance and control and toward support and learning, as well as away from the belief that there is a silver-bullet solution to the problem and toward the idea that learning *is* the solution to the problem.

Any system of social learning that we can imagine would require a different assessment and accountability structure, one that is more intentionally linked to a continuous improvement process. A wider range of important outcomes would need to be captured, and the balance between formative and summative assessments would shift. Outcome data would still be important but mainly as a signal that something in the process is not yet working as intended. Much of the measurement action would focus on designing interim assessments that would enable evaluators to pinpoint what is not working and stimulate thinking about what is needed for subsequent plan-do-study-act cycles. Such a system would also embody a different ethos, one in which some degree of failure is an expected part of confronting the unknown, and the role of assessment is less to punish and more to identify how to improve the process for the next cycle. This is not romantic, happy talk; it is a cardinal principle of the continuous improvement processes described by Deming and used across a range of industries.

As a variety of actors seek to initiate these networks, their exact configurations will vary, but we can say at the outset that the effort will require several different types of resources to succeed. One is money to pay for the coordination work—organizing meetings, finding good facilitators, helping to design and share common protocols, and so forth. A second is teacher time, which will need to be freed up for them to participate. A number of studies have noted that American teachers spend more time in the classroom and less time planning than those in other countries; there is no way that any of this work can get done without building in significant teacher time to work on process improvement. Policy can help in a variety of ways—by reallocating teaching slots, providing substitute teachers, and using other strategies to free up some teacher time. Because we do not expect all teachers to participate equally, and because we would expect more experienced teachers to take the lead, our argument dovetails with other proposals to create career ladders for teachers. By creating more time for experienced teachers to work on developing new knowledge for the sector as a whole, we are both taking advantage of what they know and creating opportunities for them to extend their reach and continue to grow professionally.

Implications for Performance, Learning, and Equity

We think that the knowledge profession strategy we propose would be significantly preferable to the current system in the areas of performance, learning, and equity. In terms of performance, a raft of studies has shown that after family background, teacher quality is the most important variable in affecting school outcomes. This strategy directly targets that lever by seeking to capture the knowledge that makes effective teachers effective, make it part of the training that all teachers receive, and create opportunities for teachers to continue to grow and share their expertise across their career trajectories. International evidence also suggests that the knowledge profession strategy we sketch here is a good bet, as PISA leaders select strong teacher candidates, engage them in lengthy practice-based training, and, in some cases like Japan, make the ongoing process of examining teaching for improvement a central part of teachers' practice.

In terms of learning, we see the system we propose as much more geared than the existing system to the kind of practical knowledge acquisition the sector needs. Rather than the current split between university researchers developing knowledge and teachers implementing it, we are proposing a more collaborative system in which the questions for research grow directly out of practice. Network improvement communities are also more attuned to variation across context: rather than simply identifying a set of core practices and asking teachers to adopt them, the network strategy explicitly seeks to examine the ways in which variation across context demands different treatments. Conjoining school-, district-, and cross-district-level learning (what we have called A, B, and C levels of learning) also permits the system to learn faster than individual units could learn on their own. For all of these reasons, we think that our strategy is a promising one for increasing the rate of learning in the system.

Finally, in terms of equity, there is always a risk that any new technology, particularly one that is built on the strengths of local schools, will exacerbate rather than narrow pre-existing differences in power, resources, and skills. However, the approach we propose is explicitly set up to do the opposite: if fifty schools are left on their own to sink or swim, you might expect the better schools to get better and the worse schools to stay the same or get worse. If these same schools were linked into a network, however, then we would hope that learning would be transferred across the network and close gaps in performance. In the longer run, if the learning developed through these networks were fed back into and became a normal part of the training and work of all teachers, performance gaps would decrease, because what once belonged only to a few would now belong to the many.

From Here to There: First Steps Toward a Changed System

History has not been kind to those seeking fundamental change to the American educational system. The institutional conservatism of the system is legendary: with only slight exaggeration, you could say that the system was set up to batch-process students, to avoid learning, and for states and districts to promulgate rules and teachers to resent them. While such a system is dysfunctional to its core, it is the system that everyone knows and works within. To achieve what we are describing would require significant changes in both culture and structure. Culturally, the mind-set of the various actors within the system would need to change: schools would need to see themselves as places that learn and create knowledge rather than simply receive it; unions would need to move away from industrial bargaining and free up teachers and schools to take responsibility for learning outcomes; districts and states would need to move away from a focus on control and compliance and instead seek to facilitate and support better work in schools; and politicians would need to build trust and public confidence in a newly improving system rather than simply scapegoating its failures.

Structurally, no one is currently responsible for doing the kinds of work we stress here. Academics research, teachers teach, administrators administer. To develop the kind of discipline-spanning learning we suggest here would require a readjustment of existing roles, as well as the creation of new infrastructure and institutions whose job it would be to coordinate this kind of networked improvement. Drawing again on the health care example, Don Berwick calls these "integrative institutions," such as his own Institute for Healthcare Improvement. As mentioned previously, one of the authors, Anthony Bryk, is president of the Carnegie Foundation for the Advancement of Teaching, which has played a similar role in education. The National Center on Education and the Economy has also sought to fill this space over the past several decades. The role of these integrative institutions is to act as a focal point for a large collective action problem, coordinating other actors in the system to devote some of their resources to creating learning networks, and also to personally supply some of the needed resources that none of the other actors can provide. The obvious risk in this strategy is that the needs of the various actors in their existing organizations will supersede their commitment to working together to create a new approach; the obvious response is that integrative institutions should start by working at a manageable scale where they can provide enough resources and impetus to move in a different direction. Alternatively, if a state, district, or charter management organization were to embrace these ideas, it would have at its disposal greater formal authority and resources to push changes across its respective system.

Furthermore, although American education changes slowly, it *does* change—just consider the way that treatment of special education students or the proportion of students graduating from high school has changed over time. There are also reasons to believe that several trends are already moving in the directions that we outline here. Most fundamentally, the shift to a knowledge-based economy and the greater demands that it places on what we ask from both students and teachers will, eventually, precipitate some kind of change to the system, or else the United States will be left far behind other countries. The growth of comparative research on the performance of educational systems is itself a factor. As it has become clear that the leading PISA countries are using strategies that focus on selecting strong teaching candidates and building their knowledge and skill, there has been increasing interest in the United States in learning from these models, including two summits sponsored by U.S. Secretary of Education Arne Duncan and the U.S. Department of Education. Some charter networks as well as leading comprehensive school design approaches have already developed, or are in the process of developing, ways to grow and share knowledge across their sites. And the creation of portfolio districts suggests that there are ways for districts to move from top-down entities that set rules and regulations to more nimble portfolio managers seeking to support the needs of diverse schools. So there are some threads already in place that support movement in the direction we outline here.

The other advantage of the networked improvement approach we advocate is that it can grow incrementally and organically. It doesn't require someone to pull a magic lever to do it everywhere all at once: charters, districts, and states can all create the kind of NICs we are describing, and, if they demonstrate their utility, you might imagine that they would grow in popularity and scope. On the Carnegie Web site, we are posting what we are learning from our initial forays into the teaching of math in community colleges, and would welcome inquiries from others who may wish to develop their own networked improvement communities.

Finally, history shows that change is unpredictable and cannot be mapped out in advance. What we are recommending is as much or more a vision or strategic direction as it is a set of particular policy proposals. If all actors, throughout the system, began to conceive their jobs as transforming an Industrial Age compliance structure into a profession of competent, skilled, and continuously learning practitioners, collectively we might finally be able to move our education system into the twenty-first century.

3

MOVING TO A MIXED MODEL

Without an Appropriate Role for the Market, the Education Sector Will Stagnate

Terry M. Moe and Paul T. Hill

STEREOTYPES ARE ALIVE AND WELL in American education reform, and nowhere is this more evident than where school choice is being discussed. All too often, its detractors characterize choice as a "free market" solution that would "privatize" education. And all too often, this depiction is reinforced by its more libertarian supporters, who do indeed see choice in these terms and are stridently opposed to a government-run education system. The framing suggests an unbridgeable chasm with markets on one side and government on the other.

As is often true of stereotypes, this kind of stark, either/or framing is not helpful. The productive way to think about school choice—and about American education reform in general—is not in terms of markets versus government, but rather in terms of markets *and* government.

Consider the American economy. Stereotypes aside, it is not even close to being a free market. Yes, it makes much use of markets. And this is a very good thing, because markets are uniquely powerful drivers of efficiency and innovation. Yet they can also generate undesirable social outcomes—due to monopoly, price fixing, externalities, information asymmetries, and the like—and precisely for that reason the government takes action, mainly via rules, to regulate the way markets operate and to harness their power to social advantage. Experts may disagree about what rules are appropriate, and the Great Recession has revealed weaknesses—in financial regulation, for example—that are still being addressed. But the *model* is one that works, not just in the United States but also in every developed nation in the world. It is a mixed model of government and markets that lies somewhere in between a free market economy and a government-run economy. It is a model in which governments try to use markets to social advantage.

The same model can readily be applied to public education, although so far it has not been. Beginning in the early 1900s, Progressive reformers designed and built an education system that was purely governmental. Markets were not well understood then, and these reformers made no attempt to take social advantage of what markets might have to offer—through, for example, more choice for families, competition among schools, and stronger incentives to perform and innovate. Instead, education was produced by government-run districts, which acted as local monopolies and were controlled via top-down hierarchies of elected officials and administrators. The same governmental structure has prevailed ever since, for roughly a hundred years.

Needless to say, this system has become familiar and normal to all Americans. What few recognize, however, is that it is also an extreme approach to public education. Just as the free market anchors one extreme and fails to capitalize on the value of government, so the all-government approach occupies the other extreme and fails to capitalize on the value of markets.

Such a system may have made sense a century ago. But today, the all-government system bequeathed to us by the Progressives is a relic of the past. And by embracing it as somehow normal and natural, we allow ourselves to be prisoners of that past.

Consider a simple thought experiment. Suppose we could go back to square one and design the nation's education system from the ground up, in any way that seemed most productive. Would we build an extreme, all-government system in which choice and competition are virtually absent? For most people who are actively involved in the nation's reform movement, the answer is clearly no.

In New Orleans, this thought experiment became reality. Hurricane Katrina wiped out the city's entire school system, along with its protective power structure. For the first time in modern history, state and local policy makers were literally free to build a new education system from the ground up in a major U.S. city. Did they try to recreate an all-government system like the one that had been destroyed? No, they created a dramatically different kind of system: a system filled with charter schools—but containing some government-run schools as well—with every child attending a school of choice, all schools competing for children, and the government providing an overarching framework of rules for admissions, funding, and accountability. What they did, in other words, was to embrace a *mixed model* of public education.[1]

A mixed model, as the New Orleans case well shows, is nothing like a "free market." It is designed by government policy makers, it operates under government rules, and it represents an attempt by government to use choice and competition to social advantage while maintaining ultimate authority. Its essence—and strength—is the balance it strikes in combining the advantages of both government and markets.

New Orleans, of course, was freed from its institutional past by a devastating force of nature, an event no one would want to see happen again, anywhere. The challenge is for other districts and states—in the absence of such devastation—to somehow escape from their institutional pasts too, and to move toward solutions that strike a better, more reasonable, more productive balance between government and markets.

With the nation camped out at the all-government end of the continuum, such a move involves the introduction of much more choice and competition. But these reforms should not be viewed as radical.

Indeed, in the grander scheme of things, they should be seen as just the opposite: as a moderating move toward the institutional center. While it doubtless seems odd to say so, it is the *current* system—the familiar, normal one—that is actually radical.

How, then, to move toward the center? There is not one best way to do it. Just as the nations of the developed world have found different paths to prosperity through different mixes of government and markets in their economies, the same can be true for American states and communities in education—with each going its own route in building a mixed system that reflects its distinctive values, concerns, and local conditions.

There is much room in the center, then, for variation and diversity. That said, what we would like to do in the pages that follow is to offer some of our own ideas about what a productive mixture of government and markets might look like, what it would mean for the operation of schools, and how it might actually be achieved.

The Building Blocks of a Mixed Model

Brute political realities weigh against the mixed model: powerful groups of established interests have long been opposed to such a change, and they will continue to use their power to resist. We'll put these political considerations aside for now, and simply discuss some of the basic building blocks that, in our view, would make for a well-functioning and sensible system.

The place to begin is by recognizing that, even if everyone simply agreed that a mixed model were desirable, a big, instantaneous shift in the institutional structure would be difficult and risky, at least in the near term. That being so, it makes sense to start the reform process by keeping the current system of district-run schools in place, working from this well-established and understood base, and triggering a movement toward the institutional center by injecting new elements of choice and competition—elements that would set off a dynamic of change. The old system would not be destroyed. It would evolve and adjust over time, incrementally, in ways that ultimately lead to a transformation. But the transformed system would also retain the more productive and valued components of the *ancien régime*, whatever they might be.

On day one, then, districts would still be running their own schools, enrolling roughly 85 percent of the nation's children, with another 11 percent in private schools, 4 percent in charter schools, and the rest homeschooled.[2] The districts, in other words, would maintain their overwhelming advantage in students, holding a near monopoly. But the reform would introduce a new framework of governmental rules designed to bring that monopoly to an end—by greatly expanding the choices available to students and forcing the districts to adapt to a new environment in which they compete for students against many other providers. What would the new rules look like? As we've said, the specifics might take various forms. But here are some basics that, in our view, would bring about a productive move to the center.

Funding

A core rule is that all money—local, state, federal—should follow the child, with the amount allotted for each student determined by his or her specific characteristics. A child from an affluent family, for example, may qualify only for her share of the base per-student funding that governments make available. A low-income child, on the other hand, would get additional amounts that reflect his share of the various state and federal programs that allot funds for disadvantaged kids. And a child qualifying for special education would get additional amounts still, due to moneys allotted for special education. Today's bureaucracies and the regulations associated with separate categorical programs would largely disappear. Each child, in effect, would have a "backpack" filled with a specially calibrated amount of education funds, and those funds would go to the school or district in which she enrolls.

In the case of choice schools—charter schools, voucher schools—this transfer of funds would be literal: when the child chooses one of these schools, governments would transfer the relevant backpack amount to that school. The operators would receive dollars and then make all decisions about spending, personnel, and the allocation of resources for their schools. In the case of district-run schools, the money would literally go to the district, and the district would decide how much is spent on (or by) each school, how personnel matters are handled, and how resources are allocated.

Overall funding levels would not be guaranteed. Choice schools and districts would be treated exactly the same in this respect: they would receive funding only for the students they enroll, and thus only to the extent that they attract a clientele.

Expanding Choice: Charters and Vouchers

The new rules would actively encourage the proliferation of charter schools, limited only by their ability to attract students, sustain themselves, and demonstrate acceptable levels of performance. Currently, the demand for these schools is enormous, and the supply is being kept artificially low. New state laws would remove all ceilings on their numbers, create new chartering authorities (among them, state and county agencies, public universities, cities), provide seed grants and loans, make public buildings available, and authorize for-profit firms to participate in their management and operation. The intention is to create a positive, nurturing framework that, over a period of years, allows the supply of charter schools to increase sufficiently to meet the demand, whatever that demand may be.

The laws would put a premium on school autonomy, ensuring that charters are kept as free as possible of traditional regulations, that they are not required to be unionized, and that they have the flexibility to organize themselves and serve their constituents as they see fit. Yet charters cannot simply be given free rein to do whatever they want. As is true in any industry, there are likely to be some schools that are poor performers, engage in improper behavior, misuse public funds, and otherwise subvert the intentions of reform. Some regulations are called for to minimize these sorts of problems and ensure that choice works to the best advantage of kids and society: charters must be held to the same academic standards as the regular public schools; their children should be regularly tested and the results made public for all to see; their admissions process should be open and fair so that all children have an equal chance of being accepted; their finances should be subject to annual audits; and crucially, charters that fail to perform at acceptable levels (as defined by the rules) should be shut down.

In addition to charters, policy would also actively support new voucher programs for disadvantaged kids. Today there are numerous voucher programs (and tax-credit-based "scholarship" programs) around the country, but most are quite small. Given the plight of these kids, their need for immediate new options, and the huge numbers of private schools willing to serve them, there could easily be voucher programs in every urban area of the country and in every state, and the programs could be significantly larger than the ones now operating. New state laws should create these programs for all children in serious educational need and give all of these children the right to a voucher, so that the size of the programs is determined by the demands of local families. The amount of the voucher should be whatever is in the student's backpack.

With a framework of this sort, the private market would attract more entrants, become much more dynamic, and offer healthier and more consequential competition for the regular public schools. In particular, once vouchers were made available to fund private education, there would be a renaissance of nonreligious private schools—whose supply is currently being suppressed because they are forced to charge students tuition, yet must compete with nonreligious schools in the public sector that charge students nothing. Vouchers would level the playing field. Once that happened, families seeking a nonreligious school would be empowered—by government money—to seek out those schools in the private sector, and the supply of such schools would multiply.

The fact that voucher schools are in the private sector, however, even if many are affiliated with a religion, does not mean that they should

71

be free from regulation. They need to be regulated in the same basic ways that charter schools are regulated with regard to academic standards, testing, the publication of test results, and financial auditing; their admissions must be consistent with social equity; and they should be kicked out of the program (that is, be disqualified for vouchers) if their performance proves inadequate.

Expanding Choice: Online Learning

Our world is in the midst of a revolution in information technology, a revolution that is fast transforming the fundamentals of human society: how people communicate and interact, how they gather information and gain knowledge, how they transact business. It is inevitable that this same revolution is ultimately going to transform the way students learn, teachers teach, and schools are organized.[3]

Even today, with education technology in its early stages, online curricula can be customized to the learning styles and life situations of individual students, giving them instant feedback on how well they are doing, providing them with remedial work when they need it, allowing them to move at their own pace, and giving them access—wherever they live, whatever their race or background—to a vast range of courses their own schools do not offer, and ultimately to the best the world can provide. By strategically substituting technology (which is cheap) for labor (which is very expensive), moreover, schools can be far more cost-effective than they are now, and thus provide far more education per dollar—which is clearly crucial as we enter an era of tight budgets.

Technology is the future of American education. The explosion of innovation and new options that this nation (and the world) is only beginning to witness has the potential, in the coming decade or two, to unleash the single greatest force for choice, competition, and dynamism that our school system has ever seen. The challenge for public policy is to design rules that embrace this information revolution, harness its energy, and take full advantage of what it has to offer, while at the same time recognizing the possible problems and guarding against them.

The driving force of technological innovation comes from the private marketplace, and thus from entrepreneurs and firms in the business of developing new software and supporting materials for curriculum—on everything from kindergarten-level reading to U.S. history to AP physics—as well as systems for managing classrooms and whole schools. The more that public policy embraces technology—by, most obviously, authorizing funding for schools that educate kids via online coursework—the bigger the market will be (in terms of sheer dollars), the more entrepreneurs and firms will enter, and the greater the potential for innovation and progress over time. As things now stand, state laws and regulations are designed around traditional classroom learning and take a very restrictive approach toward online learning. This keeps the market tiny and drags down innovation. Governments now need to reverse course, get out front, and design their regulatory systems to take advantage of what markets have to offer.

The focus here is not on schools per se. In principle, the new frontiers of online learning are equally available to district schools, charter schools, and private schools, and they can make their own decisions about how to put technology to use. Some may decide not to use it at all. Some may want to use it only for Internet research in traditional classroom settings. Others may pursue genuine hybrid models, in which students take much of their coursework online and some coursework (in music and art, say) in regular classrooms. And still others may provide their entire curricula online to students who may be located anywhere and do their studying at any time of the day or night. In putting technology to use, schools (and districts) will probably find it advantageous to contract with outside suppliers—often private firms—for their online curricula. Indeed, some may contract out the management of their entire school to an outside supplier, as many virtual charter schools today are already doing (contracting with such private firms as K12 and Connections Academy).[4] The providers of education in this future world, then, will be far more numerous and far more diverse than in today's world.

The authority over all this, however, remains with government. It is the job of government to create the right kind of framework: one that promotes the dynamism of the technology marketplace and uses and guides it to the best advantage of children. The first step is to embrace online learning by authorizing funding for schools that use its technology. *The money follows the child,* and it should make no difference whether the child is learning in a regular classroom or doing his work online, whether at a school or at home (via, say, a virtual charter). The online courses, of course, would need to meet the same academic standards as regular classroom courses. And all the other basic regulations that we described earlier for charters and voucher schools—regarding testing, financial audits, admissions, and being shut down for poor performance—would still apply.

The rise of technology and its growing importance to American education presents government with an important regulatory challenge. Traditional schooling has always been geographically bounded: kids go to school at a physical place, where they meet with teachers in classrooms. Online learning makes geography irrelevant. When children take an online class, they need not be in a particular place; they can be anywhere. So can their fellow students, who may be in another city, another state, or even another nation. And the same is true for their teachers. This is part of the astounding power of technology, and a capacity that offers enormous benefits for education. As things now stand, however, every state has its own set of regulations on everything from funding to teacher certification to academic standards, and it is impossible for virtual schools to reach their potential. While they are capable of enrolling kids across the entire nation (or the world, for that matter), any given school must now limit its enrollments and its teachers to those who physically reside within the school's state boundaries. This is a great waste, and a limitation on what technology can provide.

What the country needs is a common market in education. In our national economy, states are not allowed to levy tariffs and construct other barriers to trade; we have a common economic market, and it is hugely advantageous for economic growth and productivity. We need to follow the same approach in education. The nation needs to bring down the legal silos that prevent educational services from spreading freely across state borders. Most likely, this will require the adoption of a new policy framework (or set of inducements) by the federal government. It could also happen through agreements among the states, which have already formed voluntary compacts to set common academic standards and have often agreed to accept teachers trained in one another's universities. Yet the states would obviously need to go much further than this in coordinating their own laws and overcoming parochial interests, and the federal government—which has a responsibility for the whole that the states themselves do not—is still likely to play a pivotal role in encouraging and shaping any such agreement.

However the movement toward an educational common market comes about, it should include (at a minimum) a regulatory structure that allows schools to enroll kids who live anywhere in the country, that allows funding to follow the child across state borders, and that allows schools to hire teachers who reside anywhere and are not required to meet state-specific certification requirements. Technology is unbounded by geography. Education should be too—and it is government's job to make that happen.

Freeing Up the Districts

The existing school districts will remain in place at the start of the new system. But they will no longer have a monopoly on kids and money. They will be faced with competition from charter schools, voucher schools, and various technology providers, which will all be doing their best to attract their own clienteles.

Today's education reform movement is heavily focused on trying to hold districts and their schools accountable—through standards and tests, but also through consequences for poor performance (the reconstitution of failing schools, for example) and reforms that force districts to evaluate and pay teachers based on their performance. A rigorous, far-reaching system of accountability makes sense when the school system is a huge monopolistic organization that is run from the top down. Top-down accountability is essential to instill the right incentives and allow for effective management.

But once the districts are faced with serious competition, and once the rules guarantee that money must follow the child, there are new, very strong incentives at work and built-in consequences if those incentives are not followed. In this new educational world, districts need to perform and *earn* their clienteles, or families will simply go elsewhere and the money will go with them. Unresponsive districts will tend to wither. They do not need to be required—by their states or by the federal government—to evaluate their teachers based on performance. They do not need to be required to pay teachers based on their performance. They do not need to be required to close down bad schools. For the most part, they can simply be allowed to do what they want—reaping the rewards of wise decisions and suffering the consequences of bad ones.

Under the new system, then, higher-level governments need to let go. Districts should be granted substantial freedom to meet the competition in whatever ways they want. They can choose to do nothing and adhere to their traditional approaches to education. They can continue to run their schools through central control and try to improve them through internal reforms imposed on the schools. They can also choose to decentralize more authority to the schools themselves—giving them control over budgets, say, or over hiring, firing, and personnel rules. They can even move to a portfolio model, in which they contract with a range of groups—for-profits, nonprofits, unions, parent organizations—to run individual schools, and then manage the portfolio (ending some contracts, expanding others, entering into new ones) in the interests of better performance, and thus of attracting more students and money back to the district.

As with the choice schools, the districts must conform to certain basic rules regarding academic standards, testing, publication of test results, and admissions. And importantly, the states should not be allowed to inject additional funds to save districts from failing. Districts can reorganize (on their own tab). They can be managed differently. They can try different educational strategies—by, for example, relying more heavily on online learning. But the districts need to float on their own bottoms, spending only the money that they earn (or can raise via loans) from the students they attract. Districts have no special status in the larger system, and they deserve to survive only if families with options to go elsewhere nonetheless choose to enroll children in their schools.

Collective Bargaining

Under the current system, most districts have collective bargaining for teachers (and other employees), and most states have labor laws that sanction, encourage, and bolster it. The resulting contracts often run to more than a hundred pages, filled with restrictive work rules—on pay and benefits, but also on seniority, assignments, evaluations, prep time, class size, and countless other topics—that shape and constrain the organization of district schools, and make it difficult for district leaders or principals to create the kinds of organizations they consider most effective for educating children.[5]

Under the new system, a cardinal principle is that choice schools should be granted as much autonomy as possible to build their own organizations and provide educational services as they see fit. Accordingly, there should simply be *no state laws* regarding collective bargaining in schools run by independent providers. Collective bargaining should not, however, be prohibited. It should be a free choice. Therefore, if teachers and school operators decided to create collective bargaining arrangements for themselves, they could do so. But the laws should not promote collective bargaining, provide electoral arrangements for its adoption, make allowance for exclusive representation or the duty to bargain, or anything of the sort. Collective bargaining should arise spontaneously, on its own—and any schools embarking on this path should have to compete with other schools that have chosen to be free of unions and collective bargaining.

It is also a cardinal principle that the districts should be granted substantial autonomy. But the new system should be designed in a way that allows for the possibility that basic features of the institutionally extreme system—top-down governance, centralized control, collective bargaining—may have some value. And thus we want to allow these features to be preserved, at least in the first stages of the new system, to see if they can compete and survive in a performance-based world in which families are free to go where they want. The framework should therefore allow the states to impose (as most do now) pro-collective-bargaining labor laws on their school districts.

The acid test is whether collective bargaining makes it difficult for district-operated schools to respond effectively to competition from choice schools. If it does, then states and districts will have incentives to move away from collective bargaining as children, money, and jobs leave their schools. If collective bargaining has no effect or even proves a net positive, then states and districts will presumably decide to keep it. These are decisions they will have to make as the dynamics of choice unfold over time. Given the incentives, collective bargaining will have to prove its worth in making schools more productive, or it will be jettisoned. The framework should give it a chance, however, rather than ruling it out *ex ante*.

What Would the Mixed Model Look Like in Practice?

In moving away from the institutional extreme toward a mixed model, public policy would not be designed to create a school system that fits some sort of ideal mold. Rather, it would set up a framework of rules—regarding rights, requirements, funding, and the like—and then (with later adjustments, based on experience) let the system evolve over time. There is no magic way of dividing kids between the regular public schools, regular charters, virtual charters, private schools, and other possible alternatives. The districts' hold on America's children, now at roughly 85 percent, will almost surely be greatly reduced due to the emergence of many new choice options. But whether it will fall to 50 percent or 35 percent or some other number cannot be known in advance—and in most respects, is unimportant.

The nation's families will determine the ultimate balance. They will decide how their children—and thus, public money—get distributed across the various types of schools, depending on what they want and what the schools have to offer. The framework's job would be to ensure that the supply of schools can flexibly respond to the underlying demand of families, and that their wants and needs can be freely expressed and pursued. Its job would also be to ensure that, as this dynamic plays out, basic social values—of equity, fairness, opportunity, achievement, and the honest and effective expenditure of public funds—are met as well, and thus that markets are working to the advantage of society as a whole.

The beauty and power of the mixed model is precisely that it does *not* prescribe a "one best system," but instead gives rise to a *process* of change, growth, and development that puts a premium on quality education, effective schools, and important social values. The details of the system, then, will turn on millions upon millions of decisions by educators and families over a long period of time. And as values change, as new knowledge and technologies arise, and as the supply of school options grows and is refined by competition, the dynamic will simply continue—there is no end point, no settling down. Through it all, however, the dynamic is guided by the overarching framework, which is designed (and adjusted over time) to propel the system toward productivity and achievement.

Although we cannot say what the specifics of the new system will look like, we can talk in very general terms about how the mixed model, as it evolves, is likely to prove different from the institutional extreme that it replaces.

Schools and Classrooms

Schools will exist in a competitive environment that puts a premium on academic achievement, and they will have strong incentives to organize themselves and their classrooms in whatever ways prove productive. Different schools may do this in different ways, depending on what children they serve—their social and cultural backgrounds, their talents, their learning styles, their needs—and the evolving capacities that technology makes possible.

Some families will continue to prefer traditional schools, organized around full school days in one building, constant contact between students and teachers, and conventional teaching styles based on lectures and discussions. Especially as the new system is just getting going, families are likely to find these kinds of schools within districts, but also in the choice sector, as most charters and voucher schools will be organized from the start in this same traditional way.

Although there will probably always be a demand for these kinds of traditional schools, they face two big challenges over the long term. One is that they are highly labor intensive, and labor is extremely expensive. As technology advances, and as it can more readily be substituted for labor—with computers doing much (not all) of the teaching—these traditionally organized schools will be at a severe cost disadvantage, and their performance (per dollar) will suffer. A second challenge is that, as technology advances and becomes ever more productive, children and their parents will simply prefer a greater reliance on technology and a less traditional approach to schooling. So for both reasons, the constituency for traditional organizations will probably decline markedly over time.

There is a radically different niche at the other end of the technology spectrum. Some families will prefer virtual schools, in which all instruction is delivered online and students do not go to the same physical place. The obvious clientele is the current homeschooling community. But there are many other kids—dropouts, those needing remedial help, those who are especially talented or gifted, and those living in rural areas, to name a few examples—who are natural constituents as well. These full-time virtual schools do not have physical classrooms. Yet they do have virtual classrooms: their students take classes together, interact online, do group projects, get to know one another, and have frequent contact with their online teachers. The absence of face-to-face interaction does not erase the importance or impact of this kind of schooling; it is simply different from the traditional, a different way of doing education. And many families in the future will choose to go this route. Indeed, although technology has only begun to transform American education, some two hundred fifty thousand children are already enrolled in full-time virtual charter schools. That number will increase dramatically in the years ahead.

Children can also take advantage of online education, of course, without enrolling in full-time virtual schools. What technology does is proliferate attractive new options, allowing families to mix and match to find the combination that suits them best. With virtual options growing in availability, for example, children may take a portion of their classes at a brick-and-mortar school, and take the rest of their coursework from one or more virtual schools (or providers) that have nothing to do with the brick-and-mortar school. Families will be able to pick and choose among providers, putting together their own portfolios of schools and classrooms that enable them to pursue a wide range of interests and needs that no single school can satisfy on its own.

Technology makes this possible, giving students many more choices in customizing their educations. But this multiple-school approach is also fairly complicated, and it is fair to say that most families will want something much simpler. They will want their children to "go to school"—that is, to a physical place—and while there, take advantage of the best that both technology and face-to-face interaction have to offer. What they will want, in other words, are hybrid schools. Hybrids, in our view, are likely to be the most numerous and popular types of schools in future years—in the choice sector, but also within districts as they begin responding to the competition.

Hybrid schools will doubtless vary in their relative emphasis on the traditional and the high-tech. But as technology advances, we believe that, in the typical hybrid school of the future, students will take roughly 80 percent of their academic courses online. Nonetheless, children will still be physically "at school," and while there they will take subjects like music and art in traditional classroom settings (although computers will be highly relevant too), participate in sports and clubs, interact face-to-face with other students, and interact personally with teachers. Combining the traditional and the virtual in these ways is more than just a possibility—hybrids are already emerging in American education. Among the most notable examples are the Rocketship schools in San Jose, California, which have shown impressive early success with disadvantaged kids and are beginning to expand to other cities around the country.[6]

Again, there is no "one best way" to blend the traditional and the virtual. Educators will experiment with different combinations—different ways to use computers, to mix online learning with classroom learning, to deploy teachers, to allocate their time and money. As time goes on, some formulas will work better than others, and the better ones will thrive and be copied. Others won't work so well and will fall into disuse. Still others will be effective for some types of children but not for others and will thrive only in certain niches. But through it all, educators will have incentives to search for organizations that work, and families will be empowered to leave those that do not—thereby generating a dynamic of organizational change and diversification that moves the entire system in a productive direction.

Teachers

Under the current, institutionally extreme system, most teachers are poured into the same mold: they deliver a standardized curriculum to classrooms filled with twenty-five to thirty children. The conventional description is that all teachers "do the same job." Moreover, what teachers do at school and their conditions of employment—how much they are paid, how many hours they work, what duties they can be assigned, the role of seniority, rules that govern hiring and firing, and much more—are typically determined by collective bargaining contracts that heavily shape the organization of schooling and severely restrict what kinds of changes and innovations are allowed. Under the mixed model, almost all of this standardization and sameness will end. Teaching is destined to be a much more variegated profession, with many different roles, new opportunities, and much more freedom and flexibility.

There will be some schools, as we have said, that occupy the traditional, face-to-face niche. And in those schools, where familiar modes of classroom teaching prevail, teaching roles will be much the same as in the past. But even there, diversity will flower. Many of these traditional schools will be in the choice sector, where they will be free of collective bargaining restrictions and can be much more innovative in their whole approach to teaching: they can hire teachers who agree with the school's mission, weed out teachers who are poor performers, assign teachers to whatever duties and classrooms work best for kids, reward teachers who are especially productive, involve teachers in important school decisions (because they share the same mission), and in countless other ways depart from the traditional organization of schooling. Teachers will function much more like a team, and much less like a disparate assortment of employees who just happen to work at the same place. Above all else, even in the most traditional schools the emphasis will be on each teacher's performance—which is simply not the case under the current institutional system.

At the other end of the spectrum from traditional schools are the virtual schools that deliver all of their courses online and whose students do not go to a common physical place. These schools will have teachers too, but they will do their work entirely online from wherever they happen to be located—which typically means they will have no physical contact with their students—and their jobs will be radically different from those of traditional classroom teachers. Computers—and students, through their computers—will do much of the work. Teachers will monitor that work online, assess students' progress, grade written work, interact with students through written exchanges, structure students' interactions with one another, exchange information with parents (and involve them in the education process), arrange phone conversations for more personal contact, and so on. Online teachers will be handling many more students than the typical traditional teacher—making schooling much more efficient, dollar for dollar—and their skill sets and day-to-day activities, which revolve around the effective use of technology and virtual interactions, will obviously be very different.

Hybrid schools are likely to be the norm, however, and in those schools the new diversity of the teaching profession will be most on display. Kids will take most of their coursework online, and many of those courses will have online teachers who are not at the school at all—and indeed, are not even employed by the school (or district), but rather by the online provider that the hybrid has contracted with for aspects of its curriculum. Physically present at the school itself, though, will be teachers who monitor what students are doing on their computers, serve as tutors and troubleshooters and advisors when students have problems or need special help, and fill in the educational gaps—via personal attention—that are inevitable in a world so heavily dependent on machines. At the same time, there will also be teachers carrying out much more traditional roles—teaching art, music, and sports, leading group discussions, developing children's social skills—and whose jobs may have little to do with computers.

San Jose's Rocketship schools, which we mentioned earlier, employ a small number of highly skilled and very well-paid teachers. Indeed, the savings from technology—with students taught part of the day by computers rather than certified teachers—allows for salaries that are about 20 percent higher on average than what their peers in the district schools are paid.[7] Rocketship students learn core skills and facts online, and teachers monitor their progress daily, provide one-on-one help, assign supplementary online instruction when needed, and enrich the learning experience with class discussions and projects.

As this snapshot can only suggest, the sameness of teaching is destined to give way to a much more differentiated profession. Technology will be responsible for much of this, creating roles that never existed in the not-so-distant past. But choice and competition will also generate change, because schools will have incentives to put teachers to creative use and benefit from their vast array of skills and talents in whatever ways contribute best to student learning. In the early going, as the mixed model begins to evolve, it simply will not be clear which formulas are better than others. But over time, with freedom and experimentation—driven by incentives—new, productive combinations of technology and human input will emerge and demonstrate their value. And teaching, no longer stifled by institutional sameness, will diversify and offer new opportunities like never before.

In the process, the stultifying restrictions that now are often imposed by collective bargaining will tend to be driven out. Schools burdened by these restrictions are likely to be at a disadvantage in putting teachers to productive use, and thus, in future years, are likely to fail or simply occupy a much smaller niche in the larger population. It is possible, of course, that some form of collective bargaining could prove helpful to schools, which is why we have not proposed that it be prohibited from the outset. We want to give collective bargaining a chance to prove its worth in a competitive world. Our expectation, though, is that the only form of collective bargaining that is likely to survive the rigors of competition would be a much relaxed version that, while giving "voice" to teachers—and thus, useful input to schools—does not impose restrictions on the way schools are organized or allow forced transfers of teachers from one school to another. Collective bargaining as American education has come to know it under the current system, then, will likely cease to exist under the mixed model, leaving the schools free to build their organizations as they see fit.

In addition, with the massive substitution of technology for labor throughout the system, there will be many fewer teachers per student. Teachers, empowered by more capital (computers and online resources to enhance instruction), will individually be much more productive— the logic is the same here as in all other industries, historically—and they will be paid more as a result; in a competitive system, it is simply rational for employers to pay employees according to their productivity. Some teachers, moreover, will be more valuable than others, depending on their specific roles within their schools, and their pay will reflect that higher value. The sameness of teacher pay—the single salary schedule—will go out the window. Productivity will be rewarded. Pay will be differentiated. Teachers will have ample opportunities to move up, advance, and reap greater rewards for their contributions.

Performance, Innovation, and Equity

The current education system is not just institutionally extreme. Its performance is also disappointing. It resists genuine innovation. And it dooms disadvantaged children by segregating them in the very worst schools. The mixed model is designed to change all this.

As the mixed model evolves, and thus, as families exercise greater choice among an expanded set of options, schools will have strong incentives to adopt the most effective organizational arrangements possible—including the most productive uses of their teachers—and in seeking out such arrangements, they will have strong incentives to innovate. Schools that respond to these incentives should be a vast improvement (on average) over the schools in the existing system, and schools that do not respond—for whatever reason—will tend to attract fewer students and, at the limit, go out of business. The population of schools as a whole, therefore, should trend toward higher levels of performance and innovation.

The success of this evolution depends not simply on the introduction of choice and competition, but also on the governmental rules that shape their operation—and in particular, on getting the rules right and adjusting them over time in light of experience. The most obvious of these rules have to do, broadly speaking, with accountability. They include regular testing, the publication of performance information, financial audits, and the shutting down of bad schools. As the system evolves, then, the question is: are these rules having the desired effects?

If so, the rules can be kept as is. But if the system falls short in any respects—as is likely, given the complexity of the undertaking—changes should be made in order to engineer better outcomes.

It may well be, for example, that the publication of test score data does not provide parents with enough information to make good decisions about schools, and that something more needs to be done—such as requiring all schools to hold open houses on specific dates, or requiring them to publish detailed reports filled with relevant data on staffing, course offerings, and performance. To take another example, policy makers may decide that too many low performing schools are surviving under the new system, and that stricter criteria need to be adopted—with perhaps new agencies to enforce them—so that more of these schools are identified and closed. Yet another example: the supply of new choice schools may be increasing too slowly to meet demand, and policy makers may decide to change the rules so that seed money, loans, and buildings are more readily available and more institutions are allowed to serve as charter authorizers. The scenarios are almost endless, because the world is complicated and no framework of rules can be perfectly designed on day one. Adjustments will have to be made over time. The goal, however, is always the same: to create a framework that does a better and better job of harnessing the power of choice and competition to social advantage.

One dimension of social advantage has to do with creating schools that are high performing and innovative. Another has to do with equity: making sure that the American education system provides high-quality schools for disadvantaged kids. There is good reason to believe that, as the mixed model evolves, equity will dramatically improve. That is what the framework is designed to do—by empowering disadvantaged families to leave bad schools and seek out better ones, by ensuring that their kids have more money in their backpacks than more affluent kids do (thus ensuring that receiving schools will find them especially attractive clients and will have more funds to spend on their education), by requiring equitable admissions procedures at all schools, by taking steps to ensure that their parents are well informed about their choices, and in other ways as well. No longer will disadvantaged kids be trapped in bad schools. This is a system that is designed to make high performing, innovative schools *their* schools—and to put their families in the driver's seat.

Throughout this evolution, the advance of technology will also boost equity. With online learning, disadvantaged kids in Detroit and Appalachia—and anywhere else—can be liberated from many of the severe limitations of their own local districts, cities, and social backgrounds. They can have access, via the Internet, to the best curricula and teaching methods that the world has to offer. And computers do not care about their ethnicity, the color of their skin, or their family's income. Technology will be a huge force for equalizing educational opportunity for all kids.

Again, problems and disappointments may emerge as the system evolves. Some kids, especially in the early years, may not have ready access to the Internet. Parents may need better information. Some disadvantaged children may find that they cannot easily gain admission to certain kinds of schools. Researchers may determine that, even with the additional money in disadvantaged kids' backpacks, still more funding is necessary if the performance gaps of past years are to be overcome. In these and other ways, there may be indications of continuing equity problems, and thus of a need to change the framework of rules to engineer better outcomes. As always, it is a matter of finding the specific rules that, in shaping the operation of choice and competition, yield the desired outcomes. As the mixed model evolves, equity will surely be enhanced—but just as surely, adjustments will be needed in light of ongoing experience in order to bring about outcomes that are better still.

The power of the mixed model, as we have said, is precisely that it is not a fixed thing. And it is not a fixed thing, in large measure, because it is not stuck at an institutional extreme. It is an evolving mix of rules and dynamics, and its "place" on the institutional spectrum—the balance that is struck—is simply determined by *what works*: for performance, for innovation, for equity.

Governance

Governance under the mixed model takes two forms, at least in the early stages of its evolution. Because the education system is currently at the institutional extreme, and because we have chosen to preserve this system (initially) as a baseline for moving toward the institutional center, district-run schools will continue to be governed from the top down by states and districts. As we have discussed, these governments are free to run their schools as they see fit. They can centralize decision making, impose detailed organizational restrictions, restrict hiring and firing, maintain collective bargaining, and in general, take whatever approaches they think are beneficial. But they need to stay within the overarching framework that applies to all schools. And because they will be operating in an environment filled with other choice options, they will suffer the consequences—lower enrollments, less funding—if their approach to schooling is not effective.

So the traditional approach to governance is being given a chance to prove itself here: states and districts can stick with their "old" approach and see if it works. But in our view, there will be strong incentives for them to devolve most essential decisions to the schools themselves—where almost all the essential knowledge resides—and shift over time to much more decentralized, less prescriptive forms of governance. Most of the trappings of traditional top-down governance, then, should give way to school autonomy as the mixed model evolves, with district schools (which may turn out to be contract schools in district portfolios) evaluated on the basis of their performance but granted almost total freedom in how to achieve it.

The second form of governance is not a holdover from the past, but in fact a hallmark of the mixed model. This form of governance is exercised through the framework of rules that constrain and guide the choice dynamics of the system. We have indicated some of the basic rules that we consider important. But states will fill in the specifics, add rules of their own, and, as they do, act on the distinctive values and needs of their own people in moving toward frameworks that they consider best. Frameworks will vary across the states, then, as each state shapes—and, in light of problems and opportunities that may emerge, makes adjustments in—its own framework to govern its own schools. Although there is a key governing role for the federal government here too, particularly in trying to harmonize (aspects of) state frameworks to create an educational common market for the nation, there will ultimately be diversity across the states in the frameworks they craft for themselves. As we suggested previously, the federal government should get out of the business of funding or mandating particular services. The funds it now distributes for disadvantaged children should be included in those children's backpacks, but schools and districts will make the operational decisions—within the overarching framework of state rules—about how that money should be spent.

A guiding premise of the mixed model is that the role of these frameworks is to harness the power of choice and competition for social advantage, not to run the schools from the top down as though they are government agencies. Again, we can draw an analogy to the economy. The government does not operate business firms. It recognizes the value of having goods and services produced in a marketplace driven by choice (for consumers) and competition (among firms). It governs business firms by setting up a framework of regulatory rules that constrain and guide their behavior in the marketplace. Within this framework, decision making is radically decentralized. All the key decisions about organization, allocation of resources, personnel, and methods are in the hands of the firms themselves.

And so it should be in public education: governance is exercised through the framework—shaping it, enforcing it, adjusting it—but the schools have almost total autonomy *within* the framework to organize and operate as they see fit.

Future Prospects: The Politics of Moving Toward the Center

The existing school system is institutionally extreme and in dire need of reform. But reform necessarily comes through politics, and the many elected officials who make the government's decisions tend to be heavily influenced by considerations of power and special interest, not simply by what is best for society. The fact is, the current institutional arrangement is exceedingly well protected in the political process by powerful vested interests—notably, the teacher unions, but also the districts themselves—that have a stake in keeping the system just as it is, regardless of how unproductive or extreme it may be.[8]

We have no illusions that these vested interests would embrace a serious move toward a mixed model. Indeed, they would fight against it tooth and nail. With a vast expansion of choice options for families, it is unavoidable that children, money, and jobs would flow out of the district-run schools and into charter schools, voucher schools, and various online education providers. This is the last thing that the teacher unions and the districts want to see happen. It is no accident that both—with the unions in the political lead—have spent the last quarter-century opposing school choice and using their immense political power to block its expansion. After all this time, only 4 percent of the nation's public school kids attend charter schools, and far less than 1 percent attend private schools using vouchers.[9] Online schooling is being opposed and stifled as well. Political power has kept the lid on, with great success.

Reformers like to believe that, if only they can provide good ideas about how to improve the schools, those ideas will prevail. We do not believe that. Politics is driven by power, and the political landscape is littered with the bodies of good ideas that never went anywhere because they were threatening to, and defeated by, powerful interests. As long as the unions, in particular, remain as powerful as they are in the American politics of education, the institutional status quo will continue to be staunchly protected.

Is there any hope, then, for serious change? There are two good reasons for thinking that the answer is yes. The first is that reformers are more powerful now than ever before, and the teacher unions are more widely criticized and on the defensive. This is a major historical shift. With public frustrations gaining in intensity, and with groups representing the disadvantaged increasingly favoring big doses of choice and accountability, a reformist ferment has grown within the Democratic party—a ferment that sees the party's traditional ties to the unions as barriers to progress—and the unions have grown increasingly isolated. This will continue. One result is that, over time, the unions will be less able to block the expansion of choice options to the district-run schools. And as choice expands, children and money and jobs will leave—and the unions will lose members, resources, and power. The less power they have, the less their ability to block still greater expansions of choice—and with more choice, their power will decline further. And so on. This expansion of choice will not happen overnight, however, and there will still be plenty of mainline Democrats eager to link arms with the unions in the short term to make progress very difficult and slow.

There is a second, strongly reinforcing dynamic going on at the same time, however: the revolution in information technology, whose advance within education the unions can resist and slow but not stop. Over time, there will be more and more online options for children. As this happens, there will be a growing substitution of technology for labor, a dispersion of the teaching labor force (which will no longer be nearly so geographically concentrated in districts), and a proliferation of new education providers—all of which, as online learning becomes the norm in American education, will dramatically undermine the membership and financial resources of the unions, and thus their political power and ability to block the expansion of choice.[10]

The combination of these forces—the rising power of reformers, the ferment within the Democratic party, the transformations associated with online learning—will be mutually reinforcing, and, over a period of perhaps many years, will bring about a new politics of education that is freed from the iron grip of today's vested interests. For the last quarter-century, these interests have protected the traditional institutional system from change. But in the future, with a decline in their power and the opening up of politics, real institutional change will be possible—and a productive shift toward the institutional center can become reality.

As the mixed model evolves and a new institutional system takes shape, education will still be political. There will always be interest groups that try to influence the basics of the system—the rules that make up the governmental framework, the flow of money, the balance between government and markets—to their own advantage, and away from what is best for kids and quality education. But the same problems plague our economic system as well: powerful groups are constantly trying to shape the regulations by which the economy is governed, and the public interest is not always the winner. Even so, the kind of economic system that we have—a mixed model that seeks to benefit from the contributions of both government and markets—is the best the world has yet discovered for achieving productivity, growth, and innovation, and there is no question that it works better than an economic system that is simply run by the government. The mixed model is imperfect, yes. But it is far better than the alternatives.

So it will be with the mixed model of public education. It will always be vulnerable to political influence. It will always be imperfect. But in taking advantage of what both government and markets have to offer, it will also be far better than the extreme, all-government education system that we have now—more productive, more innovative, more equitable, and designed to evolve in the direction of whatever types of schools and forms of organization work best for kids.

4

"UNBUNDLING" SCHOOLS
AND SCHOOLING

Let's Think More Flexibly About How
to Structure Institutions and Jobs

By Frederick M. Hess and Olivia Meeks

THE TEACHER-QUALITY DEBATE today is something of an absurdist's delight. Teacher advocates insist that we should not expect miracles from teachers already doing their best to inspire, mentor, design and align lessons, differentiate instruction, craft assessments, analyze data, grade homework, connect with parents, enforce discipline, promote fitness, cultivate a love of learning, write individualized education programs, and so on. We are told that the job "is what it is," and that all we can usefully do is pay, support, and appreciate teachers more. Anything else is to rail against nature's course.[1] To those of us unmoved by this appeal, would-be reformers argue that many teachers are "ineffective" and propose plans to replace them with a couple million all-stars via the skillful manipulation of value-added assessment, new evaluation systems, and merit pay. Meanwhile, the professional development gurus insist—against all evidence, including a couple of compelling Institute of Education Sciences studies—that if we would just embrace new preparation models, they could dramatically boost the quality of teaching.[2]

We find the remedies proffered by both the would-be reformers and the professional developers to be lacking. The first envisions a death-defying search for elusive round pegs; the second, a grand scheme to shave square pegs until they fit into round holes. It strikes us that there is a third, generally ignored, option. Perhaps, rather than search madly for round pegs or try to retrofit the pegs we have, we might start asking how to alter the shape of the holes.

We could start to tackle the teacher-quality problem not by finding more superheroes able to master a hugely demanding job, or by placing boundless faith in training and professional development, but by rethinking the way we define the role so that more people might do it well. This entails "unbundling" the teaching job so that each teacher is not asked to excel at so many different things, and reimagining it in such a way that permits individual teachers to spend more time doing what they are best at.

The need to rethink the teacher's role in order to address new challenges is a microcosm of the need to rethink our broader system of schooling. Just as a reliance on the familiar pegs and labels hinders smart efforts to improve teacher quality, our casual obeisance to century-old models of schools and school systems limits our ability to use new tools, technologies, and talent to radically improve teaching and learning. In both cases, the key to tapping new possibilities is to unbundle what teachers, schools, and districts do, allowing us to recombine these functions in better, smarter ways.

Why We Need to Unbundle Teaching: The Roots of the Quality Shortage

The notion of the do-everything, lifelong teacher once made good sense—when talent was cheap and plentiful and our demands on teachers were pretty basic. Trying to retrofit this outdated model of teaching for a modern school system, however, is a fool's errand. Instead of changing the conception of what the teaching job description should be, however, many have wrung their hands at the shortage, doubling down on their calls for more full-time, lifelong teachers.

Nearly everyone has had experiences with teachers who were terrific mentors but terrible lecturers, or who might have been entertaining in front of a classroom but provided mediocre written feedback. An unbundled teaching model seeks to most effectively leverage each individual's particular skills, while relaxing the century-old assumption that every teacher should be a lifelong, do-everything employee.

A Problematic Common School Legacy

The roots of today's classrooms can be found in the Common School movement of the nineteenth century. Under the leadership of figures like James Carter, Henry Barnard, and most notably, Horace Mann, this movement sought to make schools "common," or widely open to the public regardless of social class. The ideal education system envisioned by these reformers was one defined by sameness, where all students would undergo the same cultural, social, and intellectual training—often led by low-wage female teachers—in order to establish a united, homogeneous American citizenry.

To maintain the same Common School–era classrooms as public education expanded throughout the early twentieth century, schools raced constantly to recruit and then retain more and more teachers, a pace that now requires that we hire some two hundred thousand teachers annually.[3] We have been on this path for decades: the drive to hire more and more teachers has tripled the teacher work force, from 1.1 million in the 1950s to 3.3 million in the early 2000s.[4]

In the 1950s and 1960s, even as this enormous expansion proceeded, the K–12 monopoly on female graduates was ending. This meant that the mass increase in hiring was accompanied by a steady dilution of talent. For example, the likelihood that a new teacher was a woman who ranked in the top 10 percent of her high school cohort fell by 50 percent between 1964 and 2000.[5] Meanwhile, policy makers and educators were slow to tap new pools of talent; it was not until the late 1980s that they started tinkering with alternative licensure and mid-career recruitment. It's no wonder that shortages are endemic and that quality remains a persistent concern.

The inherited notion of what teachers do has shaped key elements of the profession in the present. This includes our approach to teacher licensure, pay, and tenure. The result is that educators and policy makers are trapped in a doomed effort to nurture a world-class, twenty-first-century teaching force within the bounds of outmoded policies and practices. Instead of continuing to scrape the bottom of the talent barrel, we can save ourselves some grief by rethinking the parameters of the teaching profession and unbundling its components.

At the district level, a related inheritance is the expectation that every school system will tackle a vast array of responsibilities for every student who lives in the geographically defined catchment area. This makes it difficult for these systems to carry out any one of these responsibilities particularly well. Schools are expected to hire faculty to provide instruction for the diverse needs of English language learners, students with special needs, and gifted students; to provide physical education, extracurricular supervision, counseling, and other services; and to excel at all of the above. Once upon a time, when travel, communication, and management constraints forced most industrial enterprises to adopt the same approach, this arrangement seemed sensible enough. Now, expecting these systems to perform all of these functions at once is an anachronistic burden that makes it harder to deliver specialized services, instruction, and support across geographic boundaries.

At the school level, the familiar building block has been the "whole school." An emphasis on the school building made good sense when it was a feat to gather students and teachers in a single building and there was no other practical way to connect students with instructors, tutoring, or educated adults. Today, of course, the proliferation of online instruction, multimedia instructional programs, tutoring providers, and mentoring programs means that those old ties no longer bind in the same way. Yet, the presumption that a given building will provide an array of services and be able to serve every child excellently has been the starting point for reforms geared to accountability, funding, and equity. The result is an assurance that schools will be overburdened and have a difficult time doing anything especially well.

What Is Unbundling?

Approaches to schooling and teaching today look remarkably like they did a century ago. One would not say that about medicine, engineering, farming, or air travel. In each of these cases, dramatic shifts in the labor force, management practices, technology, and communications transformed familiar institutions and comfortable routines into more efficient and more effective versions of themselves.

These transformative gains have generally not been a product of doing the same things in the same way, only "better" or with more elbow grease. Rather, they have been the result of rethinking the way the work is done. Rather than one doctor serving as general practitioner, surgeon, ophthalmologist, and pharmacist, the profession (in concert with training and technology) evolved to permit these functions to be unbundled and then reassembled in smarter ways. This makes it possible to take fuller advantage of expertise and technological advances, though it poses new challenges of coordination.

Consider how decentralized service options, such as buying plane tickets online or using an ATM—tasks now considered mundane—have made it cheaper and easier for people to travel or access their savings. Rather than requiring travel agents or banks to hire full-time employees to handle these routine tasks during set business hours, customers can now access them at a time of their choosing. Meanwhile, this has reduced the amount of time that travel agents or bankers must devote to routine tasks, permitting a smaller number of employees to focus on tasks that take fuller advantage of their skills. In this chapter, we explore how unbundling could play out in K–12 education, where the irresistible push and pull of new tools, technology, and talent have created the opportunity to dramatically rethink and restructure schooling.

Put another way, unbundling involves finding ways to deconstruct established structures and routines and then reassemble them in newer, smarter ways. If we think of schools as evolving institutions charged with providing students with schooling—rather than as inviolate and immutable places charged with the entirety of teaching and learning—we create vast opportunities to unbundle the components of that package and customize them to better suit student needs.

There are two dimensions along which we can think about K–12 unbundling. The first is *structural unbundling*, in which we loosen our grip on the commonly held understanding of what it means to be a "teacher," a "school," or a "school system" and rethink how schooling is delivered. The second dimension is *content unbundling*, or the unbundling of the "stuff" of learning, in which we revisit assumptions about the scope and sequence of what students are taught and expected to learn, thereby paving the way for new, more varied approaches to curriculum and coursework.

In an unbundled world, today's familiar, do-everything schools give way to a shifting web of providers meeting varied needs in myriad ways. One provider might help students with writing and composition but not teach novels or literature. Another might specialize in offering rich, interactive instruction about pivotal historical periods without offering a full-scale chronological course. Others might package content from multiple online providers with in-person school faculty to offer "blended" instruction.

Recalibrating our fixed notions of "schools" and "teachers" in favor of a focus on "schooling" and "teaching" is the essential starting point in making possible a more unbundled system.

The Difference Between School and Schooling, Teachers and Teaching

Unbundling asks that we stretch our critical faculties and contemplate with fresh minds how we organize and operate schools. As Charles

Bidwell and John Kasarda elegantly observed more than thirty years ago, we tend to mistake *schools*, which are places where schooling takes place, with *schooling*, "a process that individual students experience."[6] The failure to appreciate this distinction has led us to conflate the schools we know with what schooling can and should be.

The result? Familiar arrangements are the benchmark for determining if a new model of schooling is acceptable or legitimate. This means that any number of routines from 50 or 150 years ago have come to serve as the defining features of public schooling. Our system of schooling was never designed to meet the individual needs of each student, compete for scarce talent, or leverage technological advances.

This same problem arises when we conflate "teacher" and "teaching." The act is reduced to the person inhabiting the job, and schools become places where dozens of isolated individuals are doing more or less the same job in classroom after classroom.[7] The old rules and norms have kept the traditional framework locked firmly in place, and the teaching job itself has remained remarkably undifferentiated over the last century. Across the land, from Syracuse to Seattle, a visitor can stroll into a school and be confident that all fourth-grade teachers in a school district—regardless of talent, experience, or particular strengths—will instruct about the same number of students, be required to spend about the same amount of time on each subject, and take on roughly the same number of ancillary duties. This may have made sense when little data was available to track teacher strengths or student needs, but given today's marked increase in such data, it represents a careless waste of skill and expertise.

Unbundling in Practice: Teaching

The challenge of modernizing our approach to teacher quality to match the twenty-first-century labor market demands doing more than, say, revising recruitment and compensation. Taking full advantage of talented individuals requires that we rethink the teacher's job description, specifically the management of teaching teams and the use of outside talent.

Specialization and Hybrid Teaching

Instead of thinking of each teacher as an identical cog that works the same 8 a.m.–3 p.m. shift and leads the same basic lesson plan in the same basic classroom, we need to reshape our conception of the teaching profession by focusing on specialization and team teaching. While today's school system treats most second-grade reading teachers alike, an unbundled system would allow the most talented reading instructors to focus on this strength, earn the label of expert, and, buttressed by special training and support, advise and instruct other reading teachers.

Other professions use precisely this model to ensure that they are squeezing maximum value out of their most talented and most highly trained professionals. The medical field is one such example: the American Medical Association now recognizes 199 specialties. While there are seven million medical professionals in the U.S., only five hundred thousand are physicians.[8] Those remaining are trained practitioners with talents that complement those of doctors. In a well-run medical practice, surgeons do not spend time filling out patient charts or negotiating with insurance companies; these responsibilities are left to nurses or support staff. Schools might find more thoughtful ways to employ lead instructors who have had more intensive training and complementary staff who have had less, and then apportion instructional or administrative roles accordingly.

Once schools embrace specialization among teachers, they can strategically arrange their staff. New York City's School of One is an intriguing example of how this kind of thinking can play out. School of One is a model of math instruction for grades six through eight that abandons the traditional classroom in favor of integrating multiple modalities of instruction—such as live teacher-led lessons, software-based lessons, collaborative activities, virtual tutors, and individual practice. Using an iTunes-like "playlist" (described in more detail shortly), the school identifies which learning objective a student ought to master next and then assigns students to a teacher or complementary modality for each unit based on each student's needs and learning styles. The result allows teachers to customize what a student learns each day on the basis of what he has already mastered and needs to learn, doing so with an eye toward the ways that he learns best while organizing learning to most efficiently use school resources. School of One, which is currently designed only for middle school math, enables individual teachers to focus on what they do best. In the School of One model, one member of a school math team might handle all of the instruction in a particular domain, building her expertise while allowing colleagues to similarly focus on what they do best. The integration of multiple modalities permits teachers to hand off instruction, which can be accomplished effectively via online tutoring or intensive computer-assisted exercises, and to devote more time to small-group instruction, personal coaching, and other roles that they are uniquely equipped to tackle.

Outside Talent

While segmenting and specializing the tasks of full-time teaching staff increases productivity, a fully unbundled system also seeks to tap the burgeoning pool of supplemental talent from other professions. Indeed, the Woodrow Wilson National Fellowship Foundation has reported that 42 percent of college graduates ages twenty-four to sixty express an interest in teaching.[9] This does not mean that these individuals want to abandon their current careers or are interested in getting certified through teacher training programs, but rather it suggests that they may be more interested in approaching teaching the way they approach coaching Little League or volunteering at their church. In other words, many talented individuals have an interest in teaching as something they do in addition to, rather than instead of, their chosen profession. Unfortunately, schools today have few ways to harness the talents of people whose career goals do not include being a full-time teacher.

That said, there are some organizations that have attempted to leverage such untapped community resources to augment existing staffing structures. Boston-based Citizen Schools, for example, provides afterschool instruction and career-based learning by arranging for local volunteers to work with students on a regular basis. Rather than simply mentoring or tutoring students, participants teach weekly modules that tackle complex projects with interested students. The model leverages the expertise of local professionals on a part-time (and cost-free) basis, illustrating the viability of approaches that do not wholly depend on full-time, career-long staffing. Tutor.com has also utilized outside talent in its worldwide network of on-demand tutors, most of whom are not full-time teachers. Even after their teachers go home at the end of the day, many students need further help with their studies; Tutor.com provides this extra help twenty-four hours a day. Other organizations could look to this "adjunct approach" to tap into particular expertise or retain the services of talented professionals who might otherwise depart teaching entirely when they opt to start families or pursue part-time employment.

These efforts teach us that there are ways to staff learning outside of our traditional definitions. We need to stop thinking of teaching as an all-or-nothing job staffed by solitary teachers and, instead, unbundle the conventional job description to boost productivity and better serve students.

Unbundling in Practice: Schools and Classrooms

In an era where providers of goods and services as mundane as cell phones and advertising routinely segment those services in accordance with individual wants and needs, it seems ludicrous that something as critical and innately personal as schooling is still required to fit into predetermined, time-bound blocks of instruction limited to twenty-four students at a time. Doing better requires stepping back and asking how we might more effectively tap tools, technologies, and talent to best serve students.

As has been noted by authors like Clayton Christensen, Michael Horn, and Curtis Johnson in *Disrupting Class: How Disruptive Innova-*

tion Will Change the Way the World Learns, John Chubb and Terry Moe in *Liberating Learning: Technology, Politics, and the Future of American Education*, and Tom Vander Ark in *Getting Smart: How Digital Learning Is Changing the World*, new technologies make it possible to free instruction from the constraints of geography and to customize coursework using real-time, sophisticated assessments, among other things.[10] This transformation need not come in the form of completely virtual, computer-based school systems, though examples like Florida Virtual School show that such an approach can be successful. Technology can support the use of supplemental providers who serve students outside the bounds of the traditional classroom and provide more choice within schools at the course and subject level. Bringing the power of technological innovation to bear in an unbundled classroom requires a clear-eyed assessment of virtual learning's potential benefits and challenges, as well as a strategic approach to integrating technology into the current system.

One of technology's potentially invaluable contributions to education is the way in which it facilitates unbundling and customization. Fifty years ago, if you wanted to listen to your favorite song, you would buy the LP, pop it in your record player at home, and sit through the entire album from the beginning waiting for your song to play. Like you, everyone else who wanted to hear a particular song on that record had to buy the same LP and listen through the entire record in order to hear it. However, with the advent of digital music technology like iTunes, listeners no longer have to purchase the whole album to get their favorite songs; they can buy each song individually and combine it with other favorite songs to create a customized playlist. Just as technology helped audiophiles custom-fit their music to suit their listening preferences, it can help educators custom-fit lesson plans and instruction material to best suit their students' learning preferences.

Digital learning holds the promise of enabling educators to apply this iTunes intuition to today's classroom. School of One and Florida Virtual School are demonstrating various uses of technology to deliver schooling in new ways. In addition to these two examples, Rocketship Education provides an intriguing vision of how to rethink structure and delivery. Rocketship, which operates several elementary schools in or near San Jose, California, and is slated to open several dozen new schools in the next year or two, employs a hybrid model of classroom instruction, real-time assessments, and customized supplementary services in the learning lab. Students spend their days moving from traditional classrooms, where one teacher instructs them on the conceptual component of the lesson plan, to computer lab sessions, where they work individually on the practice of these concepts with help from tutors and digital learning technology. Student progress is constantly assessed so that teachers can identify areas in which students need extra support and what modalities are best suited for their needs, all done in a manner that ensures each student can move at his or her own pace. This hybrid approach to teaching arrangements and instruction methods allows Rocketship to handle whole-class learning and individual needs separately.

Another approach would utilize technology for tasks where teachers can add only limited value. For instance, monitoring student achievement via technology might alleviate the need for teachers to devote substantial time to administering, grading, and entering data generated by formative assessments. One such example is Wireless Generation, which enables elementary school teachers to use Palm Pilots as tools in assessing and tracking early reading performance. This saves teachers substantial time in the assessment and data-entry process, and makes a wealth of easily manipulated information on student performance immediately available.

Technology has enormous potential to help carve new paths to instructional delivery. Unleashing the transformative power of the array of high-tech providers is not, and cannot just be, about the technology—it must also be about using the technology to get the most value out of instructional talent, and about the conditions in which developments will unfold.

Unbundling in Practice: Performance and Equity

The current one-size-fits-all model of schooling represents the triumph of "best practices" that held sway at the dawn of the twentieth century. The modern schoolhouse is an artifact of the Progressive Era's fascination with "scientific management" and its emphasis on efficiently educating lots of students in bulk. The result was a system geared to serving the average student, with little attention given to how the brightest or the neediest students might be well served. The practice of teaching has long entailed plowing through the scope and sequence of instruction at a clip geared to the median students, with teachers expected to "differentiate" instruction for twenty-odd children through heroic planning and classroom efforts. Unbundling enables educators to move away from a uniform scope and sequence, using a mix of traditional instruction, tutoring, computer-assisted instruction, online learning, and other provisions to craft courses of instruction that are better suited to the circumstances of each student. Greater access to high-quality nontraditional instruction for all, not just those whose parents can afford it, has the promise of particularly benefiting those children most in need. In this sense, unbundling can be a powerful lever for equity.

Meeting Kids Where They Are

A customized, unbundled model of education is by its definition going to better serve the individual needs of students, optimizing their instructional time and learning modalities so that they are best able to master subjects at their own pace. Utilizing a well-suited lesson plan or instructional strategy maximizes "on-target instruction time," which in turn will raise student performance and teacher efficiency. Otherwise, teachers are faced with the herculean task of tailoring instruction to the vastly different needs and interests of all students in the same room at the same time.

While the conventional one-size-fits-all school model serves few students well, it is especially stressful when it comes to trying to customize instruction for students with learning difficulties or behavior problems in a cost-effective fashion. Teachers are hard-pressed to provide these students with suitable, individualized instruction when simultaneously asked to serve the needs of the remainder of their twenty-five students in that period. Standardized tests and other conventional performance metrics used today do not tell us enough about where students are and what they need, and teachers lack the freedom to seek outside services that could better serve their students' individual learning styles. As a result, these kids are much more likely to get discouraged and drop out. An unbundled system, however, through its focus on individual pacing and student preferences, can be much more agile and better work around special needs so that these students stay on course for success.

Offering Performance-Based Compensation

In the same way that we neglect the needs of students who fall outside performance norms, our one-size-fits-all approach to compensation is a disservice to both high and low performing teachers. Today, teachers are paid within a step-and-lane pay scale, which values time served over performance. One-size-fits-all compensation means that we are either paying the most effective employees too little, paying their less effective colleagues too much, or, most times, a little of each. In a world of scarce talent and limited resources, this is a problem. Savvy leaders recognize the benefits of steering resources to employees who do the most good, as these are the employees whom schools most need to keep and from whom they need to wring every ounce of skill; however, contract restraints and institutional policies prevent leaders from doing so.

One approach to using talent more wisely might entail overhauling teacher schedules and student assignment so that the single exceptional English language arts instructor would teach reading to every student in that fourth grade. Colleagues, in turn, would shoulder that teacher's other instructional responsibilities. However, this is not an even swap. Excellent reading instructors are rare; we should refashion compensation to recognize their importance. If that encourages other teachers to develop their skills and pursue this role, so much the better. Districts with a plethora of talent can then revise staffing accordingly. In the end, salary should be a problem-solving tool for finding smarter ways to attract, nurture, and use talent; it should not be an obstacle to doing so.

After all, we pay thoracic surgeons much more than we do pediatric nurses—not because we think they are better people or because they have lower patient mortality rates, but because their positions require more sophisticated skills and more intensive training, and surgeons are harder to replace. By allowing pay to reflect perceived value, law and medicine have made it possible for accomplished attorneys or doctors to earn outsized compensation without ever moving into administration or management. Employing that kind of model in education would permit truly revolutionary rethinking in how we recruit, retain, and deploy effective educators. That is a far cry from today's ill-conceived proposals to slather some test-based bonuses atop existing pay scales.

Unbundling in Practice: Assessment and Accountability

It is difficult to craft quality-control systems that reflect and adapt to the seismic shift that characterizes an unbundled world. The best that policy makers can do is to select among—or combine—three basic approaches, each with its own significant limitations:

- Input and process regulation
- Outcome-based accountability
- Market-based quality control

You might have noted that these are precisely the same choices available to policy makers seeking to hold any public service accountable. Input regulation entails policy makers prescribing what entities must do to qualify as legitimate online providers. Outcome-based accountability relies on setting performance targets that providers must meet. And market-based quality control permits the universe of users to choose their preferred providers—and then trusts that market pressures will reward good providers and eventually shutter lousy ones.[11]

These are not mutually exclusive options, but together they compose the basic menu of choices for ensuring the quality of schooling (or any other public function). The difficulty is that these approaches were devised for assessing conventional institutions, not the more fluid possibilities of an unbundled world. Rather, like a Sunday suit that a teen has outgrown, they will tear, pinch, and constrict.

Regulating inputs like class size, instructional time, and staff credentials offers some minimal assurance as to what providers are actually doing, but carries a high risk of stifling potential innovation, customization, and cost-efficiency. Policing outcomes offers the opportunity to ensure that providers are delivering results that meet a given standard for pupil growth or achievement, but also encourages gamesmanship and disputes over the right metrics, while deterring providers whose service does not map neatly onto existing outcome measures. Markets offer diversity and scope for customization, but invite shoddy providers to profit, allow some families to be taken advantage of, and encourage online providers to focus more on marketing than on delivering a high-quality service.

These risks can be mitigated, if not eliminated, through thoughtful design that combines these approaches judiciously. But there is no golden mean or foolproof formula, and any promising combination will entail trade-offs.

While talk of assessment often trends toward the hypertechnical, the truth is that accountability and quality control are not technical exercises. Instead, they require fundamental judgments about how to weigh the risks and opportunities posed by mediocrity, red tape, standardized outcome measures, and markets.

Using New Tools to Gauge Quality

Empowering school leaders to organize instruction in smarter ways, or equipping families to negotiate a series of more specialized providers, requires specifying relevant and robust metrics. DC Opportunity Scholarship investigators Thomas Stewart and Patrick Wolf have observed that most parents, after visiting a few schools and gathering some information, will tire of the search and settle for a convenient choice; only about 15 percent of parents are willing to check with every provider before making a decision.[12] While this may give pause to those who suggest that nearly all families will make informed and careful decisions, it's not at all clear that families need to examine every option in order to benefit from new or more specialized options. In fact, only a limited number of consumers shop carefully for any good or service— but those quality-conscious choosers have an outsized impact on what providers do, in large part because their actions influence those of less assiduous shoppers. The challenge is to ensure that good and reliable information is readily available to those who need it.

Beyond the now-popular outcome metrics and the inevitable calls for process regulation, a number of market-friendly metrics are increasingly feasible and useful for an unbundled, multiple-provider education sector. These include:

- Professional, systematic ratings on customer satisfaction, something akin to the information reported by sources like J. D. Power and Associates. These make it easy for consumers to draw on the judgments of other users.
- Scientific evaluations by credible third parties, such as those offered by *Consumer Reports*. Such objective evaluations allow experts to put new educational products through their paces and then score them on relevant dimensions of performance, as well as price.
- Expert evaluation of services like that provided by the British School Inspectorate. Unlike input accountability, this type of evaluation focuses on revealing processes and hard-to-measure outcomes. And, unlike the *Consumer Reports* model, such evaluations draw more explicitly on informed, subjective judgment and far less on laboratory-style experimentation.

- Crowd-sourced data reflecting user experiences—essentially, drawing on the wisdom of the masses. TripAdvisor, eBay, and Amazon allow the public to readily access quality rankings, while also letting users offer detailed accounts of their experiences with providers. Unlike professional rankings, these results do not aspire to be systematic or scientific, but for that reason they are especially well suited to flagging narrow or particular concerns.

Such approaches have the possibility to hold educators accountable, promote new levels of transparency and insight, and inform the decisions that families and educators make.

Aggregating Data from Multiple Providers

The presence of multiple providers raises new challenges when it comes to gathering and collecting granular, reliable data. In an unbundled environment, where one school district is no longer tasked with trying to meet every need of every child in a geographic area, the ability of educators and families to access trustworthy data is essential. Two decades ago, education professor Frank Smith described a way to track and manage assessments from nontraditional services: students would be given an ATM card, which they would swipe after assessments at various locales and with different providers in order to track their mastery of the subject matter.[13] Thus, student performance information would create a framework for creating accountability and transparency in a system of multiple providers. Devices such as barcode-scanning cell phones make such once-futuristic ideas viable for today's students.

Indeed, the New Hampshire Department of Education, in its efforts to manage the increased number of educational options now available, has developed a system for tracking students' use of and performance in nontraditional services like internships, community service, and independent study, and then assessing their progress on competency-based exams for those contexts.[14] Such instances are cropping up across the nation. The New York City Department of Education has addressed this need for more robust data through the Achievement Reporting and Innovation System (ARIS) data warehouse, which aggregates and links a number of different data sources to better track student achievement over time.[15]

While the world of higher education is fraught with data challenges, colleges and universities show how this kind of aggregation can be managed by a "home" institution. For instance, a full-time student at the state university can take a calculus course at her local community college or another institution and have the results tracked and recognized by her institution's registrar. Third-party assessors partner with district and state governing bodies to serve as an aggregation source for students whose instruction choices sometimes fall outside the jurisdiction of any particular institution. Even among the most innovative data collection efforts, however, there is a need for much more. Recording raw scores is only a first step to understanding the full picture of student achievement.

How We Get There: Politics, Governance, and Funding

An unbundled system as outlined here has the potential to upset teachers, disrupt schools, discombobulate parents, and disturb familiar routines for providers and policy makers. Unbundling will prove feasible and workable only if the underlying regulatory barriers, governance, and funding structures are overhauled accordingly.

Political Barriers

Public education is a public activity, and therefore, inevitably governed by statutes, rules, and contracts. Understanding the source of these formal barriers—which block us from developing a more customizable, unbundled model—begins with a simple insight into the general nature of government agencies. Public policies, regulations, and the bureaucratic agencies that implement them are inevitably influenced, and frequently dominated, by active interest groups that wield influence in legislatures and at every level of the rule-making and implementation process. Those seeking to fundamentally alter established routines in schooling encounter opposition from teacher unions, major textbook companies, teachers colleges, and other key players that have evolved to fit comfortably within today's arrangements. This means that the policies required by unbundling will inevitably be controversial and will entail heated disputes.

Laws and regulations restricting teacher credentialing and teacher evaluation need to be rethought with an eye toward how they impede efforts to unbundle the teaching job. For instance, contemporary efforts to promote value-added teacher evaluation are predicated on the expectation that each teacher will be solely responsible for teaching a class of students for an academic year. If teachers team-teach, if students learn certain units or take select courses online, or if teachers are responsible for teaching students some units but not others, then these value-added metrics are unreliable. Indeed, these value-added measures become increasingly less reliable as schools and districts move to unbundled instruction.

Governance

Like today's antiquated classroom model, our school governance structures are anachronistic holdovers that have limited more innovative and flexible approaches to education. Having all-purpose governance operations focus on serving a given geographic community was common in the early twentieth century and hardly unique to schooling. In fact, until a few decades ago, it was thought natural for a given store to meet all your shopping needs, stocking everything from shoes and dresses to washers and tires. A glance at catalogs from the early 1900s shows the one-stop-shop business mentality of the era. The Sears, Roebuck and Co. catalog, for instance, features firearms, baby carriages, jewelry, saddles, and even eyeglasses with a self-test for "old sight, near sight and astigmatism."[16] However, that is no longer the way providers in most sectors are organized. A more sensible configuration would allow governance leaders to provide guidance and assistance directly to a growing population of students or across a range of schools and geographies.

Redesigning school governance will require tackling the balky vestige of an aged model and exploring how else we might, for instance, provide oversight and governance for providers educating a million kids in forty communities across ten states.[17] This is quite similar to the challenge that changing technology has posed in transportation or banking—as people or capital become more mobile, they start to seep past old regulations. Either regulatory structures adjust to that, or they stifle some kinds of provision while encouraging providers to seek loopholes—rewarding those who play fast and loose. Today, every school district is asked to devise ways to meet every need of every single child in a given area. Since they cannot tailor their services to focus on certain student needs, districts are forced to try to build expertise in a vast number of specialties and services. An unbundled approach to governance could alleviate these pressures, allowing district leadership to tailor its services to specific schools while also leveraging technology to lessen the demands of place-based governance.

Funding

Funding is another obstacle for an unbundled schooling model. Proponents of "weighted student funding" have called for ensuring that all the dollars intended to support the education of a given student follow that student to his school. Though a sensible step in its own right, weighted student funding is too limited a design for an unbundled world. It does nothing to recognize that a family may be satisfied by a given school but still have concerns about music or math instruction and wish to utilize an alternative provider for those purposes alone.

In the health care debates, for instance, even the most ardent single-payer enthusiast presumes that patients should be free to make a series of choices among physicians and providers. Yet, when it comes to schools, the most expansive vision of choice entails allowing parents to choose School A or School B. This may appeal to urban parents eager to escape awful schools; it does little, however, for the majority of parents—and especially for the vast majority of suburban parents—who like their schools overall but may wish to take advantage of a different math or foreign language program. Permitting families to redirect a portion of the dollars spent on their child through a kind of health savings account analog—in which families are empowered to spend educational dollars allotted to their child on a mix of approved providers—would address unmet needs, allow niche providers to emerge, foster price competition on particular services, and make the machinery of educational choice relevant to many more families.[18]

Unbundling requires funding systems that encourage educators, schools, and school systems to seek out the new efficiencies that result from taking apart comfortable arrangements and reassembling the component parts. While every state now features an accountability system that reports on student achievement by school and district, there is not a single state where accountability metrics gauge cost-effectiveness or return on investment (ROI). States tell parents, voters, and policy makers a lot about student achievement, but next to nothing about which schools or districts are delivering more bang for the buck. One result is that school and district leaders have little incentive to seek out new cost efficiencies. Maintaining or even boosting school outcomes while shaving costs has yielded little in the way of recognition or reward, while the headaches of trimming staff or squeezing expenditures are guaranteed to make a principal's life less pleasant. Reporting performance in terms of dollars spent, appropriately adjusted for cost of living and student demographics, should be a standard part of accountability systems and would be a critical component to assuring cost-effectiveness in a multiprovider, unbundled system.

Conclusion

The biggest challenge we face is not a lack of potential practices or good ideas, but systemic rigidity that makes it difficult to execute even smart solutions with discipline and focus. This is not unique to schooling or school systems. In the course of time, even today's most trailblazing ventures will eventually grow ossified—requiring a new wave of creative, nimble successors. If we agree that our system of schooling as it is currently configured is fundamentally unable to support and leverage new tools, technology, or approaches usefully, we must look for opportunities to create a world of teaching and learning marked by talented people pursuing new ways to more effectively serve students, teachers, and schools.

In the end, such a world will demand that we make at least four pivotal shifts. First, we must begin to think of education in terms of segmentation, not just whole schools. Second, we must begin to gauge educational quality in terms of cost-effectiveness as well as student achievement. Third, we must see that parents and educators benefit when they make choices that are cost-effective as well as educationally advantageous. Finally, we must provide both parents and educators with workable, comparable metrics by which to gauge both cost and effectiveness.

The goal here is not to develop a new model of what a good school "should" look like in 2030. Rather, it is to cultivate a system that emphasizes performance, rewards success, addresses failure, and enables schools and specialized providers to meet a variety of needs in increasingly effective and targeted ways. Too often, discussions of unbundling devolve into emotionally charged debates about the propriety of rethinking teaching and staffing, rather than asking how we can tap new opportunities to tackle new challenges in a changing world.

5

ADDRESSING
THE DISADVANTAGES
OF POVERTY

Why Ignore the Most Important Challenge
of the Post-Standards Era?

Jeffrey Henig, Helen Janc Malone, and Paul Reville

What's the Problem: Good Intentions, Poor Results

After nearly twenty years of vigorous, standards-based school reform in this nation, we still see an iron law correlation between socioeconomic status and educational achievement and attainment. The standards movement set out to eliminate this correlation, but after two decades and hundreds of billions of dollars, we have failed to reach our goal. Analyses of National Assessment of Educational Progress (NAEP) data illustrate a consistent and significant gap between low-income students and their peers. From the late 1990s through the most recently available tests, low-income students have made important gains in absolute terms, but the gaps between them and their more affluent peers have barely changed, averaging around twenty-five points (on a scale of one to five hundred for fourth-grade reading and mathematics, and a scale of one to three hundred for eighth-grade writing). The rate at which affluent children complete college has increased by 21 percentage points over the last two decades compared to only 4 percentage points for children from low-income families.[1]

Massachusetts is the nation's leading student achievement state. As the state's secretary of education, one of us (Paul Reville) can personally testify to the fact that the energy and concern remains focused on the equity issue; however, the gaps persist. While the floor of achievement has been raised for all students and some gaps have narrowed, the most recent results show that we have a long way to go. For the last four years, the gap between low-income and non-low-income students statewide has remained practically unchanged on both state English language arts (ELA) and mathematics exams for all grade levels. The proportion of low-income students scoring proficient has remained 32 to 34 percentage points behind non-low-income students. Fifth- and eighth-grade tests in science and technology show the same stubborn pattern.[2]

This powerful and enduring relationship between socioeconomic factors and student educational performance is not unique to the United States, although it is more extreme here. The 2009 Program for International Student Assessment (PISA) findings, as Iris Rotberg has noted, indicate that "close to 60 percent of the difference in reading performance between schools is accounted for by the socioeconomic status of the students attending the schools. In the United States, socioeconomic status accounts for close to 80 percent of the difference."[3] As our colleagues Ben Levin, Robert Schwartz, and Adam Gamoran have noted in chapter 1 of this volume:

> There is no reason to think that schools are immune from larger social forces, or that they can, no matter how heroic the efforts, compensate for vast inequalities in society . . . Children with health problems, poor nutrition, unstable housing, fetal alcohol syndrome, or other such issues are not playing on level ground with children who don't have these challenges. Education policy cannot be divorced from social policy more broadly.

The data supports what observers from Geoffrey Canada to Richard Rothstein have argued—that schools, on average, are too weak an intervention to overcome the obstacles that prevent many economically disadvantaged students from learning at high levels. Obviously, there are schools and students that defy the odds, triumph over the obstacles, and achieve great success, but they are the exception, not the rule. No matter how much we improve the quality of instruction, schools as currently conceived cannot, by themselves, close the achievement gap. Until we begin to systematically mitigate the problems that impede students from taking advantage of optimized schools, we cannot hope to achieve the audacious aspiration of the standards movement—all students achieving and ready for success.

We can lash ever tighter accountability measures around schools and educators; we can drown educators in data; we can, in fact, dramatically improve the efficiency and effectiveness of schools, but in the end, schools alone—especially the conventional one-size-fits-all, six hours a day, 180 days a year model (20 percent of a child's waking hours during schooling years)—cannot get the job done.[4] Schools need outside partners to assist in eliminating the barriers to effective education.

As obvious as this may seem to some, the concept of what Linda Darling-Hammond and others have called a "bolder, broader education" is threatening or repugnant to others.[5] Reformers have avoided the conversation about nonschool factors for fear of being accused of "making excuses" for students and educators, or of conceding that socioeconomic status is somehow destiny, or of nullifying the accountability system or undermining the value proposition for schools generally. For fear of these misinterpretations, we dance around the subject altogether, and as a result continue to fail to close critical achievement gaps. Couple the conceptual failures of policy makers with the general public's conservatism on matters of education, the general passivity of the education profession, and massive bureaucratic inertia, and you have the perfect prescription for maintaining the status quo even if it is manifestly failing to deliver.

Our problem is a failure to conceive a twenty-first-century education system that is capable of delivering the broad array of services and supports needed for all students to achieve proficiency. This system would not be the batch-processing, mass-production system we have inherited from the early twentieth century, when America was trying to rapidly socialize and minimally educate large numbers of immigrants and new urban dwellers so that they could be ready to serve a low-skill, low-knowledge manufacturing economy. Then, a bell curve of educational attainment served this nation very well. Now, we need a different distribution of talent: we need the overwhelming majority of our students achieving at a level previously reserved for an elite few. The old delivery system will not get us there.

What's Needed: An Education System—Not a School System

The new system will look and feel more like a health care system that differentiates among the needs of patients and prescribes for each individual the particular remedies and strategies that will help him achieve healthy outcomes. We would not give each patient the same treatment and same length of stay at the hospital irrespective of ailments, yet that is essentially what we do in education.

We need a system that differentiates among students, providing the quantity and high-quality instruction as well as enriching learning opportunities, in and out of school, that enable each student to attain mastery. But before that can happen, our education system—not the schools by themselves, but a network of schools and community/human service providers—must create a healthy platform that enables each child to attend school, be attentive, and supply motivated effort in response to quality learning challenges.

This education system, not a school system, would include a broad network of partners including families, communities, and health and human service providers. This network would be devoted to an integrated, individualized approach to healthy child development. Children's education would start early, parents would be enlisted as co-educators, and every child's life would be suffused with a myriad of in-school, afterschool, and summer learning opportunities and enrichment experiences. Schools serving large numbers of economically disadvantaged youngsters would have the capacity to reach out to agencies in the community that have the expertise and time to help students and their families solve problems that get in the way of students' attending school and supplying their best efforts.

This coordinated network of school and nonschool providers would focus on responding immediately and efficiently to the individual needs presented by particular students. The network would be charged with mitigating the problems that impede a child's capacity to attend school and be attentive and supply motivated effort when in school. Without such a frontal assault on obstacles to student success, the efforts to improve schooling in general and optimize instruction in particular will be far less effective in producing student achievement gains.

We know how to do this work. It's not a mystery. Privileged families do it all the time and regularly reproduce success. The work of supporting successful, privileged children begins with prenatal care and continues through supporting young adults well into their twenties and thirties. These children are typically stimulated and learning throughout their waking hours and all year long. They have all manner of physical and mental health supports, countless recreational opportunities, and access to technology and resources to enable round-the-clock learning. No wonder achievement gaps tend to grow over time!

We cannot institutionalize all the characteristics of a high-functioning, affluent family. But if we are serious about our education aspirations—as we must be for the health of our economy and democracy—we will have to try to do better.

Why the Past Is Not Prologue

The idea of a comprehensive approach to education is nothing new. Since the Progressive Era, the education and human services sectors have pushed to coordinate services for children and youth in poverty to alleviate barriers to learning and promote positive development. From philanthropic community schools efforts of the 1930s and 1940s (Kellogg and the C. S. Mott foundations, both in Michigan) to federal initiatives of the 1970s (1974 Community Schools Act, 1975 Service Integration Targets of Opportunity) and today (2007 Full-Service Community Schools Demonstration Project, 2009 Promise Neighborhoods), the initiatives and policies enacted over the years have engaged a variety of stakeholders—federal and state departments, local agencies, community organizations, and schools. Each time, a different configuration was designed in hopes of streamlining funding, maximizing available resources, encouraging cross-agency and cross-sector collaboration, and buttressing children and youth development across contexts. However, the success of many of these projects was often short-lived, and the attempts to coordinate services tended to fade away after a demonstration phase.

The failure to sustain or scale up such efforts speaks to both the complexity of the endeavor and to the power of the external actors and environments. A change in leadership (gubernatorial, mayoral, agency, school district, or school) could shift priorities or discourage cross-agency collaboration. An austere economic climate could trim budgets for services and reduce or eliminate funding streams for programs. Poorly designed policies and/or weak implementation could give rise to partner tensions over control and use of resources, turf, leadership, and the overall vision and direction of a coordinated initiative. And a lack of investment and engagement in evaluation research could limit the evidence base to inform ongoing coordination efforts.[6]

Given the record of high hopes, promising beginnings, and disappointing outcomes, it is easy for skeptics to ask, "Why should it be different this time around?" Part of our answer grows out of our analysis of what has gone wrong in the past. Efforts that depend too heavily on extraordinary leaders or superhuman teachers often fizzle due to burnout among founders and early conscripts. Overfascination with replicating "proven" designs closes off the continual and pragmatic process of learning and adapting to particular settings and contexts. Reliance on the abstract idea of coordination feeds an underestimation of the challenges of working across bureaucratic silos, and neglects the need to build and nurture a sustaining political constituency. Correcting for these past failures is one reason we think it is possible to do better this time around.

Another part of our answer to the skeptics is that some things *have* changed. Improved data systems make it more feasible to identify what works and assess costs and benefits that spill over the boundaries between schools and other agencies. Growing federal and state involvement brings more capacity and ability to address inequities than a highly localized system in which individual communities must thrive or fail on their own. Increased involvement of general-purpose government and leaders—mayors and governors, and state and local legislatures—makes possible cross-agency strategies that are far more difficult to initiate by school districts acting as autonomous governments with single-issue responsibilities and distinct constituencies.

Leveraging Human—Not Superhuman—Teachers as a Key School-Service Link

Students do not leave their problems, concerns, and emotions at the door when they enter the school building in the morning. While poverty in of itself does not cause low academic performance, children in low-income neighborhoods are exposed to daily stressors in both their internal and external environments, and these often manifest themselves inside the classroom.[7] Alleviating barriers to learning through quality community services has the potential to help students gain access to preventive services, interventions, and learning supports, while at the same time ameliorating teachers' informal roles as counselors, tutors, and mediators.[8] Letting teachers teach leaves service professionals to handle a variety of student needs: homework assistance, tutoring, case management, health and well-being, enrichment, and extracurricular development.

However, "letting teachers teach" is also a bit of a misnomer. While teachers do not have to provide services themselves, students benefit when teachers are cognizant of the available interventions that help children come to class ready to learn. The school-community partnership model asks teachers to be attuned to individual students' needs, to have the capacity to put a student and family in touch with needed services, and to know how these programs affect students. Further, some teachers might benefit from opening their doors to classroom aides or paraprofessionals who run afterschool and summer programs as a way to link and align instructional practices with academic supports available outside the traditional school hours. There are many models of such partnerships, ranging from full-time youth development specialists who work at schools as liaisons between teachers and external community agencies, to teacher aides, often college students or recent college graduates looking for classroom experience.

City Connects, a full-service school model, illustrates a promising case-management example. Each City Connects school hires a school site coordinator who brokers partnerships between teachers and service staff, working collaboratively to customize services for individual students. Teachers identify students in need of support to the school site coordinator, who then links the students to appropriate services. The school counselors and social workers work with students, teachers, families, and community partners to ensure that students access appropriate services and track student progress over time. An annual teacher survey shows that teachers in City Connects are overwhelmingly satisfied with the service integration, feel able to more effectively engage in instructional practice, and also note improved relationships with students' families.[9]

Having school-based or school-linked access to diverse support services does not necessitate overburdening schools with social problems or asking teachers to be Superman.[10] In fact, school-community service partnerships do the opposite—they understand that schools cannot wear all hats to support healthy child and youth development, and they recognize that many teachers already put tremendous amounts of energy into finding appropriate services or helping students outside of school. Good programs both lessen that burden and facilitate some of this work. Schools that partner with community service providers can design shared planning structures, hire a liaison or a coprincipal to serve as a direct link between the school and community providers, sign memoranda of understanding outlining the partnerships, or develop a shared data system to track individual students' academic progress and participation in the services and interventions offered by school partners. These kinds of partnerships allow for customized service delivery, delineate roles and responsibilities across stakeholders, and maximize existing human capital to serve student learning inside and outside the classroom.[11]

New technologies for record keeping, integrating data, and social networking have already reduced the implied demands on teachers or others who would serve as the interface between schools, social service agencies, and communities. The No Child Left Behind Act of 2001 (NCLB) and state systems of accountability have ignited an explosion of new software for dissecting test scores and fluidly returning diagnostic information to teachers. Similarly powerful tools could be developed and applied to evaluate and improve school-agency-community connections.

Embracing Open-Ended Learning in Place of Innovation for Its Own Sake

The reform impulse in the education sector gets much of its energy from resentment over the dominant system's seemingly stubborn and parochial resistance to change. The resentment is real—and at least some of it well founded—but it has been channeled into an undifferentiated celebration of innovation, change, and disruption as values in and of themselves. Some of this impetus toward innovation and change borrows from Joseph Schumpeter's concept of "creative destruction," and what he saw as an essential part of a functioning capitalist system, a "process of industrial mutation that incessantly revolutionizes the economic structure from within, incessantly destroying the old one, incessantly creating a new one."[12] In *Disrupting Class: How Disruptive Innovation Will Change the Way the World Learns*, Clayton Christensen, Michael Horn, and Curtis Johnson provide the most widely cited version of the argument as applied to school reform.[13]

"Shaking things up" is not the same thing as systematic experimentation, however, and "trying things out" does not in itself generate collective learning. We see no purpose in innovation for its own sake, in the celebration of creative disruption, in naïve faith in technology and entrepreneurship as the vehicles for constructive change. But diverse approaches are desirable because strategies that work for some children and some communities might not work as well for others. And, importantly, we do not yet have good information on the consequences of diverse initiatives and how those depend upon context.

The system we would like to see will draw on the conception of societal learning that Donald Campbell articulated in his vision of an "experimenting society."[14] It will embrace innovation—but innovation that is intentional, informed, and of sufficient magnitude to register outcomes against a background in which other social, economic, and political forces also are at play. It will embrace differentiation based on theoretically and pragmatically developed ideas about how interventions interact with context and specific target populations. It will adopt rigorous assessment as the primary tool for collective learning, rather than a simple faith that policy makers and the public will intuitively know when something is working. Critically, its assessment systems will consider spillovers, both positive and negative, across policy sectors. If investments in school-centered activities generate positive outcomes in other sectors—for example, in crime reduction or in more effective connections between social and health providers and families in need of their services—this should be taken into account. By the same token, so should any negative effects of school-focused strategies, or opportunity costs if a comparable investment in nonschool interventions would produce greater social gains.

Such cross-sector framing inevitably demands the adoption of a multi-indicator approach to assessment. Focusing on standardized test scores in reading and mathematics is obtusely narrow. Broadening the perspective—to include the impacts of education on such matters as the inculcation of desirable social norms; creation of adept and thoughtful citizens; development of technical skills and technological innovativeness; nurturing of personal characteristics associated with tenacity, adaptability, and hard work; stabilization of communities; dissemination of public- and mental-health-related information and services—requires a much wider palette of indicators to measure both long-term and short-term progress. Applying the principles of the experimenting society to the comprehensive conception of education that we are discussing also means taking seriously the fact that policy learning is gradual and ongoing. In the future we envision, research is employed as a critical source of feedback and guidance to policy makers; it is not manipulated to make premature, universal, or definitive claims that a certain intervention is *the* answer, providing a seal of approval that advocates that intervention's broad adoption and closes the door on newer ideas. The construction of a twenty-first-century system will require us to strike a thoughtful balance between the urgent need for near-term implementation and the longer-term process of thoroughly gathering data on which to base widescale change.

Learning What Works in the Accountability Era

In highly polarized education policy debates, those who argue against a schools-focused approach often find themselves arguing against the reigning accountability regimes. But there is a difference between standards and accountability, which we favor, and narrowly defined systems that automatically assign rewards and sanctions based on standardized mathematics and reading tests. The latter has been destructive, but the former has had some beneficial effects. The standards and accountability movement has transformed how we approach education and children and youth programs, and despite the surface tension, has begun to set the stage for a more sophisticated and mature approach to identifying which particular community and social service interventions are worth battling for. Evidence-based, data-driven decision making has become the currency for public and private investments in children and youth-centered initiatives. Anecdotal arguments are acknowledged but are no longer enough to enact policies and fund programs. And the passage of NCLB and the subsequent narrowing of the curriculum have increased pressure on supplemental child and youth service providers to link their work to student learning.

For decades, supplemental service providers' accountability structure, devised from a myriad of governmental, philanthropic, and private funders, and specific to each individual institution, largely rested on foot traffic data—how many students received immunizations, saw a counselor, or participated in an afterschool program. Although these descriptive measures still matter, the spillover effect of the accountability era within the education sector has pushed providers and those who fund them to think more broadly about the services they offer. Today, it is not uncommon for funders to employ more rigorous requirements, asking grantees to create their own organization- and intervention-level theory of change models, tie inputs to outputs, align interventions with student learning and developmental goals, and invest in longitudinal evaluations. Being held accountable for both the quantity and quality of services has engaged many service providers in a more thoughtful data-driven practice, leading the child and youth development field to ask (and answer) different types of questions about their own practice—what type of student seeks particular services; when, where, and for how long; and how are particular interventions making a difference in a student's life? This is a significant development because it enables support services to develop data-informed, targeted interventions that link to students' in-school experiences, while inculcating in students complementary proficiencies, such as life and career skills, civic responsibility, collaboration, critical thinking, and healthy physical and mental habits.

This shift has had real consequences. We know today, for example, that quality early-childhood programs can make a long-term difference in children's lives, that continuous participation in high-quality afterschool programs is associated with positive student academic experiences and learning outcomes, that summer learning loss makes a significant difference in children's reading scores, and that continuous participation in quality case-management services can impact students' grades.[15] We are aware of what environments nurture positive youth development—safe and structured settings that encourage positive peer-to-peer and child-adult relationships, and spaces that are culturally and ecologically appropriate.[16] And we understand that addressing health disparities among children and youth in poverty can positively affect their in-school motivation to learn.[17]

External collaborators are also providing an increasing array of tools and instruments for those engaging in this work. For instance, Public/ Private Ventures, which evaluates the California five-city initiative Communities Organizing Resources to Advance Learning (CORAL; a program focused on linking high-poverty students with literacy-centered afterschool programs), offers multiple tools to help program sites improve their work, including a program tool designed to align indicators with specific activities, an observation tool designed to capture evidence of lesson components, and a coaching tool designed to help staff identify goals and to assess their progress between observations. These tools are used to observe staff in practice, to offer timely feedback, and to track instructional strategies, classroom practices, and innovations. The leaders work with frontline staff to improve teaching and modeling practices, and the staff offers feedback about how useful the trainings are in meeting their professional needs.[18] This feedback loop has helped CORAL improve internal capacity and knowledge transfer. External, longitudinal evaluation results show that 88 percent of site instruction improved to a "moderate" level of quality as a result of the practice-oriented continuous learning system. Students' reading performance increased .45 grade levels in reading and was strongly related to the quality of programming received at the individual sites.[19] These intervention instruments helped to improve the quality of external supports that students receive and enabled schools to begin viewing external partners as important collaborators in children's learning experiences.

For over a decade, we have made assumptions in education about high-poverty students based on one yardstick—test scores—and have used these assessments to judge whether student improvement strategies rise or fall. If we pay attention only to the standardized tests, see outside social factors as unimportant to the work of the school, and view support services as "unnecessary add-ons," we will continue to be baffled by the growing dropout rates and low college acceptance and completion rates among high-poverty students. The emerging pockets of intentional, thoughtful experimentation that link and align in-school and out-of-school time factors, share responsibility for the whole child, and use data to improve practice tell us that a different accountability system is both possible and desired. How we get there rests in large part on our ability to design systems where cross-sector, cross-agency collaboration is welcomed and supported.

Coordinating Across Agencies and Organizations

We recognize that interagency and cross-sector collaboration is a complex endeavor and engaging in such work is no panacea. As suggested earlier, a range of political, cultural, and institutional obstacles serve as barriers to collaboration.[20] But prior efforts at coordination have helped educators and service professionals learn important lessons—namely, that shared vision, emphasis on relationships, clear roles and responsibilities, and careful planning build trust and lead to change. While there is no *one* correct way to help solve educational problems, there is a growing understanding among educators and service providers that intentional and informed experimentation offering customization and flexibility is preferable to cookie-cutter models that cast a wide net across a diverse set of problems facing students in our schools and society. We see meaningful efforts across the country, initiatives that build coordination systems across the preK–20 spectrum (e.g., Harlem Children's Zone, New York City; Children's Aid Society, New York City; Douglas and Sarpy Counties, Nebraska; Multnomah County, Oregon; Kentucky P–20 Data Collaborative). The impetus is often similar—equity of educational opportunity, a drive to level the playing field for low-income students and to offer children and youth access to customized learning experiences that could help them succeed in school, college, and life.

The Community Learning Centers (CLCs) in Cincinnati, Ohio, show how a successful coordination can work.[21] In 2001, Cincinnati embarked on a mission to coordinate and streamline resources so that every child received immediate, customized, data-driven interventions. Part of a $1 billion Facilities Master Plan was designated to link and align support services for children. With the district's support and robust local funding, schools began transforming into full-service schools, housing community liaisons and comprehensive services including tutoring, mentoring, college access, afterschool and summer programs, and social services and health clinics. To help coordinate these services, the district created CLC Partnership Networks, where like-minded agencies offering similar services work together to align goals with one another and with the district's strategic plan.

To better inform the coordination efforts, the Cincinnati school district created a data management tool so that schools and service providers could access student-level information—student ID numbers, grade levels, attendance, referrals, individualized education programs (IEPs), standardized test scores, demographic information, class schedules, enrolled services, and contact information. Providers are able to track students across time and contexts (school, agencies, programs, interventions). Struggling students are flagged by the system so that schools can coordinate with community partners and connect at-risk children to the appropriate service (be that mathematics tutoring, immunization, or a social service). The data system is coupled with student developmental asset surveys and individual program evaluations.

All agencies are held accountable for realizing the districtwide strategic plan via a "shared report card," a single measurement tool that links individual services with student academic success. There is a common expectation that every adult in the education system—be that a nurse, a sports coach, a history teacher, or a creative arts volunteer—will link his or her service outcomes to in-school learning. A 2010–2011 district report indicates that the coordination efforts are showing positive student-level outcomes in reading and mathematics scores, and that family engagement in schools continues to increase. A joined governance structure, universal access to data and fiscal resources, and a shared accountability system enables Cincinnati partnerships to collaborate, learn from each other, and quickly customize services that benefit students.

Moving Beyond Bureaucratic Silos

One lingering concern regarding coordinated service efforts is how to create shared accountability. Each service provider operates under its own institutional structure and culture, with separate goals, inputs, and desired outcomes, and with customized interventions and delivery mechanisms. Each service provider is accountable to its own set of funders, whose reporting requirements and measures of progress vastly vary, depending on the individual funder's vision, mission, and goals. Meeting in joint committees to share and evaluate data and problem-solve takes time, adds a layer of management, requires continuous staff buy-in—particularly when faced with leadership and staff turnovers—and potentially leaves organizations vulnerable to partner, funder, and public scrutiny. Given the high direct and transactional costs, skeptics wonder, why would an agency engage in shared accountability?

Multi-indicator, multi-agency information systems can be part of the solution. Today, institutions are able to track students across multiple service providers, to know which services students sought, dosages, and participation levels. At times, these data systems, depending on the partner capacity, accompany interim evaluations and data analyses to help determine student progress toward a set of provider-specific outcomes. Accessibility to data helps service agencies learn more about their clients and services offered by other partners in a coordinated system. Shared data reports send a signal to funders that individual organizations are open to transparency, and focused on improving practice and maximizing resources to sustain or scale up successful projects. Organizations participating in coordinated efforts can coalesce around shared goals because they are designed to serve the same children across contexts; the mission is solidly anchored by a focus on real families rather than on abstract appeals for partnering. The Youth Data Archive illustrates this point.

The Youth Data Archive (YDA), at the John W. Gardner Center for Youth and Their Communities at Stanford University, operates in the greater Bay Area. As a neutral third party, YDA serves as an interagency data link among school districts, community-based organizations and government agencies, county offices, community colleges, and local universities. The goal of YDA is to increase service delivery, align funding, and develop policies to support children and youth through a coordinated, cross-agency effort.[22] To inform on-the-ground practices, YDA collects a variety of data from the partner agencies—students' names, dates of birth, demographic information, parent(s) names and levels of education; school district identifiers, school attendance, grades, test scores, suspensions, graduations; juvenile justice placement; government assistance; health services access; and participation in afterschool programs. The composite of this data is then used for value-added assessments of participating programs and services, and for capturing the cumulative effect of diverse support systems on children and youth. Reports generated from this data are widely shared among county stakeholders and used as tools to change policies and practices.

YDA cultivates accountability, data transparency, and mutual reinforcement of policies through data agreements with each individual partner. By serving as a locus of primary responsibility, YDA alleviates the burden of technical elements (administrative tasks, archiving, assessments, evaluations) and encourages collaboration through shared governance. Sharing of data has allowed the partners to see things that each could not see individually. For example, in a recent analysis, YDA linked individual student data across San Francisco Unified School District and City College of San Francisco in order to identify early indicators of college success and to improve post-secondary outcomes for underrepresented students. Both the school district and City College used findings from the YDA analysis to create professional learning communities among English department staff to align expectations, and the College used YDA results to change its priority enrollment polices to ensure more equitable access to core courses. The two partners are currently in talks about developing an early warning system to keep students on track for graduation.[23]

Of course, shared accountability is not without its challenges. Massachusetts has established a Child and Youth Readiness Cabinet, chaired by the secretary of education and the secretary of health and human services and including several other major divisions of state government. The cabinet is charged with finding ways to integrate social services and supports so that children come to school ready to learn. But the early returns in Massachusetts make it clear that it is not enough to simply get people talking. One of us, Paul Reville, has taken part in great Readiness Cabinet meetings, where those around the table express and genuinely share all their good intentions, but then everyone goes back into bureaucratic silos where that energy gets rechanneled, distracted, or otherwise tamped down. To overcome such impediments, the involved parties must build capacity for the daily execution of the theory of action and, in so doing, demonstrate that the strategy works.

Building that capacity is not simply a matter of breaking old routines and traditions, but rather it entails doing new interagency work that fully engages and obligates the agencies involved. Say Yes to Education Syracuse offers an example of how the work of coordination and shared accountability could be approached.

Say Yes to Education Syracuse (Say Yes) in Syracuse, New York, is a citywide scholarship-incentive program designed to help high-poverty students get into college. Starting with kindergarten, Say Yes offers students individualized tutoring, mentors, afterschool and summer programs, college application support, as well as mental and physical health care, social workers, and family services. The underlying belief is that if students have a comprehensive support system throughout their education, coupled with financial support to afford higher education, they will be more likely to go to and complete college, uplifting themselves, their families, and their community.

To break down the existing bureaucratic silos, Say Yes first instituted operational changes—creating an advisory group, operating group, and the affiliated task forces—all guided by the Say Yes Foundation, an independent third party. The advisory group is composed of key city stakeholders who set goals, review policies, and support ongoing commitment to the initiative. The operating group—composed of leaders from the city, Syracuse University, the school district, and the county—oversees daily management of the coordination efforts. Finally, the individual task forces work within specific issue areas (family services, afterschool programs, health service, etc.).

To ensure coordination, each partner plays a specific role: universities offer research expertise and financial and resource support for students; the city recruits volunteer tutors and mentors for students and also oversees a citywide data exchange system, which allows local governmental agencies to share student data across and within each organization; the school district designs professional development training sessions to help teachers better target instruction; and the afterschool and summer program providers customize interventions to fit each individual child's needs. In addition to these specific roles, partners are encouraged to work across their domains. For example, the school district works with local universities on student transition programs and teacher preparation.

This did not come easily. Siloed institutional cultures, structures, and funding initially deterred many from reaching out to other agencies. With an independent coordinating body, Say Yes was able to begin to resolve long-standing tensions between agencies, change incentives to encourage genuine collaboration and information sharing (e.g., working with agencies to open up state and local funding streams that serve the same families), and sell the initiative as both an educational and economic benefit to attract a broader pool of funders. Say Yes was also able to overcome pushback from schools that doubted its ability to deliver on the program's promise—getting kids to college tuition-free—through a targeted marketing campaign, door-to-door community mobilization, behind-the-scenes negotiations, and the presence of willing afterschool and summer program providers.[24] Demonstration phase results indicate that the Say Yes program is making a difference in the community. The ninth-grade dropout rate declined by 44 percent since the demonstration began. The passing rate on the mathematics Regents exam increased by 30 percent. The school district gained three hundred new students, and the property values increased 3.5 percent, all in just two years.[25] An impact evaluation by the American Institutes for Research (AIR) is currently under way as Say Yes to Education Syracuse enters its third year.

How Do We Get There? The Challenges of Constructing a Twenty-First-Century System

Good plans are not enough. Once we have a new conception of an education system, we need to overcome the inevitable resistance to it. Implementation and scaling will require overcoming institutional inertia and a formidable set of cultural norms around schooling. For example, differentiating school time on the basis of need and mastery will not only be upsetting to students ("why are you punishing me by making me attend school more than some other kid?") but more importantly—because they are more powerful politically—to adults, parents, and educators who feel well served by a uniform system that standardizes time and place of schooling for all students. Differentiation is inconvenient, yet with the tools of technology, the infinite possibilities of the Internet, and widespread community resources, schooling can break out of its historic bondage to a fixed place, calendar, and schedule.

Moving beyond the changes in conception and delivery system and the associated costs, which would not be insignificant, we encounter the challenge of how to measure success. Good schools and a good education system must educate all students to high levels of proficiency in core subjects, but must also be effective at going beyond those subjects in other areas of learning like the arts and civics; in key skills like communication, collaboration, and creativity; and also in inculcating students with a love of learning. At the same time, these schools have to be effective at working with their communities to engage families and eliminate barriers to learning. How do we measure all this? How do we capture student and family engagement? Motivation? High expectations? The quality of teacher-student relationships and other key indicators of successful schools?

We need to sharpen our focus, attend to feasibility, and embark on a process that combines reform experimentation with careful monitoring of near-term progress. A key step is identifying criteria for indicators and benchmarks that government at all levels can begin to track in earnest. We would suggest three principles with which to start. First, the social interventions and outcomes measured should have a close link to schools (e.g., study the causes and consequences of low attendance rates, rather than broad indicators of community health). Second, indicators need to be quantifiable, with commitments to collect and maintain them over the long term. Third, while it is good to have a long-term vision in mind, we need to develop benchmark indicators that can provide near-term feedback on whether we are making progress.

If we are to rationalize an investment in a broader, deeper education system, we will have to be more skillful at demonstrating how such investments, if properly made, will pay off. What will the leading indicators be? How will we know if we have achieved success or are on our way to it? While the great achievement of the standards era has been a relentless, equity-driven focus on a narrow set of crucial outcomes, we have learned through two decades of experience that too tight a focus on these outcomes, as pure academic measures, will mislead us about how to close achievement gaps. To change the conversation, advocates need to get far more sophisticated about the metrics and the framing of the argument for a much more robust education system.

Research is a critical and ongoing component, not an afterthought and not just an upfront investment to determine "the best" interventions that are then launched, institutionalized, and protected. This of course requires investments, and defending research spending at the expense of direct services poses a political challenge. Paradoxically perhaps, the strongest advocates of a comprehensive approach to education can be among the most resistant to research; they worry that funding for research diverts resources to elites (universities, think tanks, well-paid technocrats within public agencies) at the expense of those with immediate and tangible needs. Two factors, however, can make systematic and ongoing research less expensive than ad hoc studies mounted on an occasional basis. First, considerations about research will factor into the original design of interventions. While randomized field trials have been oversold as the only valid design for assessing policy impacts, when used selectively and pragmatically they can provide clear feedback, are especially appropriate when there is insufficient funding or certainty to warrant universal implementation, and, while expensive, can be done more efficiently when the basic infrastructure and procedures are in place and the policy interventions are specifically designed with evaluation in mind. Second, once states and districts develop institutionalized, cross-sector databases that combine student-level information with other information on their families and neighborhoods, the marginal cost for studies of new interventions will be dramatically decreased.

A Sustaining Political and Governance Regime

Funding, governance, and politics would all have to change in order to realize the vision of a truly comprehensive approach to education, but the encouraging news is that many of the requisite changes are already under way. Three important lines of cleavage have historically characterized education policy in the United States. One is the vertical split established by a federal system that at times has set localities, states, and the national government at odds with one another. A second is an institutional cleavage within the education sector that led preK, K–12, community colleges, and universities to develop more or less independently from one another, with their own governance structures, funding, constituencies, and missions. The third is the horizontal divide that has separated education policy making into single-purpose arenas—notably, school districts—deliberately buffered from other governmental activities that deeply impact community and individual capacity and health. The existence of these cross-cutting silos likely served positive functions as the nation's education infrastructure developed, but it created a landscape that greatly complicates efforts to coordinate, build comprehensive strategies, leverage resources, exploit institutional advantages, and take into account the costs and benefits of public sector initiatives that spill outside the arenas in which their effects are normally measured.

Our vision calls for approaches that reinforce complementary efforts at the local, state, and national levels; that address the P–20 continuum; and that evaluate trade-offs and mobilize resources across a range of agencies in the education and health and human service sectors. Progress can be made within the existing formal governance systems by strong application of coordination and leadership, but hortatory appeals to school boards, superintendents, state boards of education, and chief state school officers to build bridges to other agencies are unlikely to succeed on their own. The historical lines of cleavage are strong, and under the pressure of tight budgets and stricter accountability regimes, the more natural reaction is to retreat into the well-established silos, focus on institution-specific bottom lines, and shore up traditional constituencies boasting the so-called "iron triangles" of support: interlaced interest groups, political leaders, and bureaucracies that help protect established programs and procedures and impede systemic change. Policy history presents numerous examples of efforts to work around institutional silos or to induce cooperation through deft manipulation of financial incentives for those willing to play along. Community Action Agencies and Model Cities in the 1960s, for example, tried to generate more integrated urban revitalization efforts by bypassing traditional state and local bureaucracies and creating new, more decentralized bodies that ideally would combine program and funding streams in innovative and proactive ways at the street level. This effort rested on what Jeffrey Pressman and Aaron Wildavsky call "a one-time short-run" theory of change, which falls apart when carrying ideas into practice requires sustained attention.[26]

We take these past failures seriously. Too often, stirring visions of comprehensive and rational planning and cooperation prove to be naive in their belief that resistance is purely shortsighted turf protection by entrenched and politically well-defended bureaucracies. The institutional silos we describe are not simply obstacles, and the political constituencies that protect them are not simply self-interested actors willing to sacrifice the common good in pursuit of their narrower interest and privilege. Each level of federalism, institutionalized sector of educational delivery, and bureaucratic agency organized around a specific function represents an aggregation of organizational capacity, resources, and political and social capital that is needed simply to get things done. Accordingly, we envision scenarios by which a comprehensive approach to education works its way through—rather than working around or barreling over—existing formal structures.

Our cautious optimism stems from the fact that shifts in the institutional landscape of education are making the traditional divides less daunting—making it more realistic for able leaders to develop comprehensive education strategies as part of their platforms and still get elected; to implement those strategies without having to go to war with their own agencies; and to orient their administrations around long-term benefit yet generate sufficient near-term progress to satisfy impatient funders and voters, replacing the familiar and ephemeral sprints of reform with the slow and steady pace demanded by a marathon.

Here's why we think a broader, less conventional conception of education will emerge as the commonsense framing for school and social reform.[27] First, a growing focus on outcomes and evidence will reveal the limitations of the schools-only approach. School-focused reformers proclaim that addressing education by tackling tough social problems has been tried and proved wanting. But their no-excuses accountability approaches, born in the late 1980s and gathering momentum since, have had a long time in the field and yet have failed to simultaneously ratchet up achievement levels and substantially shave achievement gaps. Second, attention to the bottom line and return on investment (which have been myopically measured within bureaucratically delimited parameters) will be expanded to capture critical spillovers among schools, social service agencies, health care, and other policy venues. When schools do what they are supposed to do—and what the public historically has asked them to do—payoffs are not limited to school performance; they include an array of human- and social-capital outcomes that help communities and the nation compete in a global economy, handle the stresses of multiculturalism, eliminate the costly social byproducts of poverty, and build a more informed citizenry. Third, major shifts in information technology and education-governance institutions will facilitate this broader-base framing and analysis. States are aggressively putting into place systems with unique student-identification codes that link information from various agencies through the years (student-level data on enrollment, demographics, and participation in specific programs), match student test data from one year to the next to calculate achievement growth, and track individual students who graduate or drop out of school each year.

Responsibility for education, at the same time, has been migrating out of the highly localized, single-purpose school districts that once determined policy—moving vertically up the ladder of federalism to include state and national government, and horizontally away from special-purpose units (like school boards) to general-purpose government (like mayors, governors, city councils, and state legislatures). Trade-offs and spillovers across policy domains are more visible in these general-purpose arenas, and the levers for addressing them more readily in reach. Traditional school boards might sense that school-based clinics or midnight basketball would create conditions more conducive to teaching, but mayors and councils are better positioned to get health departments, parks and recreation departments, and principals into the same room.[28]

Countering the Reigning Fatalism

A major challenge to a comprehensive approach is that it is quite intimidating. Mobilizing a coordinated multiservice effort appears costly, and all levels of government are facing deep and perhaps enduring fiscal stress. The comprehensive approach we are advocating is likely to take time to put in the field, and the payoffs may take time to register as meaningful improvements; making such commitments is difficult in a political system in which key decision makers are forced to think in electoral cycles of two or four years' duration. All this occurs, too, against a backdrop of diminished expectations and declining trust in government. Asked how much trust and confidence they have in the federal government when it comes to handling domestic problems, more than half of respondents (53 percent) indicated "not very much" or "none at all." Confidence rose slightly as one moved down the ladder of federalism, with 47 percent lacking trust and confidence in state governments and 30 percent in local governments.[29]

Such baseline skepticism toward government has played a major role in shaping the schools versus nonschool factor debate. A central theme of those proposing to focus on school-based strategies is that a record of failed public sector efforts to address such issues as inequality and the concentration of poverty means that continuing to do so would be tilting at windmills. As two of us (Henig and Reville) have written:

> Sure, these things matter, is the general attitude, but they are so big, powerful, and deeply ingrained that to even acknowledge their import is to risk losing focus on things like accountability, standards, tenure reform—policy levers we know how to manipulate. Attention to nonschool factors

is feared as an excuse to let bad schools and teachers off the hook. It seems to be a call for a vast increase in spending in an era in which retrenchment is the order of the day.[30]

We do not pretend that there is an easy resolution to the trust-in-government issue. One element, though, likely involves changing the ways in which political leaders define problems, endorse solutions, and use research. In the highly polarized arena of national policy debates, leaders on all sides of the major controversies find it expeditious to simplify the nature of challenges, promote silver-bullet solutions, and cherry-pick research that supports their point of view. The inevitable result is serial disappointment. The public watches one administration after another promise dramatic gains in short order and at low cost. When the results do not match the hype, when gains occur but slowly and unevenly, when we fail to meet 100 percent proficiency or zero out the achievement gap, or when costs are greater than anticipated, citizens understandably lose confidence. Our proposals put honest, systematic, pragmatic, open-ended research in a central place precisely because we believe this is the way to begin countering at least that one source of underlying skepticism.

The new data systems can help address the trust issue in another way as well. The standards and accountability movement shifted national attention from educational inputs (teacher salaries, per-pupil spending, student demographics) to educational outcomes, and for the most part that is to the good. But the hyperfocus on mathematics and reading tests as the outcome of interest has had the unintentional effect of feeding further skepticism. Anecdotes about exceptional students and school performance aside, the lesson some have drawn from NCLB and state-based standards reform is that intense effort over nearly two decades has fallen dramatically short of the stated goal of proficiency for all. Putting aside the questions of whether 100 percent proficiency is a meaningful target and whether we need to develop better ways to measure educational achievement, most theories connecting non-school-centered reform strategies to achievement outcomes recognize that there are steps along the way toward genuine success. A key step is integrating into student- and family-centered databases interim benchmark indicators that government at all levels can track in earnest, so the public can witness progress as it gradually unfolds. Better eating and exercise, greater access to health services, increasing school and community integration by race and class: these should eventually manifest in better achievement, but they can be more directly manipulated and are of value in and of themselves. In Ontario, for example, seeing signs of progress on interim indicators helped erode skepticism, boost confidence, and set the stage for further and more ambitious efforts.[31]

How We Get to a Twenty-First-Century Education System

Rhetorically, all of our states and the federal government committed long ago to the ideals of all children achieving at high levels. We just have not figured out how to get from here to there. How do we engineer an educational child-development delivery system that's strong enough to achieve our noble goals?

We have described the numerous obstacles, from inertia to scarce resources, that impede progress in building such a system. We have described past experiments—some successful, some not—and current promising practices. We have strongly asserted that the logic of standards-based reform and the disappointing data to date make it imperative that we broaden and intensify our approach to mitigating out-of-school factors that routinely impede student attendance and learning. We believe that such work is not only a moral imperative but also an essential investment in the future prosperity of our economy and efficacy of our democracy. Our moral obligations are now coincidental with our self-interest as a society. It is time to act with resolve and urgency.

We see at least three credible scenarios by which a state might break from the pack and take a leadership role in realizing our vision of a comprehensive approach to education. The first is a *court-focused* approach based on establishing the meaningful opportunity for a sound education as a legally enforceable right. Michael Rebell argues that there is a statutory and constitutional basis to claim that children have a right to comprehensive educational opportunity. NCLB, he reasons, "implicitly" establishes a statutory right in its opening paragraph, which declares that "all children have a fair, equal and significant opportunity to obtain a high quality education," and sets the goal that all children "reach, at a minimum, proficiency on challenging state academic achievement standards and state academic assessments." Rebell goes on to suggest that this implied statutory commitment is further backed by a range of equal protection cases and "dozens" of state court decisions establishing a constitutional right to a "sound basic education," some of which "have specifically held that the state constitution imposes an obligation on the state to create an education that overcomes the effects of poverty."[32]

The internal logic of the courts puts them in position to be a catalyst for changes broader than those that the more politically attuned branches would be likely to make on their own initiative. Summarizing some of the literature on "court-driven reform of educational governance," Benjamin Superfine writes:

> Given their insulation from the political process in a way that legislatures and agencies are not, the courts constitute a governmental institution that engages in a comparatively more "evenhanded" type of decision making than these other institutions. As such, the courts have been hailed as an institution more willing and able to overcome political inertia or resistance than federal or state legislatures to restructure the public school system to protect the rights of underrepresented student groups.[33]

The second scenario envisions a *bottom-up* political mobilization route that builds outward from community-based, grassroots efforts, where solving cross-sector challenges is sometimes easier and where more immediate street-level payoff can help build localized constituencies. Grassroots efforts combat cynicism with existence proofs, build relationships and trust over time, and can generate local constituencies that have seen benefits, not simply imagined them. Stanford's Youth Data Archive, for example, built slowly and "organically," fitting its strategies differently in each of the communities it focused upon. Getting buy-in from wary agencies took time, and part of the process of building trust depended on demonstrating, with small and focused studies, that research combining various kinds of information could help the agencies do what they wanted to do. "Part of the value of doing some of these analyses," a YDA representative indicated, "is to show the folks who are collecting the data that the more they collect, the deeper they can go, the better the analyses are going to be, and the more they can tell from them."[34]

The third is a more *top-down* scenario depending on strong gubernatorial leadership within a supportive national policy framework. Governors are in a better position than courts to build a political constituency for change, and in a better position than school boards and state education agencies to induce cross-agency collaboration. And to the extent that the needed reforms entail shifting priorities and resources from more to less affluent students, schools, and districts, states are better situated than cities to engage in redistribution, because they are less susceptible to the threat of wealthier taxpayers exiting. States, moreover, are the constitutional linchpin of public sector responsibility for education. They have the legal authority to mandate substate changes and commandeer local resources and capacity; local districts can petition for state support but do so as supplicants. And federal power to induce state change, while growing, is limited still by states' rights considerations and the need to incentivize change rather than mandate it, as well as the fact that federal revenues still constitute a relatively small share of public education spending.

Our top-down scenario envisions a gubernatorial candidate setting the groundwork during his or her campaign by redefining the education issue as part of a broader and long-lasting commitment to improve economic and social conditions, rather than as a function of school reform and a crisis requiring dramatic and instant change. Campaigning on such a platform will make it possible for the governor, once elected, to claim a popular mandate and have a supporting constituency to call upon when necessary to take on challenges that inevitably will emerge. While anchoring the platform in a long-term vision of educational attainment, achievement, and equity, this governor will create or build upon state and local databases to identify interim measures to serve as mileposts.

Whichever institution or level of government takes the lead, what we need now is forceful, visionary, clarifying leadership. The public must be persuaded of the logic for altering existing, comfortable school arrangements in favor of a new model: an integrated, comprehensive, interagency model that operates year-round to meet the developmental challenges facing our neediest children. The change to such a system will not occur overnight, but our leaders must generate a sense of urgency and a willingness to invest in the kind of coordination, experimentation, and evaluation we have described. The system we need, the twenty-first-century system, will meet each child where he or she is in early childhood and give that child what he or she needs to pursue a steady trajectory toward adult success. It will take long-term commitment and effort to transform the status quo into such a system. Only through such a deliberate, sustained initiative can we invent the bolder, broader system that will enable all of our children to develop into healthy, well-educated adults ready to fully participate in our society and, consequently, enjoy its benefits.

6

REDEFINING EDUCATION

The Future of Learning Is
Not the Future of Schooling

**Elizabeth A. City, Richard F. Elmore,
and Doug Lynch**

IMAGINE THIS: students choose a learning project from an array of curriculum materials and begin an individual line of inquiry. Adult tutors, who are trained by other tutors and network leaders (who organize tutors across a large number of communities), work with students in areas where they have expertise. These adults assume a variety of roles, sometimes doing what might be called conventional teaching, sometimes probing and asking questions, sometimes offering advice in areas where they have specialized expertise, but never standing and purveying knowledge in front of a group of students sitting in rows. Once the students have demonstrated mastery in their chosen inquiry project, they prepare a formal response and present it in an exhibition to fellow students, tutors, and parents. Demonstrations of mastery are based on students' ability not only to explain and justify their knowledge to a broad cross-section of adults and students, but also to teach what they know to other students who have not yet achieved mastery in their subjects. Because students who have mastered a given subject play the role of tutor to other students who are undertaking inquiry in the same area, they learn both the content they're studying and the practice of tutorials. Over time, this student learning, coupled with the training that tutors receive in the broader network, becomes a font of knowledge available to tutors and students in other schools in the network.

Or imagine this: learners select from a menu of possible domains, each of which has a set of knowledge and skills that learners must demonstrate successfully to earn a badge of accomplishment. Domains include entrepreneurship, financial literacy (with eleven subareas, including good credit, budgeting, and comparison shopper), digital arts, healthy living, and citizenship in the nation. Learners select domains based on their interests, pursue those interests in a largely self-guided way with some assistance from adult volunteers if needed, and after accumulating a number of badges, earn a rank of accomplishment.

What do these scenarios have in common? They may sound futuristic, but they are already happening. The first example is the Learning Community project in Mexico. The second is the modern version of Boy Scout and Girl Scout badges. These scenarios are all about learning. Learning is the future. Learning is now.

Schools as Portals

If learning is the future, what does that mean for schools? What exactly is school? Is it a building, or something else? One way to view school is as a portal through which some combination of information, knowledge, and learning flows.

Information, Knowledge, and Learning

One of the chief miracles of the so-called Information Age is our capacity to gather, store, and transfer raw data. So, accordingly, let's think of "information" as simply the ordered collection, storage, and transmission of data. The way information works today is that everything is essentially reduced to an ordered collection of ones and zeros. Through the magic of digital technology, we can reduce almost anything to this form, store it, and move it from one place to another. The ones and zeros have increased and continue to do so exponentially. The constraints on our ability to manipulate information are purely technical, not cognitive or intellectual—meaning that the relationship between what we can gather, and what we can know as a result of what we gather, is largely uncoupled. Put another way, we now have unprecedented access to vast quantities of information with a few keystrokes, but what we know as a consequence of this capability is another matter.

Now think about "knowledge" as information "acquired by an individual through experience or education" and "the theoretical or practical understanding of a subject."[1] Knowledge, in other words, is information plus meaning, where meaning is acquired through experience or education. Since meaning making is a habitual human activity, not just something that happens in organized education, knowledge is being created all the time through the interaction of human beings with their environments.

Next, let's add "learning." Learning might be best described as the process by which information becomes knowledge. That is, the world is full of information emanating from multiple sources, much more than anyone can process at any given time. To convert information into knowledge, human beings have to choose among competing sources, focus their attention on those sources, and construct their learning from those sources. Learning is an activity with its own special characteristics and skills, informed by experience, dispositions, and interests.

Finally, imagine a world in which the amount of information that is accessible to individuals is, as noted earlier, large and increasing exponentially. In this world, there is a set of institutions—schools and their attendant complex governance structures—that purports to, in some way, control access to this information through organized learning. One function of this institutional structure is to authoritatively say what constitutes knowledge, and it does so with an elaborate regime of curriculum standards, tests, and accountability measures. Think of this institutional structure as a portal. That is to say, in order for information to become knowledge through learning, it must first pass through this portal of legal definitions and constraints and then be converted through the intervention of adults charged with delivering knowledge to students. At each level, the system applies a series of filters—standards, tests, age-grade structures, and curricula, not to mention the knowledge and skill of educators at each level and their understanding of what officially constitutes knowledge.

As the sheer volume of information increases, the portal associated with formal schooling begins to look increasingly restrictive and, in a world of direct access to information, increasingly dysfunctional. What qualifies as "official" knowledge looks old-fashioned in an age when there are many possible portals for access to information and many possible ways to attach meaning to that information through the process of learning. Spatial constraints on learning—finding fellow learners to engage with, enlisting teachers, gaining access to divergent points of view—are no longer as important as they were when schools were the primary portal for turning information into knowledge. The authority of people who work in the established institutions of schooling becomes increasingly tenuous. When learning spreads out into social networks, the role of teacher takes many forms, only one of which resides in the institution of school. And the system's ability to monopolistically define what constitutes knowledge similarly begins to erode. The system can use its regulatory authority to "certify" certain providers as legitimate and certain bodies of knowledge as authoritative. It can also specify where people must spend their time during daylight hours until they are sixteen years old. But it cannot prevent people from making their own decisions about what and where they will *learn*.

Our current—inefficient—system depends on a portal that is increasingly small relative to the vast amount of information it is trying to accommodate. Because the system operates on principles of authoritative control over both the "what" and the "how" of learning (rather than individual choice), and is based on physical structures in fixed locations (rather than social networks), it cannot adequately handle learning that is not similarly constrained. It will not take long for people to discover that learning occurs much more efficiently in what Sugata Mitra has called "self-organizing" systems characterized by the property of "emergence," or the ability to morph into structures that were not planned in the original design but develop to meet the needs of learners in the system. "Education," he argues, is best thought of as "a self-organizing system where learning is an emergent phenomenon."[2] In this environment, a fixed structure with a small portal will either change radically or collapse.

It is important to understand that there is nothing necessarily "better" about this environment than the one we currently work in. There is no guarantee that self-organizing systems will be more responsive to individual learning differences than the schools we have, nor is there any guarantee that these systems will improve the overall cognitive performance of American students. Our argument is about the challenges posed by the shifting relationship between information, learning, and knowledge in a world in which this relationship is largely determined by institutions that ignore or actively oppose such a shift. These institutions will have opportunities to shape and design with intention emerging learning environments, but to exercise influence they must first recognize the contours of the modern world.

In addition to posing problems for the education sector, the growth of information radically changes the definition of learning. In a world in which the institutions of schooling determine what knowledge is, learning itself is relatively easy to define: it is the accumulation of authoritative knowledge, and demonstrated competence in recall and application of that knowledge. The growth of information, however, redefines learning. When the volume of possible information applicable to human problem solving is vast, and the portals available for accessing that information are numerous, learning becomes mastering the ways of imputing *meaning* to information—not recall and application of official knowledge. Skillful learning is being able to engage in the complex process of deciding what information to accept as authoritative for certain purposes and applying it accordingly, and fluently negotiating the boundary between information and knowledge.

Not the least of the transformations that will occur as a result of the new wealth of available information is a systemic shift from defining education as "schooling" to defining it as "learning." The activity of learning will become increasingly uncoupled from the institution called school. In the short term, there will be a conflict between the old definition of learning (accumulation and recall of official knowledge) and the new (fluency in the translation of information into knowledge). Soon, the social rewards will shift from the former to the latter, and the configuration of learning environments will follow.

Adoption Versus Use

When Steve Jobs died in October 2011, NPR ran the obligatory segment on his—and Apple's—impact on the education sector. The segment dealt entirely with what we would call the *adoption theory* of technology and learning, assessing impact using quantitative data about the number of machines in use rather than the ways in which they add value, or not, to the actual learning of students. This theory makes us ask questions like: *how many computers do we see in classrooms? What proportion of them are Macs? When students graduate from high school and move on to college, how many of them use Macs?* For most people, the idea of learning and technology begins and ends with the adoption theory (we have these machines called computers; they have entered the organization called school), which neglects the deeper question of how to actually use the adopted technology to enhance learning.

But, as educators, we instead ask questions like: *how will these computers be used, for what purpose, and with what effect?* Typically, as many studies have demonstrated, the promise of "new" technologies and their impact on learning is subsumed by the default culture of schooling. The machines are adapted to existing practices, and the organization continues to do what it has always done. Two of us (Richard Elmore and Elizabeth City) see the following scenarios time and time again in classroom observations. A teacher seats a group of boys with "special learning needs" in a corner and gives them laptops, while she works with the rest of the class using the blackboard. Halfway through the class, she checks in with the boys to see how they are doing and discovers that due to a malfunction, none of the laptops has access to the activity that she had planned for them. In another class in a "laptop school," the students are busily following the teacher's instructions on their computers. A student raises her hand and says that her laptop is not working. The teachers says, "No problem," pulls out a piece of paper that is an exact copy of the worksheet on the computer, and tells the student to follow along on that. In a third school, students have been released from their regular classroom to do "research" for a class project in the computer lab. Several pairs of students are unable to access important Web sites because they are blocked by the school's access policy. The teacher tells them, "Do the best you can with what you have," and the subtext is clear: "Do the research at home where your access is not blocked."

We could recite dozens of examples like these, mirroring Larry Cuban's perceptive prediction about how technology will affect schooling in the twenty-first century, which is hardly at all.[3] The problem with the adoption theory, however, is that it ignores the real impact of technology on learning by focusing on the increasingly outmoded organization called school. It is true that technology is—as Clayton Christiansen, Curtis Johnson, and Michael Horn argue—a disruptive force in the education sector, but the disruption is not occurring through the impenetrable fog of organized schooling.[4] Instead, it is occurring in the environment around schools. The real criterion for the impact of technology on learning is "use": technology is a means, not an end. When we think about Steve Jobs's impact on education, instead of counting computers and other devices, we could instead look at the kind of learning that his company's technology has enabled.

A focus on use rewrites the adoption script: we have these machines called computers. Outside of the organization called school, we use them to access knowledge, to pursue interests, and to learn with others and on our own. The activity called learning is increasing exponentially as a consequence of access to knowledge unmediated by the organization called school. The proportion of that activity that will occur in the organization called school in the future will decline dramatically.

From Encyclopedia to Wikipedia

One of the most striking features of the current use of technology is the shift in the authority of knowledge and the role of the individual learner in relation to that authority. The evolution of the encyclopedia illustrates this shift. Who among us enjoyed reading the encyclopedia as a child (and is not afraid to admit it)? What better way to spend a rainy day than choosing a volume of the *World Book Encyclopedia* from the bookshelf, opening it to any page, and just reading? How wonderful was it to believe that all of the essential knowledge in the world was contained in those volumes? There was a sense that if you could just read every volume, A to Z, you would know most of what was worth knowing, and you could trust the encyclopedia as the definitive source. If you had a research paper to do at school, it was always best to start with the encyclopedia and then go search for the teacher-required additional two resources as supplements.

Encyclopedias had a good reign as king of knowledge. The earliest surviving encyclopedia—the *Naturalis Historia*—is almost two thousand years old, written by Pliny the Elder, a Roman statesman in the first-century A.D. Pliny the Elder did not survive the eruption of Vesuvius, but his encyclopedia did. Encyclopedias in other eras and countries followed, though they had to be hand-copied and thus were used by a very small number of people. Everyone else relied largely on experience and personal interactions for access to information and knowledge. The invention of the printing press by Johannes Gutenberg in 1440 meant that texts, including encyclopedias, could be printed more cheaply and made more accessible to a wider array of people, though it took until the eighteenth century for the modern version of the encyclopedia to emerge, and encyclopedias were still expensive to produce and purchase.

These days, printed encyclopedias are having a hard time keeping up with the explosion of knowledge. If students have a research paper to do for school, where do they start? Wikipedia. The words themselves are instructive. The "pedia" part comes from the Greek word *paideia*, which translates as "child-rearing, education." "Encyclo" comes from the Greek *enkyklios*, which translates literally as "training in a circle" (as in the "circle of arts and sciences"), or "general education." Thus, *encyclopedia* means "general education"—the place where you can get all the knowledge you need in a contained circle. "Wiki" comes from the Hawaiian word *wikiwiki*, which means "quick."[5] Thus, *Wikipedia* means "quick education"—the place where you can get whatever information you need quickly. *Wiki* has also come to mean something else—a Web site that people can contribute to, often resulting in collaboratively constructed knowledge. You can use Wikipedia for quick education, *and* you can contribute to Wikipedia. In January 2001, seven people contributed to the English version of Wikipedia; by November 2011, that number had climbed to 737,628 people.[6] This is a huge shift in where authority lies for construction of knowledge.

There is an accompanying shift in the role of the consumer/learner. Because everyone can be part of the knowledge-producing authority, the learner has to decide how much authority to lend to that knowledge—that is, how much to believe it. As Wikipedia has grown, a major challenge has been figuring out how to ensure that information is trustworthy. Though Wikipedia has editors, it is a heavily self-regulated enterprise, as it has to be because of the operation's scale. There are 3.8 million articles on the English-language version of Wikipedia as of November 2011, and this number is increasing every day.

Wikipedia itself recognizes this role of the learner in its FAQs for schools:

> Wikipedia's objective is to become a compendium of published knowledge about notable subjects. The reliability of Wikipedia articles is limited by the external sources on which they are supposed to rely, as well as by the ability of Wikipedia's editors to understand those sources correctly and their willingness to use them properly. Therefore, articles may or may not be reliable, and readers should always use their own judgment. Students should never use information in Wikipedia (or any other online encyclopedia) for formal purposes (such as school essays) until they have verified and evaluated the information based on external sources. For this reason, Wikipedia, like any encyclopedia, is a great starting place for research but not always a great ending place.[7]

How did we learn about Pliny the Elder and his unfortunate encounter with Vesuvius? Wikipedia, of course, with a search for "history of encyclopedia."[8] How about the derivation of *encyclopedia*? We searched Google for "etymology of encyclopedia" (after trying "what does encyclopedia mean?" and getting definitions but not word history), and then clicked on a couple of links until we found what we wanted and decided it sounded right based on prior knowledge.[9] Those searches were quick, done with a computer and Internet connection, and did not require a school or a teacher to either provide a portal to the information or help translate it into learning. The authority of knowledge here resides in a social network rather than in official institutions. Clearly, people are finding Wikipedia useful for a "quick education"—the site gets 9.5 million views per hour, and that is just the English-language version. We "know" this because we believe Wikipedia's self-reports of usage statistics.[10]

The More Things Change, the More They Stay the Same?

Even with all that use, Wikipedia has not made much of a dent in the sturdy institution of school. Why is school so impervious to change, much less improvement, and why do we think it will be different this time?

To the first question, we do not dispute that schools are remarkably stolid institutions. While this is increasingly blamed on educators, we would argue that there are multiple forces inside and outside of schools that make them perfectly rational in their unyielding approach to weathering reform. We are not the first to argue this (see David Tyack and Larry Cuban, for example), and our colleagues in this volume take on some of these forces.[11] In his book on educational entrepreneurship, Frederick Hess explains the shortcomings of traditional reform, arguing that it is often akin to patching a building in that it builds upon current structures, people, and systems.[12] The result is that we end up with a "new" system that looks pretty much like the old one. The problem with this approach, if you follow the metaphor to its logical conclusion, is that when buildings are continually patched, they ultimately lose their structural integrity.

Schools are conservative in nature. Systems of education throughout the world have not seen significant improvement in terms of pedagogy in a long time. Historically, pedagogies have been the most efficient and effective ways of facilitating the kind of learning that allowed a student to earn a diploma and secure a job to make a decent living. American schools have been quite good at preparing people for low-cognitive-demand, repetitive tasks (e.g., assigning twenty-five math problems for homework that are all variants of the same problem—if you can do one, you can do them all). As economists Richard Murnane and Frank Levy argue, computers have replaced many of these "routine" tasks and the accompanying decent-paying jobs (e.g., filing and assembly line work). Today's economy (much less a thriving democracy) requires complex communication and problem solving.[13] Though Murnane and Levy called these "the new basic skills" fifteen years ago, there is little evidence that American schools are yet places where all or even most students are learning those skills.

Many educators understandably take a "this too shall pass" approach, hunkering down to avoid being battered by reforms that churn without moving learning forward. However, we do not think the networked learning revolution represented in part by Wikipedia will pass, whether or not educators join in.

The networked learning revolution will ultimately impact schools precisely because it is mostly bypassing schools. There is a lot of learning going on outside of schools.[14] The policy debate has been centered on changing the "formal learning environment" and has largely ignored the much larger "informal learning environment."

This informal sector is much freer of constraints. Constraints limit innovation; it is hard for an existing system to effect its own transformation. The more we try to engineer innovation to look and feel like what we recognize in formal systems, the less likely we are to evolve solutions that will work. This phenomenon has certainly proven relevant outside of education in business. Successful organizational reinventions are considered an anomaly (GE and IBM are the only two such cases in the Fortune 1000); in fact, one-third of the companies listed in the 1970 Fortune 500 vanished by 1983. There are very few old companies around today (e.g., Shell, IBM, GE). Whole industries that were thriving a generation ago have died; think tobacco and video stores. Economist and Harvard Business School professor Theodore Levitt suggests that an organization's ability to adapt, as well as its cohesion, tolerance, and control over its governance, are key to survival.[15] If these traits are indeed requisite with success in our society, it does not bode well for schools. Much more common is to see one set of goods fade into oblivion (e.g., any sort of Hi-Fi system or video device) while a newer system emerges that better meets the needs of society (the iPad). Christensen, Johnson, and Horn have argued reasonably that this is how things play out time and again.[16]

For a more institutional example of innovation's relationship to a venerable establishment, let's go back to the same printing press that made encyclopedias (and the knowledge contained within) more accessible. The institution most affected by the emergence of the printing press was the Catholic Church. Before the printing press, in the Christian world, religious knowledge was mediated through the portal of the Catholic Church and the men it ordained as interpreters of that knowledge. When the disruptive technology of the printing press emerged, bibles became more widely available and could be interpreted without an authority sanctioned by the Catholic Church. The Protestant Reformation ensued, and there is now a plurality of Christian denominations. We predict that something similar to this pattern will happen with schools: a revered institution that is working well for some people and not as well for others will be challenged as alternative, unmediated pathways to knowledge open up. Like the Catholic Church, schools may not disappear entirely, but they will no longer be able to claim a monopoly on what is worth knowing and how to know it.

In the future, people will have many more choices about how, and whether, they want to engage the institution called school, and for what purpose. We are less interested in protecting the franchise of school as the location of learning than we are interested in the long-term impact of the migration of learning into the world and the many forms it will take.

The Future Is Here; We Just Don't See It

The future of learning is here, and it is already happening. The shift from schooling to learning allows us to look for learning outside of current formal systems of schools, and to explore what schools might evolve into if we accept the premise that learning is here to stay and is ubiquitous. To build on the comparison of informal and formal learning, think of mapping a variety of learning experiences on a two-by-two continuum of how formal the learning is and where it takes place. Formal learning is largely inside schools and informal learning is largely outside schools, but it does not have to be that way, as described in several of the "futures are now" examples in the following sections. While there are many examples of individual schools in the U.S. embracing the future of learning, we are most interested in what we can learn from systems and organizations that are approaching learning on a broader scale. To that end, the following examples draw from both inside and outside of schools, and range from formal to informal.

Networks of Learners

Two examples of school systems embracing a different kind of learning are in Mexico and Australia. The Learning Community project, which we described in this chapter's opening, is currently operating in nearly six hundred rural schools in Mexico and will soon be expanded to nearly seven thousand schools across the country.

The state of Victoria in Australia comprises a system of sixteen hundred schools, roughly five hundred thousand students, and covers a land area about the size of Minnesota or Michigan. There are no local school districts in Victoria; all schools are governed as a unitary state system, with a relatively light regional structure. If you are a principal in Victoria, there are exactly two people between you and the person responsible for the whole system on the organizational chart. Because the system is necessarily light on control and overhead, it relies primarily on cultural means to produce its high quality and high student performance. The central idea in Victoria is to shape the overriding values and focus of the system, to provide support to schools consistent with that focus, and to increasingly use networks of schools to create and reinforce a culture of high performance.

In 2010, the Victorian system launched a technology initiative called the Ultranet (http://www.education.vic.gov.au/about/directions/ultranet/default.htm), an online resource to connect networks of learners, both teachers and students, and provide access to knowledge and learning, unbounded by geography. The system is ambitious in its architecture, and its rollout was accompanied by the predictable glitches of a leading-edge innovation. The Ultranet provides a single learning platform, a flexible interactive space that includes teacher-built curriculum materials, content and performance standards, and various forms of professional development materials for teachers and school leaders, as well as interactive spaces where students and teachers can communicate with their peers in other settings. Underneath the Ultranet, however, is a single big idea: learning will, in the future, happen through networks of learners—teachers and students—operating outside the constraints of the physical structure called school. Issues of population density; of urban, suburban, rural locations; of proximity to the primary nodes of knowledge will, over time, be diminished by the rich interactions of learners with common purposes. The role of the state—the "system"—is not to control and contain this learning, but to provide the infrastructure to support it. With the Ultranet, Victoria already has the vision and infrastructure to provide relatively unmediated access to learning for every student and teacher in the system, but the question remains whether its policy makers have the stamina to support it over time.

Structured learning. We are not suggesting that the transformation of learning means that all learning will be informal and self-directed. There are numerous examples that suggest a role for more formal learning experiences. A well-established example is in the U.S. military. The elite components of the military (Navy Seals, Green Berets, Army Rangers) have one thing in common: their primary designation as teachers. They spend a majority of their time designing and delivering state-of-the-art learning both to other members of the U.S. Armed Forces and to foreign military. In this model, the master becomes the teacher, and all special operations units have a primary responsibility of training. In addition, the military learning approach emphasizes experience (e.g., simulations and practice) combined with a significant feedback loop that also provides formal opportunities for continuous intraorganizational learning (what the military calls *after action reviews*).

On-the-job training is not strictly the purview of the military: U.S. employers spent $126 billion on employee learning and development in 2009, roughly equivalent to what all of higher education spent ($125 billion in 2009).[17] In any given year, 40 percent of all working adults are enrolled in career or job-related courses or apprenticeships.[18] As well, the single largest area in which companies focus their learning and development is remediation, with some 60 percent of budgets on average going to fix what the formal system failed to accomplish. Even when learning is relatively formal, it is migrating out of formal educa-tion institutions and into areas that involve experiential learning and ready application.

Mastery. While not all learning focuses on mastery, monitoring mas-tery will probably be an important part of schools' function in a future learning environment. Fortunately, we already have some cases illustrat-ing what this might look like. For example, the Boy Scouts and Girl Scouts have been evolving their system of badges that aspiring scouts can accrue for one hundred years. While Girl Scouts can still earn badges in cooking and camping, they now can also earn badges in dig-ital arts, financial literacy, local food awareness, and "netiquette" (as a badge within "manners"), as well as "make your own" badges, in which they pursue interests not captured by the current badge system. The Boy Scouts acknowledged and celebrated the ways that their merit badges have changed over time by offering four historical merit badges in 2010 for the one hundredth anniversary of the Boy Scouts of America: car-pentry, pathfinding (without a GPS!), signaling (with flags), and track-ing (animals). While Boy Scouts can still earn badges in hiking and first aid, they can also earn badges in nuclear science, entrepreneurship, robotics, and disabilities awareness. The Scouts set both a curriculum and an assessment system that allow for credentialing and promotion of their scouts. The John D. and Catherine T. MacArthur Foundation is now supporting the development of digital badge systems to inspire, support, and recognize lifelong learning. The concept is similar to scout-ing: people acquire skills and knowledge in a variety of settings, many of them informal, throughout their lifetimes, and it can be helpful (for personal motivation, for employers, etc.) if there is some signal of the acquisition of that skill and knowledge. In the MacArthur Foundation merit badge system, which is still in the early stages of development, the assessing agency is some formal organization, like a community group, company, or college. Once the agency affirms that the badge is earned, the recipient collects badges in an online CV. Digital badge systems in development include science, technology, engineering, and math; manufacturing; young adult library services; and wilderness explorers. One could imagine systems of schools adopting similar approaches.

In the world of corporate learning, the American National Standards Institute (www.ANSI.org) and its international mirror organization, the International Standards Organization (www.iso.org) recently released standards for certifying nonformal learning. They recognize that any "high quality" learning has some design elements—some attention paid to the learner, the method of instruction, and the expertise of the designers and "subject matter experts," and a system of evaluating the process and the outcomes. This approach has now been adopted by some fifty countries and organizations (not only corporate learning organizations, but also nonformal learning organizations such as dance schools, scuba diving schools, and language schools). These organizations can now get a stamp of approval whereby they demonstrate that they are "certified" as delivering what they promise, even though the promise delivered varies significantly based on learner, content, and teleology.

The world of higher education offers another intriguing example, Thomas Edison State University. This public, regionally accredited college in New Jersey offers degrees, but does not offer courses or employ faculty. Instead, it has evaluators who assess the varied learning experiences of its adult students. Students present College-Level Examination Program® (CLEP) scores, Council for Adult and Experiential Learning (CAEL) portfolios, American Council on Education's College Credit Recommendation Service (CREDIT) feedback, and individual courses taken at any host of institutions. The Thomas Edison State University evaluators map out that individual learning against a proposed associate's or bachelor's degree and either identify gaps that the student must learn in some structured way or award the degree.

Lifewide Learning

Rather than talk about "lifelong learning," a popular mantra in education vision statements and what schools are allegedly preparing children for, Joseph Blatt at the Harvard Graduate School of Education and many of his colleagues talk about "lifewide learning," which is an explicit acknowledgment that learning can and does happen in every facet of life, particularly in those hours beyond school. Media plays a large role in lifewide learning. Though television in its early days was primarily for entertainment, *Sesame Street*, which premiered in 1969, demonstrated that shows for children could be entertaining *and* instructional. Today, there are a plethora of shows and channels—as well as other media forms such as computer and video games—devoted to learning for both children and adults. A recent study by the Kaiser Family Foundation found that youth ages eight to eighteen spend approximately seven and a half hours a day using media, which is more than they spend in school each day.[19] And the youth are spending about 180 days in school per year, while they are using media every day. In other words, youth are devoting more than double the time to consuming media than they are spending in school.

Beyond media, many other institutions and organizations have learning as a core part of their mission and embrace pleasure as intermingled with learning. Take museums, for example. The American Association of Museums estimates that annually 850 million people visit museums in the United States. According to the Association's definition, the primary raison d'être for museums is "education and enjoyment." Similarly, the National Park Service counted 281 million "recreational" visits in 2010. Of those visits, 34 million were to historical sites (national historical parks, national military parks, and national battlefield parks), and the National Park Service devotes millions of dollars to programming and educational services for people of all ages.[20]

But What About . . . or, What Is School for, Anyway?

To the extent that learning displaces schooling rather than schools reinventing themselves and becoming portals of lifewide learning, you might be wondering what will happen to all of the other services that schools provide. After all, schools serve a number of other functions that society values—sometimes more than learning. These functions include socializing, credentialing, safekeeping, and sorting.

The first two are the easiest to imagine in a future learning world, and in fact, that world might do them better than current schools do. Socializing, or learning to collaborate and work with others, particularly across differences, is likely to be at the core of any future learning, whether networked or individual. Preparation for participating in a democracy would no doubt be stronger if learning relied on individuals exercising agency and analyzing information wisely in relation to others, whose views and knowledge might differ.

Credentialing has historically been an important function of schools, but a high school diploma already means a lot less than it used to. Attainment still matters, but there is an increasing emphasis on actual learning in the job market—what you know and are able to do. The focus is shifting in higher education, too, which will make a college diploma less valuable than the learning that graduates can demonstrate. The trend is toward proficiency—what we've called "mastery" throughout this chapter—and future learning will likely rely on it heavily as the primary indicator of what has been learned.

The other two functions will probably look quite a bit different in a future learning world. The custodial function of schools is essential. If schools do not serve that function, something else has to, as all three authors (who are also working parents!) appreciate. We understand the need for a safe place for children to be during the day that does not necessarily rely on their parents' presence during work hours. We can imagine a world that has multiple such safe places, whether in existing school buildings, in businesses, or in community venues, and that deploys adult resources differently so that children actually could be in those places for parents' full working day, rather than until midafternoon. Sugata Mitra provides a compelling vision of alternative ways to organize the physical setting for children to learn together—all the way from conventional school to holes in the wall to a physical structure he created as a minimally mediated environment for small groups to learn.[21] There is a wide variety of ways we can ensure the care and welfare of children in learning. Many dilapidated school buildings are getting replaced, which presents an opportunity to design spaces for "lifewide learning" that are also safe places where we'd feel comfortable leaving our children for eight to ten hours—or even four hours, if that is the schedule that worked for our families. At the moment, most of those brand-new buildings are designed for old learning.

Though we are not convinced that future learning would necessarily raise the level of U.S. performance globally or reduce the variability in performance among U.S. students, we do think that future learning will sort students differently than current schooling does. Despite the valiant (and in small pockets, successful) efforts of many educators to make race, class, and learning differences not be the greatest determinants of both attainment and achievement in our current system, the fact is that schools perpetuate the deep inequities in American society. This is not acceptable, whether you choose to make a moral or economic argument.

One substantive difference between the shift we envision and the current status quo is that learning will be much more the responsibility of the learner. This could create much greater equity of opportunity than exists now, reward agency and motivation, and focus on performance as a means of measuring accomplishment rather than on the ability to enact the superficial activities of school. All of these—performance, motivation, agency, and equity—are important features of a democracy in which all citizens can meaningfully and thoughtfully contribute. However, there's no guarantee that when given the opportunity, learners will embrace it and know what to do with it.

Students whom our schools currently tend to serve least well—students living in poverty; students whose first language is not English; students with special needs; students who learn better through their hands than their heads; students of African American, Hispanic, and/ or Native American heritage; students without a strong support system at home—have the most to gain or lose in any fundamental transformation of "school." This means we will need to have conversations about what supports are necessary to help all students be successful. We will also need to challenge some current assumptions about high-poverty students of color needing schools to serve a more custodial function in order to succeed.

"Custodial" does not have to mean low-level, structured, and, to put it bluntly, a version of middle-class white behaviors. Interestingly, as a practical matter, many of the ways advantaged people learn are already consistent with the future learning we are describing. Good private schools encourage arts, sports, and pursuits beyond traditional academics and give students opportunities to develop and follow their interests. Graduate school and adults pursuing their own interests outside of formal schooling also look a lot like the world we're describing. As a society, we have often assumed that poor children and children of color are not ready for this kind of high-agency, enriched learning, and that they must instead learn some "basics" first (i.e., boring recall tasks, or as we often see in classrooms, tasks that don't even scrape the bottom of Bloom's taxonomy). As school breaks down as a primary mediator of learning and opportunity, one of the things we are most looking forward to is children showing us what they are really capable of.

The Transformation of Learning

As learning migrates out into the world, and as use—not adoption—becomes the primary determinant of technology's impact on learning, we will face an enormous collective-goods problem: whether individual choices about learning benefit society as a whole. This problem has an interesting structure, since it does not really offer a choice point for public policy makers. Learning will migrate whether we choose to treat it as a public policy problem or not. In other words, left to its own devices, the migration of learning from the increasingly outmoded structure called school to the world at large will happen whether we choose to try to influence it or not. The collective-goods problem hinges on access.

Inequality of access to learning could be the major determinant of the social impact of transformation in learning. This issue is complicated by the fact that the prevailing ideological temper of the United States seems to not acknowledge the existence of collective goods, let alone how they might be affected by individual choice in a learning system.

Learning is becoming more and more ubiquitous, and a significant portion of it is located outside of schools. The availability of relatively cheap technologies offering direct access to all types of knowledge dramatically increases students' choices of what, with whom, and how they learn. The greater availability of more external educational resources and a less stringent regulatory environment suggest to us that outside of schools is where the action will continue to be. That said, this evolution will not happen in a vacuum. The extent to which this shift is perceived as competitive or complementary to the formal system will dictate what happens within it and its schools.

In the 1960s, Sloan professor Theodore Levitt wrote an interesting piece that told the story of the buggy whip.[22] In it, the "best" producer of buggy whips, not recognizing that the auto industry was emerging, continued to make good buggy whips. The producer grabbed almost a 100 percent market share of what became a very small market.

We could envision schools and school systems becoming the learning equivalent of the buggy whip. Certain students and their families will find the old system more comfortable or more suitable and elect to stay with it for their educational needs. However, over time, the more effective and more efficient offerings will come to dominate a new learning market that will evolve into a decentralized formal system. This will be compounded by the fact that—similar to what happened with the savings and loan industry, which used to have a large number of local providers, or to the old Ma Bell system—technology will force a national system of regulation and also will blow apart the system of local finance. What family, for example, will want to live in a high-tax neighborhood for its school district when it can instead consume the very best learning from an eclectic array of providers that is not limited by geography? In this scenario, schools will simply fade away.

However, if school systems begin to realize that they do not need to control every step of the learning process, they can use that as an opportunity to reinvent themselves. Rather than developing and delivering all learning to a limited group of students, systems could be student solution providers that aggregate, coordinate, and leverage disparate learning activities based on students' needs. We can see hints of such a system in Joel Rose's School of One and in the system of schools approach in New Orleans.[23] If the political will is there, we envision this as the "best" scenario for the various stakeholders in learning.

A less radical approach might focus more on shifting from a compliance orientation to a learning orientation. The mundane world of compliance training offers a perspective on what it would take for organizations to make this shift. Historically, compliance or safety training has been housed, designed, and managed by organizations' legal counsel. The goal was simply to demonstrate to the certifying agency (e.g., the U.S. Securities and Exchange Commission or the Occupational Safety and Health Administration) that the training had taken place. The "student" spent the obligatory time in a seat at the training session, and any tests were geared toward checking that the student had comprehended the training rather than demonstrating any sort of competency. More recently, some organizations have framed compliance as a learning issue rather than a legal issue. In other words, rather than simply providing training on sexual harassment in order to meet some court-mandated order, the firm actually buys into the notion that a positive and safe work environment increases productivity. As a consequence, its design, delivery, and evaluation have changed (i.e., moved away from a "check the box" model to an assessment of knowledge or skill attainment), and the responsibility for the learning lies with a human resource/development department.

While the compliance training example is not as radical as one where learning is completely unmediated by a central organization, it offers a window into what a shift from compliance to task-based learning might look like for schools. We could imagine a process that certifies entities and requires them to articulate and document their approach to learning for particular students, an approach that might simply include integrating a wide array of nonformal learning into a coherent curriculum. Given the evolutionary track record of many systems, it's quite possible that this process will uncover other, more able, producers of education. Take, for example, GE, which has been a fairly vocal corporate citizen advocating for improved education. It spends roughly 2 percent of its $42 billion operating budget on learning in its organization. Within the world of corporate training, Crotonville (its leadership development center in Ossining, New York) is seen as the mecca, and Steve Kerr, its first CLO (chief learning officer), who oversaw it for then-CEO Jack Welch, is viewed as the oracle; one need only Google either to get overwhelmed by the praise. In addition, all of its philanthropy goes toward schools in areas where it has facilities. Given that the company has expertise and contributes significant resources to learning, is it such a leap to imagine that a new sort of "Fordism" would emerge whereby it might get certified to run charter schools in its facilities for employees' families? Such systems would not compete with learning happening in nonformal settings, but rather, would augment it to provide some of the traditional school functions such as socialization and keeping children safe and off the streets. One could imagine all sorts of iterations. The school becomes analogous to a platform with multiple portals for learning. If the "curriculum" were a movie, one might watch it at home, on TV, or elsewhere on a smartphone or tablet.

There is a lot of learning going on inside and outside of schools, formal and informal. School could become less and less relevant as a narrow, fixed portal. Or, it could allow the lines between "inside" and "outside," between "formal" and "informal" to blur, becoming an organizing platform for a flexible set of portals.

In the future, will schools be different? Will they be better? Will learning be different? Will it be better?

Learning will be different. Answers to the other questions depend on whether we recognize how learning is changing all around us and shift from thinking about schools as the single portal through which all important learning flows. This shift will not happen overnight, but now is an exciting opportunity to embrace and accelerate learning.

Whatever the learning pathways, learners and all the people who support them—from communities to educators to policy makers—will need to ask and answer questions about learning and then figure out the role of schooling based on those answers. We nominate the following set of questions:

- How does learning work?
- How are learners different?
- What is worth learning?
- What kind of knowledge matters?
- How is it best learned?
- How do we know it is being learned?
- How do we improve learning at scale?

If we are serious about having all children learn, we cannot leave it entirely up to each child to decide whether to do so. A model that relies solely on individual motivation is going to produce widely variable results. But we can also think back to the Mexico example, in which individuals are learning and then becoming leaders who make learning a collective enterprise, in which everyone benefits from the motivation and accomplishments of others. We must consider the role of adults in this kind of system. Helping children be ready to learn (e.g., promoting their physical and emotional health), providing support and accountability to motivate learning, offering ideas about what might be worth learning, and sharing expertise produce an educational system that serves students and answers the seven questions we have just offered.

Let's return to our encyclopedia/Wikipedia example for a moment, and let's focus on the "pedia" part. Remember that "pedia" comes from *paideia*, the Greek word for child rearing, which is sometimes also translated as education. In the 1980s, education philosopher Mortimer Adler wrote *The Paideia Proposal*, a slender treatise on education reform. Adler posited several core principles, including:

- All children can learn.
- Therefore, they all deserve the same quality of schooling, not just the same quantity.
- The quality of schooling to which they are entitled is what the wisest parents would wish for their own children, the best education for the best being the best education for all.
- Schooling at its best is preparation for becoming generally educated in the course of a whole lifetime, and schools should be judged on how well they provide such preparation.
- The three callings for which schooling should prepare all Americans are: (a) to earn a decent livelihood, (b) to be a good citizen of the nation and the world, and (c) to make a good life for oneself.
- The primary cause of genuine learning is the activity of the learner's own mind, sometimes with the help of a teacher functioning as a secondary and cooperative cause.[24]

It should not just be professional educators asking and answering the seven learning questions or determining how to live the Paideia principles. There is power in asking and answering such questions. In the learning system of the future, power has to be shared with the coproducers of learning—namely, students and communities. We invite you to share in the answers, to help shape quality, lifewide, active-mind learning for all children.

7

THE COURAGE TO ACHIEVE
OUR AMBITIONS

Five Pathways for the Future

Jal Mehta

THE ESSAYS IN THIS VOLUME offer some significantly different paths forward for American schooling. In a field replete with cycles and fads, what we provide here is not a new set of ideas du jour, but rather an assertion that if we want to achieve significant improvements in performance we will need to make significant changes in the underlying structure of American schooling. While it is tempting to think that if only we find the right program or figure out how to scale this or that pilot we will have much better schools, the record suggests that feeding new reforms through the existing system is unlikely to achieve the results we seek.

In the pages that follow, I briefly outline the limits of current reform strategies, suggest five pathways that would alter major dimensions of the American school system, and then consider these pathways in light of the values we aspire to for schooling. My overall argument is that if we want schools that are not in the middle of the pack internationally, that do not produce huge gaps in outcomes by race and class, and that are the schools we would aspire to for our own children, we need to fundamentally change at least one dimension of the American school system.

So Little Real Reform, So Little Real Change

The past three decades have produced a wide array of efforts aimed at reforming schooling in the United States. Since *A Nation at Risk* sounded the alarm in 1983, we have seen a blitzkrieg of reforms—virtually every idea, it seems, has found a champion in a foundation, district, or state.[1] But, if we step back a bit, we observe that, from the perspective of the more significant changes proposed here, much of this activity has simply reinforced our existing system. Very little has actually been *re-formed*; rather, what was previously formed created the contours into which new "reforms" were applied. Consider four examples, drawn from across the ideological spectrum.

The Standards Movement

Perhaps the most powerful school reform movement in America since the 1980s has been the standards movement. First sweeping across the states and then becoming encoded in federal law, standards promised to clarify goals, measure results, and impose accountability. Advocates argued that standards had the potential to unify a highly disparate and localized system, and to force schools to prioritize instruction. But while standards have effected a significant change in governance (from local to state to federal) and have arguably had success as a political movement (in getting many actors in the system to focus on improving academic outcomes), they have not been able to fundamentally change the performance of the system. Two leading standards advocates, Robert Schwartz and Paul Reville, say in this volume that while they still believe in standards, they think that standards are at best necessary but not sufficient to generate the significant improvements in performance we seek.

Why haven't standards had more of an effect? The answers are complex and will be discussed at more length shortly, but perhaps the most basic observation is that by themselves standards do not fundamentally change much in terms of the relationship between teachers, students, and learning. Under standards, we still have the same kids, in the same schools, for the same school day, with the same teachers, with the day split up in the same way, with much the same set of tracked courses, and with the same level of parental support. Teachers have new goals to shoot for, but they do not have any new skills with which to meet those goals. The one real change under 2001's No Child Left Behind Act (NCLB) is that there are public consequences for failing to get more students above a proficiency bar in reading and math, and therefore more schools have devoted more of their time and attention to those subjects and those tests. Standards essentially sought to wring more out of the existing system. The result, at best, has been some progress toward the measured indicators (particularly in math) but little of the significant improvement that we aspire to. At worst, the high-stakes accountability we have seen under NCLB has narrowed learning and further bureaucratized education, taking the "one best system" erected in the Progressive Era and reinforcing its emphasis on compliance through top-down mandates from districts, states, and the federal government.

Performance Pay

Another reform that has become increasingly popular in recent years is paying teachers for performance. Again, what is revealing here is the way that these "reforms" are layered into the existing system: teachers are still teaching the same number of students, in the same schools, aiming at the same goals, and with the same knowledge and skills they had before. We aren't changing their roles; we aren't rewarding them for coming up with new and better ways to teach that could be shared. All we're doing is reallocating small amounts of money across existing teachers, based on their students' test scores (and sometimes other factors). Performance pay may or may not be a good idea, but it is undoubtedly a *small* idea—it doesn't really seek to reshape any of the major aspects of schooling.

Charter Schools

In one sense, charter schools are potentially a more radical reform, in that they create a space outside of the regular public system in which schools are freer to experiment with new practices and ideas—at least, this was the idea when they were created. But the result has again been a kind of conformity with the norm: much of the research on these schools suggests that they don't look much different from the public schools down the road—same age-graded classrooms, same subjects, same roles for teachers, same levels of teacher training and skill. Organizational sociologists call this *isomorphism*—the tendency of all entities in a field to copy one another, even in the absence of regulations requiring conformity or any evidence that the replicated practices are working. (There is a subset of charters that has in some ways been more different; we return to them later in this chapter.)

Twenty-First-Century Skills

The latest reform is "twenty-first-century skills." In some ways, this example poses a greater challenge to the school system than the previous ones: while there is nothing particularly "twenty-first century" about asking students to think critically or engage in higher-order problem solving, it would represent a fairly radical shift if schools actually and consistently prioritized these ends. I cannot tell you how many classrooms I have visited in schools—city, suburban, and rural; charter and regular public—in which students are still being given worksheets and asked to do no more than recall information. If all of these classrooms became places where students were really asked to think, it would be a major change. But there is no reason to think that this is likely to happen; the mechanism through which twenty-first-century skills are being pursued is very twentieth century—creating yet another set of standards and new assessments to match. The jury on these new standards is still out, but past experience suggests that twenty-first-century skills are likely to be assimilated into the existing structure. Schools are more likely to change reforms than reforms to change schools, as David Tyack and Larry Cuban famously put it.[2]

Overall, while we have been busy over the past three decades, we have not fundamentally changed much of the existing system, and some efforts have actually reinforced that system. As a result, while some have characterized the period as one of "so much reform and so little change," it might be more accurate to say, "so little real reform," and, not surprisingly, "so little real change."

Why Can't the Existing System Realize Our Goals?

As has been frequently noted, our existing system dates to the Progressive Era and was neither designed nor intended to do what we ask of it today. At the time of its creation, increasing waves of students were overwhelming the capacity of one-room schoolhouses, and a bureaucratic system seemed to promise a way to develop a more organized and efficient approach to schooling. Bureaucracy was seen as an antidote to patronage and nepotism, while command-and-control managerial systems were at the cutting edge of business practice. Most students were not expected to finish high school, let alone go to college; up through the 1960s, one could acquire a decent job on the basis of simply graduating from high school. While there were significant inequalities in that system in terms of race, gender, and class, these were not widely seen as public problems. Schools were explicitly in the business of sorting students, which was accepted practice. In a variety of ways, we had much lower expectations for schooling, and, as a result, schools were more able to realize those expectations.

Over the past forty years, and particularly in the past twenty-five, our expectations of our schools have increased dramatically, and the existing school system has been unable to adapt to meet these new and more ambitious aims. The combination of the civil rights revolution and the shift toward a knowledge economy has created pressure for all schools to prepare their students for college-level work. These new imperatives have arrived during the same period that many more occupational choices have opened up for women, the traditional mainstay of the teaching profession; consequently, the system is trying to accomplish more with less. Deindustrialization of cities and out-migration of advantaged families to suburbs have also concentrated poverty and increased the challenge for many schools that still reside in the urban core. By the end of the last century, bureaucratic systems of top-down control were seen as highly inefficient and unresponsive, but these organizational forms persist. In short, the challenge has become more difficult, our ambitions have grown, and the inertial pull of the organizational system within which we work has come to be seen as increasingly dysfunctional.

Why specifically is our existing school system unable to realize ambitious goals? While the authors of the previous chapters do not entirely agree, they do highlight a number of similar themes. Among them are:

- *Much of what passes for reform does not get at the instructional core.* At the end of the day, it's the triangle between the students, the teachers, and the material that counts. If your reform doesn't change that triangle, it's not likely to change student outcomes.
- *Bureaucratic systems are out of touch and not oriented toward learning.* Our ideologically heterodox group was virtually unanimous on this point: the bureaucratic system in which public schools work is more focused on compliance with rules from above than with supporting improvements in practice.
- *Teachers just do not possess the needed expertise to create good schooling consistently.* Chapters 1 and 2, in particular, argue that the core problem is American teachers' lack of sufficient expertise to consistently generate quality practice. The authors contrast the situation in the United States to international examples

where teaching is a more selective profession and training is more extensive.

- *The system is too standardized.* A familiar but important point—one-size-fits-all programs that do not capitalize on the varieties of student and teacher motivation are likely to be alienating and unlikely to fit the great variety of problems they are seeking to address.

- *Cycling priorities from above are not conducive to long-term strategies of improvement.* As described most sharply in Frederick Hess's book, *Spinning Wheels,* leadership at the top tends to cycle, with each new superintendent embracing a new set of priorities, only to be replaced in a few years with yet another cycle.[3] This pattern produces distrust and a "wait it out" attitude from teachers and schools, and eliminates the possibility of sketching a long-term strategy for improvement and change.

The aforementioned points are probably familiar to those who have read the school reform literature. The underlying ethos of these critiques is more reformist than revolutionary: the implication is that the existing system could work if only administrators were more attuned to practice, teaching were more professionalized, or political priorities were set over the longer term. However, some of the authors also advance more radical reasons why the system does not work:

- *The job of teaching is just too hard.* As Frederick Hess, Greg Gunn, and Olivia Meeks argue, "If most people can't do a job well most of the time, you can make the job easier, or split it into multiple pieces, or lean more heavily on tools. Any of those strike us as a more promising route than holding a casting call for 3 million superheroes."[4] We ask teachers to know content, to instruct 125–175 students, to take care of both their academic and social needs, as well as to prepare, grade, and handle administrative responsibilities. Perhaps that's just too much if we want students to achieve at a consistently high academic level.

- *Schools are too insular, too isolated from the larger world.* As Elizabeth City, Richard Elmore, and Doug Lynch argue in chapter 6, learning is moving much faster outside of schools than in them. While knowledge in the world continues to expand rapidly, teachers and students are largely stuck with the tiny sliver of it that is approved by states, districts, boards, and schools.
- *Schools cannot do the job alone.* As Jeffrey Henig, Helen Janc Malone, and Paul Reville argue in chapter 5, unless students—particularly high-poverty students—are given significant social support for the hours they are not in school, the job of schooling will remain too difficult to consistently succeed.

Given this litany of challenges, it should not be surprising that our past reform strategies have not generated more significant improvement. For all that they aim to change, what is significant is what they do not change. Pilot programs do not scale up because they do not fundamentally change any of the features of the existing system. *In sum, we put reforms through our existing system and when they don't work as we'd hoped, we ask what's wrong with the reform—when we should instead be asking what's wrong with the system.*

Five Paths for the Future: Transforming, Replacing, Reassembling, Expanding, or Dissolving the System

So how might we get out of this dead end and think anew about how to create a better school system? These essays make clear that if we want significant improvement, we need not just to reform the system but to rethink the assumptions of the system. It is tempting in a frenetic reform environment to focus on what is immediately doable, particularly since so many advocates are sure they know what we need to do. The problem is that we've been following this course for decades, and all the rush-rush winds up yielding merely more of the same. While fundamental rethinking may seem frustrating and unduly slow, we believe that its value will be appreciated only in retrospect. That's the nature of significant change.

This is a volume dedicated to the long view. What would it mean to design a better system that might have a reasonable prospect of helping all students learn at higher levels?

Across the essays, there are five paths to fundamental change: *transforming, replacing, reassembling, enlarging,* or *dissolving* the existing system. Each perspective brings to light a set of constraints or boundaries that we are reluctant to challenge and considers what it would mean to reform the system without them blocking our way. My discussion of these paths draws on the essays, but I have taken the liberty to combine certain ideas and add others in order to present starkly the choices that confront us.

Transforming the System: Following the International Path, from Bureaucratic Hierarchies to a Knowledge Profession

The essays in chapters 1 and 2 make the case that the core of the problem in the U.S. system is that it is staffed by people who just don't know how to do the work well enough. The international evidence they cite suggests that leading systems draw teachers from the top third of their distribution, give them extensive practice-based training, and create opportunities for their ongoing professional development. The second essay finds fault not only with the people but also with the knowledge pipeline, contending that we need to develop and draw upon more usable knowledge as we train a core of more talented people. In short, the argument here is that we have relied upon bureaucratic mechanisms to solve what is essentially a knowledge and expertise problem, and that there is no shortcut to actually increasing the knowledge and expertise across the system. For historical reasons, the American educational field has failed to professionalize; only by creating a true profession will we be able to generate consistently high-quality results. The problem is that we keep feeding reforms through a failed structure—so we need to change the structure to a more professional one.

The implications of making this choice would not be soft talk about professionalism. It would mean rethinking all aspects of the human capital pipeline: attracting more able applicants into the field, creating more extensive field-based training, lengthening the time to tenure and making tenure a high bar of demonstrated teaching effectiveness, and providing continued opportunities for growth and professional development for practicing teachers. Parallel to the development of people would be the creation of a new knowledge infrastructure, which would grow out of practice but play a similar orienting role for the profession that knowledge plays in more established fields. Over time, mastering this knowledge would become the *sine qua non* of membership in the profession. That, in turn, would ensure a consistency across teachers and schools that is sorely missing in the present environment.

From one point of view, this proposal is the least radical one. Our basic governance system could remain unchanged, schools would still look like schools, and most students would still go to the physical building down the road. But what happens *inside* these familiar structures would be radically transformed. Teachers would teach on the basis of developed and shared knowledge about good practice rather than depending solely on whatever wisdom they could acquire individually. Power relations would change to be more akin to what we find in medicine: rather than being seen as the lowest rung on an implementation chain, teachers would be considered experts in their field and so possess a degree of professional power. As with countries in which ministries of education have greater control over the education system, increased professional power could serve as a counterweight to political efforts to toss education about like a political football. In turn, this stability would allow the new system to develop the long-term perspective and consistent priorities that have marked the improvement trajectories of higher performing nations.

A significant part of what makes this approach so daunting and hard to realize in the American context is cultural. The approach emphasizes professional expertise, collective control over standards of entry to the field, and trust that schools and teachers are using their power for the collective good. The United States is a society with a marked skepticism of professional expertise, a strongly individualistic culture, and a rampant distrust of government in general and the school system in particular. It is no coincidence that the American strategies of school reform have been long on measurement, accountability, and evaluation of individual teacher performance, while international leaders have emphasized training, developing the collective capacities of teachers, and giving teachers autonomy to utilize their skills. Any effort to move toward a professionalizing strategy of reform will need to confront these cultural obstacles and make a case for the strategy in ways that resonate with Americans.

At the same time, there are a number of developments that might give hope to those championing a professionalizing approach. The criticisms that the professionalizers raise about the failure of state bureaucracies can find common cause with market critics of these same bureaucracies. The findings of international studies that suggest the need to draw more talented students into teaching are consistent with American beliefs in the power of meritocratic selection. (Indeed, when I share this finding with public audiences, it is always one of the most resonant points.) American medicine has been the envy of the world (not American health care and policy, but the underlying system of producing doctors and the science that supports the field), and thus remains a powerful example. The creation of the Program for International Student Assessment (PISA) and the increasing interest in the policy community in international examples—particularly countries that fare better than the United States on common metrics—are providing fresh momentum to these ideas. And, finally, this approach has the virtue of already having succeeded at some scale: what it proposes is not something that works in pilot programs and needs to be scaled up, but a systemic approach that has already produced results. The question is whether the century-old American bureaucratic system can be transformed into this kind of twenty-first-century education profession.

Replacing the System: Reform from the Outside In

A second possibility is that the system constructed in the Progressive Era will gradually be replaced by a new set of actors and institutions. As Steven Teles and I have argued elsewhere, each institution that serves a major function in the current system faces challengers seeking to replace it:

> Charter operators like KIPP, Green Dot, and Achievement First are competing with traditional public schools; Teach for America, The New Teacher Project, and a variety of other alternative certification providers are creating new routes for entering teachers; charter networks have created their own teacher preparation institutions like Teacher U in New York and the High Tech High Graduate School of Education in California to replace traditional education school training; foundations like the Broad Foundation and the Walton Foundation are actively funding economists and others from outside of the usual educational research world to do what they view as more rigorous analysis; state-level advocates like ConnCAN and its spin-off 50 CAN, and national organizations like The Center for Education Reform and the Alliance for School Choice are developing political support for their alternatives; and superintendents like Alan Bersin, Paul Vallas, and Michelle Rhee have run districts as if the bureaucracies they administer are, at least in part, their enemies. A longstanding cartel now has an active challenger. While numerically still small in comparison to the much larger traditional cohort, these challengers have received enormous media attention, have considerable influence in a number of major cities (e.g., Washington, D.C., New York, and New Orleans), and have increasingly had their ideas incorporated into federal policy.[5]

There are at least two variants of the replacement scenario. One is what we might think of as "open markets." The idea, which is described in greater detail by Terry Moe and Paul Hill in chapter 3, is that by opening up the provision of education to a much greater array of providers, new methods will emerge, and the market will decide which succeed and which fail. The role of the regulatory structure is not to pick winners and losers, but to create a fairly open and fair playing field in which providers can compete for parent and student attention. The popularity (if not always the efficacy) of charter schools and the growth of home schooling show that there is considerable appetite among the public for creating new options. While to date there is not evidence that charters on the whole outperform regular publics, Moe and Hill argue that in the much longer run, newer providers will find ways to meet parent and student demand that we can hardly imagine today. Particularly with the possibilities afforded by technology, they argue, the labor-intensive traditional structures of teaching will give way to more efficient, Web-based ways of delivering content. Without rehashing familiar arguments about choice or market-based systems, it is worth simply noting that there is not yet evidence that new providers, in general, outperform old ones; however, it's hard to know whether this would change if more choice were given to parents and a national market were created for schooling.

The other version of the replacement scenario—and the one that has caught much of the media and public attention—is what we might call the "reform community" vision. Its starting point is the fact that there already is a subset of these new providers whose students are showing higher levels of success by conventional metrics. In this view, the goal should be to expand their reach. Ironically, we had a few members of these self-identified reformers as part of our Futures group at the outset, but they are not represented in this volume because the immediacy of their work superseded their desire to join us in writing about the future. But in meetings they argued that the future was already here and that they were in the process of creating it every day. The question was how to scale their efforts to reach an increasing number of high-poverty kids. While still numerically very small, this community has ambitions to make its operators the preferred schools in many of the nation's cities, and, thus, in a sense, to replace the existing system when it comes to high-poverty students.

What is most heartening about these developments is the energy and optimism that this mostly young group of people has brought to the field; their determination to create functioning examples of successful practice rather than to write papers or engage in philosophical debates; and their careful and detailed attention to the nuts and bolts of practice and the principles of continuous improvement. The success of the Knowledge Is Power Program (KIPP), Achievement First, and other "no excuses" schools in helping high-poverty students who enter their schools several grade levels behind to leave those same schools at grade level or above is a remarkable credit to their hard work and shows that demography is not destiny. Even acknowledging that those schools have some advantages in recruiting students, fairly careful lottery studies have shown that the elite among these charters are having a substantial impact. These schools feel like they are part of a different culture than that in most urban public schools—a more coherent one with more optimism about what students can achieve, more attention to data, more frequent and relevant coaching and feedback to teachers, and more autonomous school leaders. They are also, in my experience, much more interested in both developing and "begging, borrowing, and stealing" usable knowledge, as they carefully study what is working in their schools and try to learn from other schools in their networks. All of this is to the good; when given the warrant to start over and freed of a century's worth of regulations and inefficiencies, these operators have come up with new and much-closer-to-practice ways of developing effective schools.

There are at least two major sets of challenges to this version of replacement: one about the model itself, and one about scaling it. The problem with the model itself, as a number of critics have increasingly noted, is that the pedagogy used by the "no excuses" schools tends to focus more on building basic skills and less on helping students do more advanced and conceptual work. Many classes in these schools tend to be highly micromanaged; everything from how students sit to how they write is carefully prescribed. Work in good high schools, in college, and in the workplace is not like that: tasks are more open-ended; self- and internal motivation is important; and you must be able to work in groups, and most critically, to think independently and creatively. To their credit, a number of charter operators recognize this problem and are trying to devolve more authority to students as they get older. But there is a very real question of whether a model that was essentially created to make students more disciplined and focused on basic academic work can be transformed into one that helps students think openly and critically.

Even if we put aside questions of pedagogy, these schools continue to face the question of whether they can scale. The essential model is highly human-capital-intensive—it requires finding lots of young, talented people who are willing to work extremely long hours and be intensely improvement-oriented, despite little initial training and very modest pay. There is limited innovation here in the model of how schooling is produced; it's mostly just *more*—more hours, more care in the details of implementation, and more work on the part of both teachers and students. Not surprisingly, burnout is a problem for many of the young teachers. And the careful emphasis on ensuring quality also acts as an impediment to scale—good charter networks grow slowly so that they can ensure the quality of each new school. New programs run by schools to train teachers are also tiny islands in the vast ocean of teacher training.

Recent years have suggested that one possible next step for these reformers may be to extend their reach by integrating their work into the existing system. Networks like New Visions for Public Schools, Expeditionary Learning, and the Mass Math and Science Initiative, which partner with districts and schools rather than running their own charters, provide a hybrid model that is somewhere between a charter management organization and a conventional district. In the longer run, even greater scale would be possible if conventional districts and states were to adopt more of the practices that characterize the work of the reform community. And there is interest in this among enlightened leaders on the traditional side, who are trying to create pilot schools, in-district charters, and other hybrid forms. However, because much of what differentiates the reformers is their culture and human capital, there is a substantial risk that efforts to transfer the work into a more traditional context would result in the loss of much of what makes their schools effective.

Reassembling the System: Putting the Parts Together Anew for the Twenty-First Century

If the reform community wants to replace the existing system with a parallel one that it hopes would be better, chapter 4 goes one step further by suggesting the "unbundling" of the system, or reassembling it anew. The core idea here is to break apart the composite structures that make up schooling today. Rather than have a school that offers math, science, English, and history, have a school function as a general contractor, bringing in different organizations that excel in teaching the various subjects. Some of these subjects might be taught online rather than in person, or through a combination of online practice and in-person coaching. Teachers might specialize also—some might teach lots of small discussion sections, while others would teach large lectures; some might teach fractions to all upper elementary students, as opposed to teaching a range of math subjects to one fourth-grade class. Schools might function more like hospitals, with star teachers analogous to doctors and a range of support personnel performing functions that do not need to be done by teachers. Students would also be able to create much more customized learning experiences, as they might choose different providers in different content areas or, within content areas, use unbundled materials that would allow them to proceed at their own pace. (In a pretechnological version of this, I was offered a math curriculum in middle school that included numerous booklets at different levels of math; students moved sequentially through the booklets, at different paces, and the teacher checked the work and offered help as needed.) An unbundled world is one that allows, and invites, real creativity in determining how to assemble the core elements of schooling in a way that is responsive to the diversity of student needs and teacher skills, creating a much more flexible system than the batch-processing factory model that has governed us for the past century.

One virtue of this approach is that it offers a different, and potentially more compelling, tack to address the question of scale. Those who focus on scaling often emphasize that we have certain programs or schools that work well, and so the question is how to get more of them. The unbundlers, by contrast, say that if we reimagine how we fundamentally organize the work, scale will no longer be such a daunting challenge. Specifically, rather than trying to find 3.6 million highly knowledgeable, competent, and creative teachers, they argue, we might be able to find a much smaller number of Sal Khans, who could make really good, widely available lessons in different subjects, and then a larger group who would build relationships with students and help them when they are confused.[6] While the examples that unbundling proponents cite are at the moment still in their infancy, the potential for scale may actually be greater than the more widely discussed approaches (like the "no excuses" charters).

It is hard to offer an overall appraisal of this set of ideas because it is both so new and so far-reaching in its implications. Moe and Hill, as well as Hess and Meeks, rightly suggest that what they are calling for is not a new "one best system" but rather a new architecture or framework within which a variety of forces will play out. They are not insensitive to the need for public accountability, and they begin to sketch how governance, finance, and assessment and accountability systems would need to evolve in a mixed-market unbundled system.

What is clear at this point is that this unbundling would be a distinctly American approach to school reform, for both better and worse. As our sole international representative, Canadian Ben Levin, said in frustration at one of our meetings, "The things that Rick [Frederick Hess] is talking about—no one does it that way." Why, Levin wondered, would we consider creating a radically new system when there are proven ways from international leaders to take the existing system and make it perform at higher levels? With real kids' lives at stake, wasn't it close to irresponsible to revamp everything when there are established practices that would improve outcomes? In his reply in an

Atlantic piece a few months later, Hess asked why so much attention was being paid to the international leaders. Did America really want to go the way of Finland or Singapore—hadn't we become the world's superpower by relying on our own ingenuity, dynamism, and diversity to devise smarter, better ways of doing things? And as a large and diverse country with a distrust of federal authority and a decentralized political structure, weren't we better off freeing people to develop lots of different solutions than to try to impose one good one across the land?

To be more precise, the virtues of the unbundled model are specialization, markets, and choice. Such a system would likely be more customized for students and for teachers; there would be more options not only in terms of which schools to go to but also which programs to choose. The hypothesized improvements in performance would derive largely from specialization (as providers focused on one thing, they would become better at it), and market mechanisms (good providers would succeed, and bad ones would fail). The weaknesses of the vision are the flip side of this coin: fragmentation, lack of attention to common concerns, and the inequalities that decentralization can perpetuate. Most of what we know to date suggests that good schools don't function like general contractors; rather, they try to integrate teachers and students into a common school culture. One could argue the same for the system as a whole: if parents and students are choosing courses like iTunes playlists, who is responsible for ensuring that American schooling plays the function it traditionally has aspired to as a guarantor of common experiences, values, and knowledge? And most of what we know about choice systems and markets of all types suggests that they work better for the more advantaged and more informed. If such a system expanded the number of options that parents and schools could choose, would it aggravate rather than diminish socioeconomic disparities?

Of course, unbundlers can and do reply that the current system already has all of the weaknesses that are only hypothesized in the one they propose, and that therefore a new set of arrangements at least deserves a shot. Whether the pros outweigh the cons, only time will tell.

Expanding the System: Linking Schooling and Society

A fourth possibility is that we're just asking too much from schools, and that we will not see consistently better academic performance unless schools are complemented by an equally robust out-of-school support system for students. If each of the previous three pathways tried to rethink schooling, this one seeks to rethink the relationship between school and outside of school. Henig, Malone, and Reville offer a vision of an integrated educational system in which the services for students do not stop at the schoolhouse door. Directly taking on reformers who say that to consider out-of-school factors is to "make excuses" for schools, they argue that school versus out of school is a false dichotomy, and that a smart and sensible strategy would pair efforts to improve students' lives in schools with efforts to improve their lives out of school.

There are a number of reasons to find this analysis compelling. Academic studies have confirmed what most parents already suspect: surveys from the Coleman report have made it clear that more of the variation in student performance is due to families than to schools.[7] Students also differ greatly in the amount of "summer learning loss" they suffer. Some studies have found that poorer and more affluent students learn at about the same rate during the academic year, and that the widening gap in academic performance is due almost entirely to differences in summer experiences. Further, a good portion of the black-white test score gap emerges even before students enter school. From a variety of perspectives, it is clear that extra-school factors are critically important in explaining school performance.

We might also think that if we could create significantly more equality in out-of-school conditions, it would make the job of teachers in schools more reasonable and, particularly for teachers who work with low-income students, more possible. The international evidence cited in chapter 1 suggests that PISA leading nations have more robust welfare states or specifically provide support for out-of-school needs within the school, or both. Leading "no excuses" charter schools famously ask for almost around-the-clock commitment from their teachers; perhaps such heroic efforts would not be as necessary if extra-school support were more regularly provided. To borrow an apt analogy from my former student Lindsay Wheeler, current efforts at school reform are like boats trying to reach shore in the face of a tremendous hurricane; rather than trying to find one hundred thousand preternaturally talented boat captains (principals), wouldn't it be easier to reverse the tide so that even moderately talented guides could bring the boats ashore?

The challenge, of course, is knowing how to reverse the tide, or even whether it is reversible. The idea that students need support out of school as well as within is at least as old as Jane Addams and Hull House (1889), and the idea that students need support before they start school is at least as old as Head Start (1964). A range of programs has been tried through the years to meet the needs of students after school and during the summer. These efforts have either been done on the relative cheap (Head Start) or have been a motley patchwork (afterschool and summer efforts); they have not, thus far, been able to significantly narrow the gaps in life chances between more and less advantaged students. There have been model programs, such as Perry preschool and the Abecedarian project, but scaling them has proven to present many of the same challenges as scaling good schools in the K–12 sector.[8]

To put it another way, the analysis of the problem is compelling, but finding a viable solution at scale continues to be vexing. There seems to be little public will in the United States for the kind of government largesse that would be needed for a full-scale attack on child poverty, and limited ideological support for a significantly expanded governmental role in children's out-of-school lives. To their credit, the authors are well aware of these challenges and suggest that a carefully targeted, data-driven effort might provide a way to integrate school and nonschool services in a way that would be feasible in an age of austerity. They also rightly note that the growth of general-purpose executive government may facilitate these shifts. The question, of course, is whether such an integrated system can, within limited means, solve the problems of creating quality services at scale that have plagued both school and out-of-school sectors in the past.

Dissolving the System: What Would Happen If We Let Them Go?

A fifth possibility is that the system needs to be dissolved entirely. Chapter 6 is motivated by two observations that run in opposite directions. The first is that schools are places frozen in time—still passing out textbooks in the age of e-readers; still using computers as screens for worksheets rather than connectors to the world of learning; still employing committees of adults at the state, district, and school levels to decide what should be learned rather than opening up learning to the learners themselves. The second is that the world of information outside of school is literally growing faster than anyone can take it in: Google is digitally archiving much of the world's reading materials; MIT is giving away its lectures for free. It has never been a better time to be a learner—as long as you aren't spending your day cooped up in school. As Richard Elmore succinctly put it in an early paper for this project, "Learning outside of schooling is exploding; learning inside of schooling is imploding."

The gap between these two worlds is what chapter 6 explores. And the authors conclude that the restricted "portal" represented by the school, where a small fraction of available knowledge is certified and passed on to students, will, over time, be overtaken by the outside world of virtually limitless access to knowledge and information. This more open world will not only give more people access to knowledge, but will also empower many more of them to be creators of knowledge, as Wikipedia, the blogosphere, and the rest of Web 2.0 have already shown. The authors predict that, eventually, schools will either have to adapt to these realities or be replaced by other institutional forms that are more suited to them. While the authors acknowledge that some kind of physical space staffed by adults will be needed to assure working parents that their children are safe during the day, they see no reason that such a space has to look like a conventional school and suggest that it may be much more multifocal and suited to a variety of specific purposes than the school buildings of today.

Historically minded readers will recognize that there are antecedents to this argument in Ivan Illich's 1960s-inspired call for *Deschooling Society*.[9] Illich, channeling Rousseau, argued that a number of the major social welfare institutions that were tasked with helping people were in fact simply controlling them, and that their attendant bureaucracies made them unresponsive to the needs of the clients they were purportedly serving. Elmore and City have both worked with the American school system for a number of years, and this piece represents a sense, at least on Elmore's part, that the system is fundamentally unable to make the changes needed to serve its charges. Given the open-access possibilities created by the Internet and the ways in which some non-school organizations have moved to reorganize the realm of learning to take advantage of this new world, you can see why City, Elmore, and Lynch argue that the future of learning is not the future of schooling.

Underneath the particulars of this vision is an optimistic view of the human being as interested learner—someone who wants to learn but is limited in her ability to do so by the conventional structure of schooling. The vision's fundamental virtues are its emphasis on intrinsic motivation, deep inquiry into subjects that are of interest, and its linking of students to the web of knowledge accumulating around any given topic. It avoids the false dualisms that Dewey warns of by creating opportunities to integrate knowledge about theory with knowledge about practice; it opens up possibilities for interdisciplinary inquiry; and it much more closely reflects the way in which adults learn in depth about subjects that they care to pursue. This approach also has the virtue of being egalitarian in its conception. As the authors note, many of these opportunities are already offered to students in good private schools, colleges, and graduate schools; we simply need to make similar options available to all students.

As with the other approaches, the challenges to this vision mirror its strengths. While it is true that there is an increasing number of homeschooled students and an increasing interest in Web-based learning, the vast majority of parents are fundamentally conservative in their notions of schooling, especially since conventional credentialing is so important for economic advancement. In addition, there are many vested political interests that benefit from preserving the existing system and that will be hard to displace in this call for whole-scale change. If those obstacles were overcome and this approach were put into practice, there would still be questions about whether more conventional means are necessary to push students to learn in subjects that they don't find interesting initially. Many would argue that some degree of external motivation at the start can lead to intrinsic motivation once students begin to acquire some familiarity and competence in a subject. There are also developmental questions about how such a system might work for younger students, who are not yet ready to take on responsibility for their own learning. And, finally, there is a fear that shifting so much agency onto students could widen imbalances between more and less advantaged students, with initial gaps growing over time as the more advantaged students disproportionately leveraged the resources at their disposal.

In my view, a middle-of-the-road approach might actually be the best-case scenario for this vision. If parents, students, and those responsible for the school system were to take these arguments seriously, they might move to significantly open up schools to outside forces, empower students rather than treating them as passive subjects, and give students access to the world of learning that is now at all of our fingertips. At the same time, concerns about equity and more conventional notions of schooling might suggest more of a role than was proposed by the authors for teachers to act as skilled facilitators, guiding and scaffolding the work of learners as they seek to link the growing webs in their heads with the web of knowledge. (Not coincidentally, this mirrors what Dewey proposes in *Experience and Education*.)[10] Such an approach might also connect to the more commonplace desire to replace seat-time with mastery, allowing the reformers' ideas to link to a much broader constituency. The hope is to preserve the immediacy of the desire to free students and give them direct access to the world of learning, while creating a supporting structure that realistically helps all students make such connections.

Assessing Our Choices

If You Want to Change Results, Change a Significant Part of the Structure

Despite the differences in the visions, the five paths share a number of key attributes. The most important is that each fundamentally challenges at least one taken-for-granted tenet of our current system. The international path keeps the overall structure and governance of schools the same, but changes who is working in the schools and what they know. The "reform from the outside in" path is not particularly radical in its design of schools, but it seeks to replace a variety of current institutions (teacher training institutions, traditional education foundations, traditional education research, traditional public schools) with new institutions that do those same functions in what it hopes will be better ways. The unbundling path is less about replacing people and more about reassembling all of the parts of the system in a way that is more varied, functional, and efficient. The schooling and society vision seeks to challenge the boundary that separates school time from out-of-school time and offers an integrative vision of an educational system. The final vision questions the entire rationale of schools as they currently exist, and asks whether we need a new set of institutions that would be more suited to connecting people to the exploding range of available knowledge. None of these is moving deck chairs on the *Titanic*. If we want significant improvement, the authors argue, chances are that we will need to do at least one of the following: *change who is doing the work and what they know; create new institutions to replace the functions of the current ones; change the elements, roles, and structures in which people work; expand the boundaries of the work beyond schools; or, finally, create an entirely new educational infrastructure around the prin-*

ciples of student agency and open access to knowledge. After four years of planning, writing, and talking among education professionals who have more than six hundred years' worth of combined experience with the current system, the authors have concluded that without change in at least one of these dimensions, we will not achieve the kind of significant improvement that we profess to seek.

Intersections, Complementarities, and Tensions

The visions also share two other important commonalities. The first is that all of the authors are fundamentally committed to significantly higher standards for all students. During one of our meetings, we visited two New Orleans charter schools that had been consistently praised in the local and national reform conversation. What we saw there was, frankly, disturbing: schools were ordered, yes, but the level of instructional challenge to students was consistently low; there was much teacher talk and not much student thinking; and, memorably, there was one young woman who kept telling her charges to switch seats every twenty seconds as she called out a series of simple math problems. Despite the heterodox nature of our group, there was a clear, shared sense that if this was what was being touted as progress, we had a long way to go. All of the visions here advocate worlds in which all students are engaged in deep learning, in high-level academic content that taps their intellect and curiosity. In our discussions, there was the usual diversity of views over what people should learn, the trade-offs between depth and breadth, and even whether a four-year college was the appropriate goal for all students. However, there was universal agreement that the level of intellectual challenge for students currently is far too low; all of the visions seek to move from high standards in theory to high standards in practice.

Speaking of practice, the other major commonality in the visions is the shared judgment that the current system exists more for historical, inertial, and political reasons than for its ability to realize better practice on the ground. All of the visions, in one way or another, seek to reformulate aspects of the system to be more attuned to the needs of schools and students. The international and knowledge profession essays (chapters 1 and 2) emphasize growing knowledge out of practice and making it a central part of training; the outside-in reformers (chapter 3) are looking to new models to figure out what works for real students; the unbundling vision (chapter 4) advocates letting schools and students decide how to deploy human resources in ways that solve problems on the ground; the schooling and society essay (chapter 5) goes to some lengths to describe how an expanded system could also be a more responsive system; and the final approach (chapter 6) suggests removing the middlemen entirely and trying to connect students much more directly to knowledge. Any approach worth trying, the authors collectively argue, needs both to embrace truly high standards and to be highly attuned to the needs of practice.

There are also important ways in which the visions the authors sketch could complement one another. Narrowing the scope of teaching might make it easier to find more expert practitioners. Supporting kids' out-of-school needs would make it easier to teach. Taking advantage of the explosion of knowledge likely requires new kinds of roles. Developing more professional expertise among teachers creates the kind of quality control up front that would permit more market-type mechanisms at the site of delivery. If we are really trying to think about how to create a better system, we need to think about these dimensions in combination, not in isolation.

At the same time, there are real differences in what the authors propose that are worthy of sustained debate. Three major tensions stand out. The first is about whether we actually already know what to do and must simply confront the challenge of creating the political and institutional support to do it, or whether we need new ideas for new times. If you imagine these views arrayed along a continuum, the international path, authors think that there is a fairly clear set of lessons from the world's leading nations, and that the major challenge is to translate them to the American context. The schooling and society essay explicitly warns against innovation for innovation's sake but invokes the idea that well-designed experiments are important for accumulating knowledge. The knowledge profession essay suggests that we need much more knowledge about practice if we are going to improve, and therefore must build a new networked infrastructure to surface, capture, and evaluate this knowledge. And the unbundling and learning essays suggest that we are moving into a radically new world, and that we are going to need very differently configured institutions to respond to it. Whether we are in a world of known knowns, known unknowns, or unknown unknowns really matters for how we think and act. It also suggests different policy tools: if you know what you want, there is no reason not to use the various policy levers available to try to achieve it; if you believe that we don't or can't yet know what will work, you would create ecosystems or greenfields in which a variety of approaches can take root.

A second major tension concerns the nature of what it means to teach. Here the contrast is greatest between the knowledge profession and international path essays and the unbundling approach. The authors of the knowledge profession and international path essays imagine teaching as complex, stimulating, and fulfilling work. They think it should be a career for bright people, one that promises both personal and intellectual rewards. They are sympathetic to the need to provide outlets for teachers to grow over time, to expand their reach in what they know and how they teach, and ultimately to create and disseminate knowledge as well as to receive it. This is an attractive vision, but one that is far from the current reality and will be difficult to realize across 3.6 million teachers. The authors of the unbundling essay, on the other hand, suggest a much more differentiated profession, with a subset of teachers, perhaps, filling the preceding role, but with many other personnel in the system doing less skilled work to support the work of those teachers. They also suggest that even good teachers might become much more specialized—teachers of fractions, as opposed to elementary school teachers or even math teachers. While this differentiated world looks radically different from our current one, it might actually be one in which it would be easier to do well because it would require fewer top-flight people. But, at the same time, it might undercut what we actually want—kids would be spending more time with people who are less talented and skilled, and it might be harder to attract good people into a field that asks less of them.

Governance: Exit, Voice, or Loyalty

A third tension is about the nature of public governance and who decides important questions of public schooling. Three of the six essays—the ones on unbundling, the mixed-market model, and learning versus schooling—envision giving considerably greater choice over learning to students and their parents. In Albert Hirschman's famous framework, these are proposals that emphasize "exit" over "voice" and "loyalty"; the emphasis is on particular students and parents choosing arrangements that best suit them as opposed to more collective governance.[11] Much of what they suggest pushes beyond the usual debates over school choice, as in these models students might be choosing providers within schools, or even putting together a menu of providers without a school at all.

These developments pose a considerable challenge to the longstanding conception of common schooling as a unifying American institution. If a student in Minnesota is taking one online class from Boston and another from Bangladesh, who is responsible for the student's learning? In an unbundled world, do we even seek to ensure that schools (or whatever replaces them) provide a common experience that represents the Horace Mann–like aspirations for American schooling?

Those who support expanded choice have a number of reasonable replies to this line of argument. The first is that the current system already violates any real norms of common schooling because residential segregation in the housing market creates marked homogeneity in schools by race and class. Choice partisans might argue that our current combination is particularly unjust: we do have markets in housing, which creates advantages for those who have more money, but we don't

have markets in schooling, which means that if you car
in a desirable district, you are stuck with what's offered b
the district you can afford. Second, while the current system is democratic in its design, in practice it falls far short of the ideal: school board
elections have extremely low turnout and are often swayed by interest groups; multiple levels of the system create incoherence by steering
schools in different directions; and the current system creates a cum-
bersome bureaucracy that makes it difficult for schools to realize any
goals well. Third, there are real motivational benefits to choice and real
costs to common (read: standardized) experiences: in a country as large
and diverse as ours, we are better off providing different educational
environments than trying to create a one-size-fits-all solution.

It is not my place to try to resolve the debate about choice; it is rather
to frame it and make clear the alternatives that face us. There may be
technical solutions to some issues—for example, designing mastery-
based oversight assessment systems that would allow students to learn
from a variety of providers but also create some assurance that those
students have learned a reasonable amount. There may also be com-
promise solutions: a district might adopt a portfolio system that gives
schools considerable latitude to develop their own curricula, but that
district or the state might simultaneously mandate certain common requirements representing core knowledge that all students should master. But even so, there is still a question of principle: if we empower
students and parents as much more active choosers and move away
from the common institutions that have defined schooling in the past,
we will be shifting from voice to exit—a shift that may or may not be
good for our students and, collectively, for our democracy.

Goals, Purposes, and Values: To What End?

The pathways laid out here also need to be assessed against the goals
and values we hold for our schools. The descriptions are long on organizational design and short on the content toward which that design aims. This was intentional: the authors are not philosophers, but

they do have professional experience in thinking about school system design; what they could have brought to a discussion of values would have been more from their perspective as citizens than as experts. But as citizens who have a stake in the school system, we all need to weigh the question of whether these various pathways will realize our values and aspirations.

At a minimum, we might expect that everyone could agree that schools should do what the Paideia proposal outlines: prepare students for a decent livelihood, prepare them to be citizens, and prepare them to live a good life.[12] More aspirationally, we might draw on Howard Gardner's recent book, which suggests that successful schooling would teach students to discern truth, recognize and create beauty, and understand goodness (as qualities of character and community).[13]

Any of the paths advocated in this book could conceivably be directed toward these goals and values. But it is striking that none of them explicitly speaks to these overriding considerations. Painting with a broad brush, you might say that the current American educational landscape is overly focused on a single value—preparing students for economic success, as measured by their basic math and reading test scores. Although the common core standards reflect an increasing recognition that we will ask more of students in the future, this "more" does not necessarily speak to the wider array of values previously listed. Unless organizational designs are suffused with these fundamental values and purposes, they may realize higher performance by conventional measures, but they will not create the kind of rich and well-rounded education that we should be aspiring to. In my view, any strategy for the future worth pursuing must take as a central starting point the need to create this richer kind of education; otherwise, we will just be designing a new mousetrap to capture fundamentally limited educational aims.

It is also worth noting that in a country as large and diverse as the United States, there are bound to be considerable differences in what people value. It is hard to imagine that any system will succeed without building in some space for this pluralism. A number of the proposals emphasize giving families choice over providers and letting students direct their own learning, and, in so doing, explicitly honor diverse visions of educational ends and purposes. While the question for these visions, as stated earlier, is how to preserve the *e pluribus unum* function of the school system in the face of greater choice, the question for the more statist visions is how to respond to the pluralism of values, which is an essential feature of our democracy.

The Alex Test: A Parent's View

When we started this project in 2008, I did not have any children. In the years since, my wife Cheryl and I were lucky enough to have a wonderful son, Alex, who as of this writing is fifteen months old. Dewey famously said that what the wisest parent would want for his or her own child is what the community would want for all of its children. That is not entirely true, because different families have different values, but Dewey's claim does force us to think about these questions in a more personal way, a perspective that provides an important counterbalance to the system-level focus of this book. It also forces us to confront whether the schooling we are envisioning for "other people's children" is the same as what we would want for our own.

What Cheryl and I want for Alex is a place that is challenging, humane, and kind. We want it to get him interested in learning, to teach him to read, and to ignite what we hope will be lifelong passions for math, music, art, or whatever he finds of interest. We want the teachers there to care about him personally, to help him when he struggles, and to challenge him when he excels. We want them to create an environment that is warm and nurturing, where there are both high expectations and permission to try and fail. We want him to realize that there is a world beyond our neighborhood, and to be surrounded by other students with differing perspectives, life experiences, and backgrounds. From the beginning, but especially as he gets older, we want him to do authentic work—work that is challenging, meaningful, and linked to the great traditions of human learning. We want him to learn how to cooperate, to respect the Golden Rule, and to develop a moral identity. And we want him to be able to play, to join teams, and to develop his body as well as his mind and spirit. While we recognize that no school will achieve all of these things all of the time, we want him to be in the hands of competent, mature, and secure adults who can model the kinds of virtues that we hope to instill in him.

I can imagine ways that any of the paths outlined herein could achieve what we want for Alex. But the personal perspective does raise certain sets of considerations other than those that some of these visions set out to address. In particular, when real children are at school, we care as much about their social well-being as their intellectual well-being; Debbie Meier's point about putting children in the company of wise adults seems increasingly essential.[14] To achieve that, a number of the visions would need to balance other virtues with the ones they describe: efforts to grow the scientific knowledge for teaching would need to be balanced with the kind of warmth and love that children need; efforts to incorporate technology would need to be balanced with face-to-face interaction; efforts to organize around students' individual interests and desires would need to be balanced with helping them to understand the needs of the group. From the parent's perspective, school is an extension of the home, and as we rethink the structure of schooling, we must remember that the schools of the future, no less than schools today, will need to help students grow across multiple dimensions—mind, body, spirit, and soul. President Obama said in his inauguration, "These things are old, these things are true." As we rethink the structures of schooling, we need to ensure that the schools of the future are designed to realize these longstanding virtues.

Acting on the Long View: The Politics of Significant Change

This is a book for those who believe ideas matter. This is not an actionable agenda in the short term. Even in the medium term, the best we can hope for is to create room for ideas to unfold. However, it's also invariably true that no system changes by ideas alone. Institutions are conservative; people benefit from existing structures. The schools are public institutions; we all have a say. Change will come only through politics—people championing new directions and arguing for different kinds of institutions and structures.

The good news is that there is a tremendous amount of energy already in the system. Lots of people recognize its failings and are trying to create something better. But we argue that a lot of this energy is misdirected, building upon a failing system rather than trying to create a new, fundamentally better one.

At the same time, the authors of our most radical vision (chapter 6) say, "the future is already here, and we can't see it." It is true that there are glimmers and examples of virtually everything we talk about here somewhere. We hope that people will build upon some of these early efforts and create more sustained change.

Across our volume, we see not only different visions, but also different theories of change that, in many ways, parallel the visions. One strand is that powerful actors could get behind ideas and create sustained change. For example, as chapter 1 suggests, Teach for America, the National Board for Professional Teaching Standards, the National Governors Associations, and the Council of Chief State School Officers could come together behind a substantially revamped human capital policy. This avenue is probably most likely for the first set of ideas, which keeps the system intact but seeks to change the people, skills, and knowledge within it. A second strand is neither top down nor bottom up but from the side: foundations or other for- or nonprofits could pursue one of these sets of possibilities consistently—developing proof points, funding research, and building advocacy. The Hewlett Foundation's work on "deeper learning" is one example of how a focused but multipronged foundation strategy might work.[15] And a third approach is more decentralized and bottom up, where lots of people (everyone from states to mayors to networks to schools) would create examples of unbundling or boundary-spanning systems, and trust that diffusing and franchising would do the work of creating scale. And, as always, these strategies can be combined: governments can seed people to work bottom up; local advocates can work to create a policy framework that is viable.

The key is keeping an eye on the longer view. We can cycle through lots of programs of the moment, put lots of effort into carefully evaluating small reforms, and express disappointment when, yet again, these modest efforts fall short of the high aspirations we have for our schools. Or, we can make a bigger bet (or a series of bigger bets) with a longer view and make a significant enough change to the structure to actually yield the results we seek. PISA leading nations did not get there overnight, but they were able to make substantial changes in their outcomes with a concerted and long-term strategy. Imagine a world in which a state decided to significantly raise the entry requirements for becoming a teacher, and single-handedly created an example of a profession filled exclusively with top-third talent. Or one in which a foundation decided to put all of its efforts into creating the kind of knowledge infrastructure that undergirds medicine and other strong professions. Or one in which a city decided to commit all of its resources to providing Harlem Children's Zone–like cradle-to-college support for all of its students. Or one in which a city and a state created the kind of ecosystem in which a variety of entrepreneurs could create new forms of schooling, one that would enable parents and students to customize an education suited to their interests and skills. Or one in which a network of schools decided to organize its work anew for the twenty-first century, beginning not with schools as we know them, but with the possibilities of the knowledge economy as their organizing point. All of these worlds are possible, and some are even beginning to emerge. The question is whether we will be courageous enough to make the significant changes we need to achieve the schools that we aspire to.

Appendix

THE FUTURES OF SCHOOL REFORM PARTICIPANTS

Larry Berger, Chief Executive Officer, Wireless Generation

Anthony S. Bryk, President, The Carnegie Foundation for the Advancement of Teaching

Stacey Childress, Deputy Director of Education, Bill & Melinda Gates Foundation

Elizabeth A. City, Lecturer on Education and the Executive Director of the Doctor of Education Leadership Program, Harvard Graduate School of Education

Richard F. Elmore, Gregory R. Anrig Professor of Educational Leadership, Harvard Graduate School of Education

Adam Gamoran, John D. MacArthur Professor of Sociology and Educational Policy Studies, University of Wisconsin–Madison

Michael Goldstein, Founder and CEO, MATCH School

Louis M. Gomez, John D. and Catherine T. MacArthur Foundation Chair in Digital Media and Learning, University of California, Los Angeles

Paul Goren, Lewis-Sebring Director, Consortium on Chicago School Research

Greg Gunn, Lecturer, Harvard Graduate School of Education, Cofounder of Wireless Generation

Kaya Henderson, Chancellor, District of Columbia Public Schools

Jeffrey Henig, Professor of Political Science and Education, Teachers College, Columbia University

Frederick M. Hess, Resident Scholar and Director of Education Policy Studies, American Enterprise Institute

Paul T. Hill, John and Marguerite Corbally Professor, Center on Reinventing Public Education, University of Washington

Michael Johnston, Colorado State Senator, District 33

Brad Jupp, Senior Program Advisor for Teacher Quality Initiatives, U.S. Department of Education

John B. King, Jr., Commissioner of Education and President of the University of the State of New York

Ben Levin, Professor and Canada Research Chair in Education Leadership and Policy, Ontario Institute for Studies in Education, University of Toronto, Canada

Susanna Loeb, Professor of Education, Stanford University

Doug Lynch, former Vice Dean at the Graduate School of Education, University of Pennsylvania

Helen Janc Malone, Advanced Doctoral Candidate, Harvard Graduate School of Education

Olivia Meeks, a Research Coordinator, District of Columbia Public Schools

Jal Mehta, Assistant Professor of Education, Harvard Graduate School of Education

Terry M. Moe, William Bennett Munro Professor of Political Science, Stanford University

Mark Moore, Herbert A. Simon professor, Harvard Graduate School of Education

Paul Reville, Massachusetts Secretary of Education and a Senior Lecturer on Education, Harvard Graduate School of Education

Andrew Rotherham, Cofounder and Partner, Bellwether Education Partners

Stefanie Sanford, Director of U.S. Program Advocacy and Policy, Bill & Melinda Gates Foundation

Robert B. Schwartz, Francis Keppel Professor of Practice of Educational Policy and Administration, Harvard Graduate School of Education

Marshall "Mike" Smith, former Senior Advisor to the U.S. Secretary of Education, U.S. Department of Education

James Spillane, Spencer T. and Ann W. Olin Professor of Learning and Organizational Change, Northwestern University

Dacia Toll, Co-CEO and President, Achievement First

The members listed here participated in at least one meeting of the group. The thoughts expressed in this volume represent the view of the chapter authors and not the members as a whole.

NOTES

Introduction

1. National Commission on Excellence in Education, *A Nation at Risk: The Imperative for Educational Reform* (Washington, DC: U.S. Department of Education, 1983).
2. Frederick M. Hess, *Education Unbound: The Promise and Practice of Greenfield Schooling* (Alexandria, VA: Association for Supervision & Curriculum Development, 2010).

Chapter 1

1. Bobby D. Rampey, Gloria S. Dion, and Patricia L. Donahue, *NAEP 2008: Trends in Academic Progress* (Publication No. NCES 2009-479) (Washington, DC: U.S. Department of Education, 2009), http://nces.ed.gov/nations reportcard/pdf/main2008/2009479.pdf.
2. Michael O. Mullis, Ina V. S. Martin, and Pierre Foy, *TIMSS 2007 International Mathematics Report* (Chestnut Hill, MA: TIMSS & PIRLS International Study Center, Boston College, 2008), http://timss.bc.edu/timss2007/intl_reports.html; Organisation for Economic Co-operation and Development, *Strong Performers and Successful Reformers in Education: Lessons from PISA for the United States* (Paris: Organisation for Economic Co-operation and Development Publishing, 2011), http://www.oecd.org/data oecd/32/50/46623978.pdf.
3. Yossi Shavit, Richard Arum, and Adam Gamoran, eds., *Stratification in Higher Education: A Comparative Study* (Palo Alto, CA: Stanford University Press, 2007); Vivien Stewart, "Singapore: A Journey to the Top, Step by Step," in *Surpassing Shanghai,* ed. Marc S. Tucker (Cambridge, MA: Harvard Education Press, 2011), 113–140.
4. Andrew C. Porter and Adam Gamoran, *Methodological Advances in Cross-National Surveys of Educational Achievement* (Washington, DC: National Academies Press, 2002), http://www.nap.edu/catalog.php?record_id=10322.
5. Pasi Sahlberg, *Finnish Lessons: What Can the World Learn from Educational Change in Finland?* (New York: Teachers College Press, 2011).

6. Organisation for Economic Co-operation and Development, *PISA 2009 Results: What Students Know and Can Do—Student Performance in Reading, Mathematics and Science I* (Paris: Organisation for Economic Co-operation and Development, 2010), http://www.oecd.org/document/53/0, 3746,en_32252351_46584327_46584821_1_1_1_1,00.html; Mona Mourshed, Chinezi Chijioke, and Michael Barber, *How the World's Most Improved School Systems Keep Getting Better* (London: McKinsey & Company, 2010), http://ssomckinsey.darbyfilms.com/reports/EducationBook_A4%20SINGLES_DEC%202.pdf.

7. Ben Levin and Michael Fullan, "Learning About System Renewal," *Journal of Educational Management, Administration and Leadership* 36, no. 2 (2008): 289–303; Ben Levin, *How to Change 5000 Schools* (Cambridge, MA: Harvard Education Press, 2008); Mourshed, Chijioke, and Barber, *World's Most Improved School Systems*; Organisation for Economic Co-operation and Development, *PISA 2009 Results*; Sahlberg, *Finnish Lessons*.

8. Adam Gamoran et al., *Transforming Teaching in Math and Science: How Schools and Districts Can Support Change* (New York: Teachers College Press, 2003); Anthony S. Bryk et al., *Organizing Schools for Improvement: Lessons from Chicago* (Chicago: University of Chicago Press, 2010).

9. Organisation for Economic Co-operation and Development, *Lessons from PISA for the United States* (Paris: Organisation for Economic Co-operation and Development, 2011), 170, http://www.oecd.org/data oecd/32/50/46623978.pdf.

10. Richard Rothstein, *Class and Schools: Using Social, Economic, and Educational Reform to Close the Black-White Achievement Gap* (New York: Teachers College Press, 2004).

11. Richard Wilkinson and Kate Pickett, *The Spirit Level: Why Greater Equality Makes Societies Stronger* (London: Penguin, 2009).

12. Organisation for Economic Co-operation and Development, *Learning for Jobs* (Paris: Organisation for Economic Co-operation and Development, 2010), http://www.oecd.org/edu/learningforjobs.

13. Programs of Study Joint Technical Working Group, *Programs of Study: Year 3 Joint Technical Report* (Louisville, KY: National Research Center for Career and Technical Education, 2011), http://136.165.122.102/mambo/content/view/45/54/.

14. James R. Stone III, Corinne Alfeld, and Donna Pearson, "Rigor and Relevance: Testing a Model of Enhanced Math Learning in Career and Tech-

nical Education," *American Education Research Journal* 45 (2008): 767–795; W. Norton Grubb, *Leadership Challenges in High Schools: Multiple Pathways to Success* (Boulder, CO: Paradigm Publishers, 2011).

15. William C. Symonds, Robert B. Schwartz, and Ronald Ferguson, *Pathways to Prosperity: Meeting the Challenge of Preparing Young Americans for the 21st Century* (Cambridge, MA: Harvard Graduate School of Education, 2011), http://www.gse.harvard.edu/news_events/features/2011/Pathways_to_Prosperity_Feb2011.pdf.

16. Levin, *How to Change.*

17. Anthony S. Bryk and Barbara L. Schneider, *Trust in Schools: A Core Resource for Improvement* (New York: Russell Sage Foundation, 2002); Anthony S. Bryk et al., *Organizing Schools.*

18. Ben Levin, "Theory, Research and Practice in Mobilizing Research Knowledge in Education," *London Review of Education* 9, no. 1 (2011): 15–26.

19. James March, "Exploration and Exploitation in Organizational Learning," *Organization Science* 2 (1991): 71–87.

20. Carnegie Forum on Education and the Economy, *A Nation Prepared: Teachers for the 21st Century: The Report of the Task Force on Teaching as a Profession* (Washington, DC: Carnegie Forum on Education and the Economy, 1986).

21. For example: Thomas J. Kane, Jonah E. Rockoff, and Douglas O. Staiger, "What Does Certification Tell Us About Teacher Effectiveness? Evidence from New York City," *Economics of Education Review* 27 (2008): 615–631; Steven G. Rivkin, Eric A. Hanushek, and John F. Kain, "Teachers, Schools, and Academic Achievement," *Econometrica* 73 (2005): 417–458; S. Paul Wright, Sandra P. Horn, and William L. Sanders, "Teacher and Classroom Context Effects on Student Achievement: Implications for Teacher Evaluation," *Journal of Personnel Evaluation in Education* 11 (1997): 57–67.

22. Teacher Performance Assessment Consortium, http://aacte.org/index.php?/Programs/Teacher-Performance-Assessment-Consortium-TPAC/teacher-performance-assessment-consortium.html.

23. William C. Symonds, Robert B. Schwartz, and Ronald Ferguson, *Pathways to Prosperity.*

24. Michael D. Shear and Daniel de Vise, "Obama Announces $12 Billion Community College Initative," *Washington Post,* July 15, 2009, http://www.washingtonpost.com/wp-dyn/content/article/2009/07/14/AR2009071400819.html.

Chapter 2

1. David Tyack, *The One Best System* (Cambridge, MA: Harvard University Press, 1974); Raymond Callahan, *Education and the Cult of Efficiency* (Chicago: University of Chicago Press, 1962).

2. Jeffrey L. Pressman and Aaron Wildavsky, *Implementation: How Great Expectations in Washington are Dashed in Oakland* (Berkeley, CA: University of California Press, 1973); Richard Elmore, *School Reform from the Inside Out* (Cambridge, MA: Harvard Education Press, 2004); Charles Payne, *So Much Reform, So Little Change* (Cambridge, MA: Harvard Education Press, 2008).

3. Jonathan Supovitz, "Can High Stakes Testing Leverage Educational Improvement? Prospects From the Last Decade of Testing and Accountability Reform," *Journal of Educational Change* 10 (2009): 211–227.

4. Michelene Chi, Robert Glaser, and M.J. Farr, eds., *The Nature of Expertise* (Hillsdale, NJ: Lawrence Erlbaum, 1988); James Cimino, "Development of Expertise in Medical Practice," in *Tacit Knowledge in Professional Practice*, eds. Robert Sternberg and Joseph Horvath (Mahwah, NJ: Lawrence Erlbaum, 1999), 101–119; Carol Livingston and Hilda Borko, "Expert-Novice Differences in Teaching: A Cognitive Analysis and Implications for Teacher Education," *Journal of Teacher Education* 40 (1989): 36–42.

5. Jal Mehta, *The Allure of Order: The Troubled Quest to Rationalize a Century of American Schooling* (New York: Oxford University Press, forthcoming); Dan Lortie, *Schoolteacher: A Sociological Study* (Chicago: University of Chicago Press, 1975); Andrew Abbott, *The System of the Professions* (Chicago: University of Chicago Press, 1988); David Cohen and Susan Moffitt, *The Ordeal of Equality: Did Federal Regulation Fix the Schools?* (Cambridge, MA: Harvard University Press, 2009); Joshua Glazer, "Educational Professionalism: An Inside-Out View," *American Journal of Education* 114 (2008): 169–189.

6. Ellen Lagemann, *An Elusive Science* (Chicago: University of Chicago, 2000); Jal Mehta, "Inverting the Pyramid of School Reform," *Harvard Education Letter* 26, no. 6 (November/December 2010); Donald Berwick, "The Science of Improvement," *Journal of the American Medical Association* 299, no. 10 (2008): 1182–1184; Anthony Bryk, "It Is a Science of Improvement," *Education Week*, Futures of School Reform blog, March 31, 2011, http://blogs.edweek.org/edweek/futures_of_reform/2011/03/it_is_a_science_of_improvement.html.

7. Lee Shulman, *The Wisdom of Practice: Essays on Teaching, Learning, and Learning to Teach* (San Francisco: Jossey-Bass, Inc., 2004).

8. See David Cohen, *Teaching and Its Predicaments* (Cambridge, MA: Harvard University Press, 2011) for a detailed analytic account of the dilemmas of practice and the skills and knowledge entailed in expert teaching.

9. Berwick, "Science of Improvement"; Atul Gawande, *The Checklist Manifesto: How to Get Things Right* (New York: Metropolitan, 2010).

10. Michael Huberman, "The Model of the Independent Artisan in Teachers' Professional Relations," in *Teacher's Work: Individuals, Colleagues, and Contexts*, eds. Judith Warren Little and Milbrey Wallin McLaughlin (New York: Teachers College Press, 1993), 11–50.

11. A personal observation offered by Jay Featherstone and recounted by David Cohen.

12. For an interesting account along these lines, see Donald J. Peurach and Joshua Glazer, "Reconsidering Replication: New Perspectives on Large-Scale School Improvement," *Journal of Educational Change* Online (October 2011).

13. Marc Tucker and Andreas Schliecher, "Lessons for the United States," in *Strong Performer and Successful Reformers in Education: Lessons From Pisa for the United States* (Paris: Organisation for Economic Co-operation and Development, 2010).

14. Anthony Bryk, Louis Gomez, and Alicia Grunow, "Getting Ideas into Action: Building Networked Improvement Communities in Education," *Frontiers in Sociology and Social Research* 1, no. 1 (2011): 127–162. In addition, we note that many reform efforts are rooted in neither of these strategies but rather in analyses of extant evidence yielding support for some proposed policy or practice. In their most rigorous form, these arguments are rooted in careful statistical modeling of large descriptive data sets. In its most casual form, extant evidence is mustered in support of some pre-existing conclusion. This descriptive research, when rigorously carried out, is a solution-hypothesis-generating activity. Some problem analysis has occurred and logical conclusions drawn. At times, this can be a useful precursor to the activity of interest in this chapter—the actual development of a professional knowledge base.

15. Peurach and Glazer, "Reconsidering Replication."

16. David S. Yeager and Gregory M. Walton, "Social-Psychological Interventions in Education: They're Not Magic," *Review of Educational Research* 81, no. 2 (2011): 267–301.

17. Cathy Caro-Bruce et al., eds., *Creating Equitable Classrooms Through Action Research* (Thousand Oaks, CA: Corwin Press, 2007).

18. Eileen Ferrance, *Action Research* (Providence, RI: Brown University, Northeast and Islands Regional Educational Laboratory, 2000).

19. Anthony S. Bryk and Louis M. Gomez. "Ruminations on Reinventing an R&D Capacity for Educational Improvement," in *The Future of Educational Entrepreneurship: Possibilities of School Reform*, ed. Frederick M. Hess (Cambridge, MA: Harvard Education Press, 2008), 181-206; Anthony S. Bryk, "Support a Science of Performance Improvement," *Phi Delta Kappan* 90, no. 8 (2009): 597–600; Louis M. Gomez, Kimberly Gomez, and Bernard R. Gifford, "Educational Innovation with Technology: A New Look at Scale and Opportunity to Learn," *Educational Reform: Transforming America's Education Through Innovation and Technology* (Whistler, BC: Aspen Institute, 2010); Bryk, Gomez, and Grunow, "Getting Ideas." See also Anne K. Morris and James Hiebert, "Creating Shared Instructional Products: An Alternative Approach to Improving Teaching," *Educational Researcher* 40 (2011): 5–14.

20. W. Edwards Deming, *Out of the Crisis* (Cambridge, MA: MIT Press, 2000); Joseph M. Juran and Joseph A. De Feo, *Juran's Quality Handbook: The Complete Guide to Performance Excellence*, Sixth Edition (New York: McGraw-Hill, 2010).

21. Gerald J. Langley et al., *The Improvement Guide: A Practical Approach to Enhancing Organizational Performance*, Second Edition (San Francisco: Jossey-Bass, 2009); Berwick, "Science of Improvement."

22. Charles Kenney, *The Best Practice: How the New Quality Movement is Transforming Medicine* (New York: Public Affairs, 2008).

23. At the center of quality improvement are a few simple but powerful ideas that IHI puts into action in health care. The ideas are fairly straightforward, but they are rarely consistently applied in health care (or education or other settings); it is the relentless emphasis on their execution that is important. First, they attend to practice. The focus of their work is the on-the-ground commerce between health care professionals and patients. Second, as an organization they strive to take large and diffuse problems and work to break them down into specific processes that are susceptible to measurement, experimentation, and improvement. Third, IHI recognizes that most, if not all, complex problems in health care do not have a single root cause. They are the result of systemic interactions. So, IHI seeks to address the system in which the problem is embedded. For example, if patients are mov-

ing between providers in their follow-up visits after being discharged from the hospital, there can be a "white space" where no one is responsible for their care, which leads to higher-than-needed levels of hospital readmission for these patients. This is a problem that links macro factors like the structure of funding reimbursement for patients, meso factors like the organizational needs of different providers, and micro factors like the need to create trust between patients and doctors. Fourth, once they have some purchase on the problem, IHI works toward a proposed solution pathway or intervention that is specific enough to be doable, but systemic enough to take on the various parts of the problem. Finally, to make progress they develop a set of evidence-oriented inquiry methods that will allow them to measure whether or not the changes are creating improvement. A relentless focus on these principles and respectful working collaborations with hospitals and other health care organizations has allowed IHI to have demonstrable traction on difficult healthcare problems.

24. Douglas Engelbart, *Improving Our Ability to Improve: A Call for Investment in a New Future* (IBM Co-Evolution Symposium, 2003).
25. Ibid.
26. Bryk, Gomez, and Grunow, "Getting Ideas."
27. G. E. Moore, "Cramming More Components onto Integrated Circuits," *Electronics*, vol. 38, no. 8, April 19, 1965.
28. James Hiebert, Robert Gallimore, and James Stigler. "A Knowledge Base for the Teaching Profession: What Would It Look Like and How Can We Get One?" *Educational Researcher* 31, no. 5 (2002): 3–15.
29. A common version of this is the plan-do-study-act (PDSA) cycle. See Langley et al., *Improvement Guide.*
30. *Lesson study* is a pedagogical inquiry process that originated in Japan in which teachers jointly plan, observe, analyze, and refine actual classroom lessons called *research lessons* (http://www.lessonresearch.net/). In our work with community colleges, each college has a lesson study community. All the lesson study communities share common data protocols and are committed to sharing their results.
31. The technical terms for this are *pedagogical knowledge* and *pedagogical content knowledge.*
32. Michael Barber and Mona Mourshed, *How the World's Best-Performing School Systems Come Out on Top* (London: McKinsey & Company, 2007): Rachel Curtis and Judy Wertzel, eds. *Teaching Talent: A Visionary Framework for Human Capital in Education* (Cambridge, MA: Harvard Education

Press, 2010); Dan Goldhaber and Jane Hannaway, eds., *Creating a New Teaching Profession* (Washington, DC: The Urban Institute Press, 2009); Mehta, *Allure of Order*, chapter 10.

33. Victoria, Australia, has built what it calls the "Ultranet," an online platform that allows for statewide sharing of ideas and materials among teachers across schools, as well as places for students to view online activities and parents to access information to support their children's education. See http://www.education.vic.gov.au/about/directions/ultranet/whatis.htm for more information.

Chapter 3

1. See, for example, Dana Brinson et al., *New Orleans–Style Education Reform: A Guide for Cities, Lessons Learned 2005–2010*, (New Orleans, LA: Public Impact and New Schools for New Orleans, January 2012), http://www.newschoolsforneworleans.org/guide/.

2. See the Digest of Education Statistics 2010, National Center for Education Statistics, http://nces.ed.gov/programs/digest/. See also the charter school data provided by the National Alliance for Public Charter Schools, http://dashboard.publiccharters.org/dashboard/home.

3. See Terry M. Moe and John E. Chubb, *Liberating Learning: Technology, Politics, and the Future of American Education* (San Francisco: Jossey-Bass, 2009); Clayton Christensen, Curtis W. Johnson, and Michael B. Horn, *Disrupting Class: How Disruptive Innovation Will Change the Way the World Learns* (New York: McGraw-Hill, 2008); and Paul E. Peterson, *Saving Our Schools: From Horace Mann to Virtual Learning* (Cambridge, MA: Harvard Education Press, 2010).

4. See, for example, provider K12's description of its services and state-by-state listing of charter and district-run schools served, http://www.k12.com/schools-programs/online-public-schools. See also John Watson et al., *Keeping Pace with K–12 Online Learning 2011: An Annual Review of Policy and Practice* (Durango, CO: Evergreen Education Group, 2011), http://kpk12.com/.

5. See Terry M. Moe, *Special Interest: Teachers Unions and America's Schools* (Washington, DC: The Brookings Institution, 2011).

6. See, for example, California Department of Education, API Growth and Targets Met, Rocketship Mateo Sheedy Elementary, http://api.cde.ca.gov/Acnt2011/2011GrowthSch.aspx?allcds=43104390113704. See also the Rocketship Education Web site, http://www.rsed.org. And see Jason

Tomassini, "Rocketship Education to Take Off in Milwaukee," *Education Week*, February 29, 2012, http://blogs.edweek.org/edweek/marketplace k12/2012/02/rocketship_education_to_take_off_in_milwaukee.html. On hybrid schools more generally, see Watson et al., *Keeping Pace*; see also Heather Staker, *The Rise of K–12 Blended Learning: Profiles of Emerging Models* (Mountain View, CA: Innosight Institute, 2011), http://www.innosightinstitute.org/blended_learning_models/.

7. Jina Moore, "John Danner Shoots for the Stars with Rocketship Charter Schools," *Christian Science Monitor*, September 1, 2011, http://www.csmonitor.com/World/Making-a-difference/Change-Agent/2011/0901/John-Danner-shoots-for-the-stars-with-Rocketship-charter-schools.

8. The political argument in this section, along with its implications for reform, is discussed and documented at length in Moe, *Special Interest*.

9. The charter school figure is from the National Alliance for Public Charter Schools at http://dashboard.publiccharters.org/dashboard/home. The figure for vouchers is computed from data provided by the American Federation for Children at www.federationforchildren.com/existing-programs. The Maine and Vermont "tuitioning" programs were not included, nor were programs that simply allow parents to take tax deductions or credits for educational expenses when paying their income taxes.

10. The impact of technology is also discussed in Moe, *Special Interest*, but for a more detailed treatment of the political implications of technology for American education, see Moe and Chubb, *Liberating Learning*.

Chapter 4

1. We'd like to offer our deepest thanks to Taryn Hochleitner, for her invaluable research and editorial assistance.

2. Michael S. Garet et al., *Impact of Two Professional Development Interventions on Early Reading Instruction and Achievement* (Washington, DC: Institute for Education Sciences, 2008), http://ies.ed.gov/pubsearch/pubsinfo.asp?pubid=NCEE20084034; Michael S. Garet et al., *Middle School Mathematics Professional Development Impact Study Findings After the Second Year of Implementation* (Washington, DC: Institute for Education Sciences, 2011), http://ies.ed.gov/pubsearch/pubsinfo.asp?pubid=NCEE20114024.

3. Glenda Rakes, Brenda Gulledge, and Thomas Rakes, "Quality Assurance in Teacher Education: Warranty Programs," *National Forum of Teacher Education Journal* 16, no. 3 (2005–2006): 1, http://www.nationalforum.com/Electronic%20Journal%20Volumes/Rakes,%20Glenda%20C%20Quality

%20Assurance%20in%20Teacher%20Education%20Warrenty%20
Programs.pdf.

4. U.S. Department of Education, Institute of Education Sciences, National Center for Education Statistics. *Digest of Education Statistics, 2001.* Publication No. NCES 2002-130. (Washington, DC: National Center for Education Statistics, 2002), 76, http://nces.ed.gov/pubs2002/2002130.pdf.

5. Susanna Loeb and Michelle Reininger, "Public Policy and Teacher Labor Markets: What We Know and Why It Matters," *The Education Policy Center at Michigan State University* (April 2004): 18.

6. Charles Bidwell and John Kasarda, "Conceptualizing and Measuring the Effects of School and Schooling," *American Journal of Education* 88, no. 4 (1980): 401–430.

7. Larry Cuban, *How Teachers Taught: Constancy and Change in American Classrooms 1890–1990* (New York: Teachers College Press, 1993).

8. Bureau of Labor Statistics, "Occupational Employment and Wages, 2008," Table 1, http://www.bls.gov/news.release/pdf/ocwage.pdf.

9. Peter D. Hart Research Associates, Inc., *Teaching as a Second Career*, (Washington, DC: Woodrow Wilson National Fellowship Foundation, 2008), http://www.woodrow.org/images/pdf/policy/Teaching2ndCareer_0908.pdf.

10. Clayton Christenson, Michael Horn, and Curtis Johnson, *Disrupting Class: How Disruptive Innovation Will Change the Way the World Learns* (New York: McGraw Hill, 2008); Terry M. Moe and John E. Chubb, *Liberating Learning: Technology, Politics, and the Future of American Education* (San Francisco: John Wiley and Sons, 2009); Tom Vander Ark, *Getting Smart: How Digital Learning Is Changing the World* (San Francisco: John Wiley and Sons, 2011).

11. Frederick M. Hess, "Quality Control in K–12 Digital Learning: Three (Imperfect) Approaches," in *Creating Healthy Policy for Digital Learning: A Working Paper Series from the Thomas B. Fordham Institute* (Washington, DC: Thomas B. Fordham Institute, 2011).

12. Thomas Stewart and Patrick Wolf, "The Evolution of Parental School Choice," in *Customized Schooling: Beyond Whole-School Reform,* eds. Frederick M. Hess and Bruno V. Manno (Cambridge, MA: Harvard Education Press, 2011), 95.

13. Frank L. Smith, *New American Secondary Schools Ventures (Grades 7–14)* (unpublished manuscript, St. John's University, 2009).

14. New Hampshire Department of Education, "Supporting Student Success through Extended Learning Opportunities," http://www.education.nh.gov/innovations/elo/success.htm.

15. Jon Fullerton, "The Data Challenge," in *Customized Schooling: Beyond Whole School Reform,* eds. Frederick M. Hess and Bruno V. Manno (Cambridge, MA: Harvard Education Press, 2011).
16. History of Sears Catalog 2010, http://www.searsarchives.com/catalogs/history.htm.
17. Jeffrey R. Henig and Frederick M. Hess, "The Declining Significance of Space and Geography," *Phi Delta Kappan* 92, no. 3 (November 2010): 57–61.
18. Chester E. Finn Jr. and Eric Osberg, "Reframing the Choice Agenda for Education Reform," in *Customized Schooling: Beyond Whole School Reform,* eds. Frederick M. Hess and Bruno V. Manno (Cambridge, MA: Harvard Education Press, 2011), 27–48.

Chapter 5

1. Greg J. Duncan and Richard J. Murnane, "Economic Inequality: The Real Cause of the Urban School Problem," *Chicago Tribune,* October 6, 2011, http://articles.chicagotribune.com/2011-10-06/news/ct-perspec-1006-urban-20111006_1_poor-children-graduation-rate-gap; National Assessment of Educational Progress, http://nces.ed.gov/nationsreportcard/.
2. Massachusetts Comprehensive Assessment System, http://www.doe.mass.edu/mcas/results.html.
3. Iris C. Rotberg, "International Test Scores, Irrelevant Policies," *Education Week* 31, no. 3 (September 14, 2011): 32.
4. Beth M. Miller, "Out-of-School Time: Effects on Learning in the Primary Grades," *Action Research Paper,* no. 4 (Wellesley, MA: National Institute on Out-of-School Time, 1995).
5. The Broader, Bolder Approach to Education, http://www.boldapproach.org/index.php?id=01.
6. Charles Bruner, "Thinking Collaboratively: Ten Questions and Answers to Help Policy Makers Improve Children's Services" (working paper, Washington, DC: Children, Youth and Families Education and Research Network, 1991), http://www1.cyfernet.org/prog/comm/98-thinkco.html; Joseph M. Bryson, Barbara C. Crosby, and Melissa Middleton Stone, "The Design and Implementation of Cross-Sector Collaborations: Propositions from the Literature," *Public Administration Review* (December 2006): 44–55; Barbara Gray, *Collaborating: Finding Common Ground for Multiparty Problems* (San Francisco: Jossey-Bass, 1991).
7. Brian Jacob and Jens Ludwig, "Improving Educational Outcomes for Poor Children," *Focus* 26, no. 2 (Fall 2009): 56–61; Lisbeth Schorr and Daniel

Schorr, *Within Our Reach: Breaking the Cycle of Disadvantage* (New York: Anchor, 1988).

8. David C. Berliner, *Poverty and Potential: Out-of-School Factors and School Success* (Boulder and Tempe: Education and the Public Interest Center & Education Policy Research Unit, 2009), http://epicpolicy.org/publication/poverty-and-potential.

9. City Connects, http://www.bc.edu/schools/lsoe/cityconnects/.

10. Robert J. Chaskin and Harold A. Richman, "Concerns About School-Linked Services: Institution-Based Versus Community-Based Models," *The Future of Children: School-Linked Services* 2, no. 1 (1992): 107–117; Larry Cuban, *As Good As It Gets: What School Reform Brought to Austin* (Cambridge, MA: Harvard University Press, 2010).

11. Howard Adelman and Linda Taylor, "School Improvement: A Functional View of Enabling Equity of Opportunity," August 2011, http://smhp.psych.ucla.edu/pdfdocs/functions.pdf; Robert L. Crowson and William L. Boyd, "Achieving Coordinated, School-Linked Services: Facilitating Utilization of the Emerging Knowledge" (working paper, Washington DC: Office of Educational Research and Improvement, and Philadelphia: National Research Center on Education in the Inner Cities, 1994); Robert L. Crowson and William L. Boyd, *New Roles for Community Services in Educational Reform* (Philadelphia: Mid-Atlantic Lab, 1999).

12. Joseph A. Schumpeter, *Capitalism, Socialism and Democracy* (New York: Harper, 1975), 83 [originally published 1942].

13. Clayton Christenson, Michael Horn, and Curtis Johnson, *Disrupting Class: How Disruptive Innovation Will Change the Way the World Learns* (New York: McGraw Hill, 2008).

14. Donald T. Campbell, "Methods for the Experimenting Society," *American Journal of Evaluation* 12 (1991): 223–260.

15. HighScope Perry Preschool Study, http://www.highscope.org/content.asp?contentid=219; Robert C. Pianta et al., "Kindergarten Teachers' Practices Related to the Transition to School: Results of a National Survey," *The Elementary School Journal* 100 (1999): 71–86; Patricia A. Lauer et al., "Out-of-School-Time Programs: A Meta-Analysis of Effects for At-Risk Students," *Review of Educational Research* 76, no. 2 (2006): 275–313; Joseph L. Mahoney, Heather Lord, and Erica Carryl, "An Ecological Analysis of After-School Program Participation and the Development of Academic Performance and Motivational Attributes for Disadvantaged Children," *Child Development* 76, no. 4 (July/August 2005): 811–825; Marco

A. Muñoz, *Outcome-Based Community-School Partnerships: The Impa.. oj the After-School Programs on Non-Academic and Academic Indicators* (Louisville: University of Kentucky, 2002), http://www.eric.ed.gov:80/PDFS/ ED468973.pdf; Deborah Lowe Vandell, Elizabeth R. Reisner, and Kim M. Pierce, *Outcomes Linked to High-Quality Afterschool Programs: Longitudinal Findings from the Study of Promising Practices* (Irvine: University of California, and Washington, DC: Policy Studies Associates, 2007); Karl L. Alexander, Doris R. Entwisle, and Linda Stefferl Olson, "Lasting Consequences of the Summer Learning Gap," *American Sociological Review* 72, no. 2 (April 2007): 167–181; City Connects, *The Impact of City Connects Annual Report 2010* (Boston: Boston College Center for Optimized Student Support, 2010), http://www.bc.edu/content/dam/files/schools/lsoe/cityconnects/ pdf/CityConnects_AnnualReport_2010_web.pdf.

16. Jacquelynne Eccles and Jennifer Appleton, eds., *Community Programs to Promote Youth Development* (Washington, DC: National Research Council and Institute of Medicine, Committee on Community-Level Programs for Youth, 2002), chapter 2, http://www.nap.edu/catalog. php?record_id=10022.

17. Charles E. Basch, *Healthier Students are Better Learners* (New York: The Campaign for Educational Equity, Teachers College, 2010).

18. CORAL, http://www.ppv.org/ppv/initiative. asp?section_id=23&initiative_id=29.

19. Amy Arbreton et al., *Advancing Achievement: Findings from an Independent Evaluation of a Major After-School Initiative* (Philadelphia: Public/Private Ventures, 2008), http://www.ppv.org/publications/assets/225_publication. pdf.

20. Louise Adler and Sid Gardner, eds., *The Politics of Linking Schools and Social Services*, The 1993 Yearbook of the Politics of Education Association (Washington, DC: The Falmer Press, 1994).

21. Community Learning Center Institute, http://clcinstitute.org/; Cincinnati Public Schools, http://www.cps-k12.org/community/CLC/CLC.htm.

22. Youth Data Archive, http://gardnercenter.stanford.edu/current_initiatives/ youth_archive.html.

23. Kara Dukakis (associate director, Youth Data Archive), interview by Helen Janc Malone, September 23, 2011.

24. Gene I. Maeroff, *Education's Central Role in Mobilizing Community Transformation: A Report to the Say Yes to Education Foundation* (Washington, DC: Cross & Joftus, 2010).

25. Say Yes Syracuse, http://sayyessyracuse.org.

26. Jeffrey L. Pressman and Aaron Wildavsky, *Implementation: How Great Expectations in Washington Are Dashed in Oakland* (Berkeley and Los Angeles: University of California Press, 1973).

27. Jeffrey R. Henig and Paul S. Reville, "Outside-In School Reform: Why Attention Will Return to Non-School Factors," *Education Week*, May 25, 2011; and a series of associated blog posts on the *Education Week* Web site, "The Futures of School Reform" http://blogs.edweek.org/edweek/futures_of_reform/.

28. For a fuller consideration of the evidence for, and implications of, the growing role of general-purpose governance and politics in education policy, see Jeffrey Henig, "The End of Educational Exceptionalism: The Rise of the Education Executives in the White House, State House, and Mayor's Office" (paper presented at Rethinking Education Governance in the Twenty-First Century Conference, Center for American Progress, December 1, 2011), http://www.edexcellencemedia.net/publications/2011/20111201_RethinkingEducationGovernance/Henig-FordhamCAP-Governance-ConferenceDraft.

29. Gallup, "Trust in Government," http://www.gallup.com/poll/5392/trust-government.aspx.

30. Henig and Reville, "Outside-In School Reform."

31. Ben Levin, *How to Change 5000 Schools: A Practical and Positive Approach for Leading Change at Every Level* (Cambridge MA: Harvard Education Press, 2008).

32. Michael A. Rebell, "The Right to Comprehensive Educational Opportunity," *Harvard Civil Rights-Civil Liberties Law Review* 47, no. 1 (2011).

33. Benjamin Michael Superfine, "Court-Driven Reform and Educational Opportunity: Centralization, Decentralization, and the Shifting Judicial Role," *Review of Educational Research* 80, no. 1 (2010): 112.

34. Lynn Olson, "Cross-Agency Project Tracks Students' Data to Tackle Policy Issues," *Education Week* 27, no. 34 (2008): 8–9.

Chapter 6

1. Oxford Dictionaries Online, s.v. "knowledge," http://oxforddictionaries.com/definition/knowledge?q=knowledge; James Gleick, *The Information: A History, a Theory, a Flood* (New York: Pantheon, 2011).

2. Sugata Mitra, "Can Kids Teach Themselves?" (paper presented at LIFT 2007), http://www.youtube.com/watch?v=xRb7_ffl2D0.

3. Larry Cuban, *Teachers and Machines: The Classroom Use of Technology Since 1920* (New York: Teachers College Press, 1986).

4. Clayton Christensen, Michael B. Horn, and Curtis W. Johnson, *Disrupting Class: How Disruptive Innovation Will Change the Way the World Learns* (New York: McGraw-Hill, 2008).

5. Wikipedia, "Wiki," http://en.wikipedia.org/wiki/Wikipedia:FAQ/Schools#What_does_wiki_mean.3F.

6. Wikipedia, "Wikipedia Statistics," http://stats.wikimedia.org/EN/TablesWikipediansContributors.htm.

7. Wikipedia, "FAQ/Schools," http://en.wikipedia.org/wiki/Wikipedia:FAQ/Schools.

8. Wikipedia, s.v. "encyclopedia," http://en.wikipedia.org/wiki/History_of_encyclopedia#cite_note-naturalis-11.

9. Online Etymology Dictionary, s.v. "encyclopedia," http://www.etymonline.com/index.php?term=encyclopedia.

10. Wikipedia, "Wikipedia Statistics," http://stats.wikimedia.org/EN/Sitemap.htm.

11. David Tyack and Larry Cuban, *Tinkering Toward Utopia: A Century of Public School Reform* (Cambridge, MA: Harvard University Press, 1995).

12. Frederick Hess, *Future of Educational Entrepreneurship* (Cambridge, MA: Harvard Education Press, 2008).

13. Richard F. Murnane and Frank Levy, *Teaching the New Basic Skills: Principles for Educating Children to Thrive in a Changing Economy* (New York: Free Press, 1996).

14. U.S. Department of Education, *Transforming American Education: Learning Powered by Technology* (U.S. Department of Education, Office of Educational Technology, 2010), 17; James A. Banks et al., *Learning in and Out of School in Diverse Environments: Life-Long, Life-Wide, Life-Deep* (Seattle: NSF LIFE Center and University of Washington Center for Multicultural Education, 2006), 9, http://life-slc.org/docs/Banks_etal-LIFE-Diversity-Report.pdf.

15. Theodore Levitt, "Marketing Myopia," *Harvard Business Review* 38 (1960): 45–56.

16. Christensen, Johnson, and Horn, *Disrupting Class.*

17. American Society for Training and Development, *2010 State of the Industry Report,* http://www.astd.org/content/research/stateOfIndustry.htm; U.S. Department of Education, National Center for Education Statistics, *Condition of Education* (Table A-50-4. 2004–05 and 2008–09 Integrated

Postsecondary Education Data System, Spring 2006 and Spring 2010), http://nces.ed.gov/programs/coe/tables/table-rep-4.asp.

18. U.S. Department of Education, National Center for Education Statistics, *Digest of Education Statistics* (Table 434, 2010), http://nces.ed.gov/programs/digest/d10/tables/dt10_434.asp.

19. The Henry J. Kaiser Family Foundation, *Generation M²: Media in the Lives of 8-to-18-Year-Olds* (Washington, DC: 2010), http://www.kff.org/entmedia/upload/8010.pdf.

20. National Park Service Public Use Statistics Office, *Annual Summary Report for 2010,* http://www.nature.nps.gov/stats/viewReport.cfm?selectedReport=SystemSummaryReport.cfm.

21. Sugata Mitra, "The child-driven education," *TEDGlobal 2010,* July 2010.

22. Levitt, "Marketing Myopia."

23. See, for example, http://schoolofone.org/ and http://en.wikipedia.org/wiki/New_Orleans_Public_Schools.

24. Paideia Active Learning, http://www.paideia.org/about-paideia/philosophy/.

Chapter 7

1. National Commission on Excellence in Education, *A Nation at Risk: The Imperative for Educational Reform* (Washington, DC: U.S. Department of Education, 1983).

2. David Tyack and Larry Cuban, *Tinkering Toward Utopia: A Century of Public School Reform* (Cambridge, MA: Harvard University Press, 1995).

3. Frederick M. Hess, *Spinning Wheels: The Politics of Urban School Reform* (Washington, DC: Brookings Institution Press, 1999).

4. Frederick M. Hess, Greg M. Gunn, and Olivia M. Meeks, "Maybe The Square Peg Will Do," *Education Week,* May 11, 2011. This essay was a predecessor to the piece in this volume.

5. Jal Mehta and Steven Teles, "Jurisdictional Politics: A New Federal Role in Education," in *Carrots, Sticks, and the Bully Pulpit: Lessons From a Half-Century of Federal Efforts to Improve America's Schools,* Frederick M. Hess and Andrew P. Kelly, eds. (Cambridge, MA: Harvard Education Press, 2011), 197–216.

6. For more on Sal Khan, see http://www.khanacademy.org/

7. James S. Coleman, *Equality of Educational Opportunity* (Washington, DC: U.S. Department of Health, Education, and Welfare, Office of Education, 1966).

8. Greg J. Duncan, Jens Ludwig, and Katherine A. Magnuson, "Reducing Poverty Through Preschool Interventions," *Future of Children* 17, no. 2 (2007): 143–160.

9. Ivan Illich, *Deschooling Society* (London: Calder and Boyars, 1971).
10. John Dewey, *Experience and Education* (London and New York: Macmillan, 1938).
11. Albert Hirschman, *Exit, Voice, and Loyalty: Responses to Decline in Firms, Organizations, and States* (Cambridge, MA: Harvard University Press, 1970). Hirschman pointed out that there is often a dilemma for how individuals should respond to an organization or other entity that they are a part of: they can express "loyalty" to the organization, they can use "voice" to try to change the organization, or they can "exit" the organization and look elsewhere. This framework is often used to compare more democratic and collective modes of decision making (loyalty and voice) with market-oriented individual choice (exit).
12. Paideia Active Learning, http://www.paideia.org/about-paideia/philosophy/.
13. Howard Gardner, *Truth, Beauty, and Goodness Reframed: Educating for the Virtues in the Twenty-First Century* (New York: Basic Books, 2011).
14. Deborah Meier, *In Schools We Trust* (Boston: Beacon, 2002).
15. See http://www.hewlett.org/programs/education-program/deeper-learning.

ACKNOWLEDGMENTS

We, the editors, would like to thank all of the contributors to the project, many of whom wrote in this volume, and all of whose names are listed at the back of this book. You stuck with us when it wasn't clear exactly where we were going or when we would arrive. You did so in good spirits, sharing your perspectives and wisdom, and listening carefully even to those with whom you did not agree. We hope that this volume shows that the whole can, indeed, be more than the sum of its parts, as the possibilities you lay out for the future range more widely than any one of us could have imagined, and the collective analysis of the limits of current thinking is more powerful than any one critique could be.

We couldn't have done our work without significant support from the following institutions and individuals. Jal Mehta and Robert B. Schwartz work at the Harvard Graduate School of Education, the rare academic institution that not only does not limit, but actually encourages, its professors to step back from the specifics of research and try to develop ideas and knowledge that might help the field inch forward. We'd also like to thank our students, who pushed our thinking, told us what was relevant and what was not, and who we trust will create a better future for schooling than we could possibly imagine. Frederick M. Hess is director of education policy at the American Enterprise Institute and is, as always, hugely grateful for AEI's generous and rock-ribbed support, its intellectually dynamic culture, and the leadership and friendship of AEI's president, Arthur Brooks. We owe a huge debt to Helen Janc Malone, the project manager for the entire project: without her tireless work and attention to detail on all fronts, the project would not have come off. She is a rising star in her own right, and we were extremely lucky to have her captaining this ship. We also want to thank current and former AEI employees Olivia Meeks, Taryn Hochleitner, and Rebecca King for their intellectual contributions, tireless efforts, and invaluable support in making this final product the success that it is. We would like to thank everyone who helped to host our New Orleans visit, particularly the schools (which need to remain anonymous) for their openness in sharing their work. We want to thank the following graduate students, who took careful notes and gave their thoughts at one or more of the meetings: Hilary Bresnahan, Joseph Doctor, John Roberts, Tai Sunnanon, Amy Wooten, and Jennifer Worden. We also express our considerable appreciation to Zachary First of the Drucker Institute for his excellent facilitation of our last meeting. Jal would also like to thank his assistant and friend, Matt Tallon, who is always there to solve the inevitable last-minute problem, and does so with such speed, accuracy, and aplomb that it is hard to remember how I ever managed without him.

As we moved toward publication, we again found ourselves in highly skilled hands. We published some of this work initially in a series and blog in *Education Week*, and we want to thank Elizabeth Rich and her team at Ed Week for seeing the potential in this project and getting our ideas into print at an early stage. Our authors found that blogging ideas and getting feedback from the *Education Week* community was a very stimulating way to develop the ideas in a knowledgeable public forum, and so we particularly appreciate Elizabeth's vision and enterprise in launching the *Futures* blog. Similarly, Joan Richardson at *Phi Delta Kappan* saw potential in some of our work around "unbundling," and her decision to publish five of our essays gave needed early legitimacy to our work. Caroline Chauncey of Harvard Education Press was a critical friend and thought partner to the project. She attended all of our meetings and discussions, and provided absolutely essential feedback about where we had something new to say and where we were just reinventing old truths. She exemplifies what an editor can be: someone who is highly knowledgeable and intellectually engaged, close enough to the work to understand it but retaining enough distance to tell us which of our "insights" might be of interest to an actual reader. She was also resolute in her conviction that, no matter what other media we might use to express these ideas, a book was still the form for serious writing—and that conviction is one reason that this book exists.

Finally, we would like to thank the William Flora Hewlett Foundation and the Spencer Foundation for their generous funding of the Futures of School Reform initiative.

ABOUT THE EDITORS

Jal Mehta is an assistant professor at the Harvard Graduate School of Education. His primary research interests are in understanding the relationship between knowledge and action; substantively, he is most interested in the policy and politics of creating high-quality schooling at scale. Mehta received his PhD in sociology and social policy from Harvard University. His dissertation, *The Transformation of American Educational Policy, 1980–2001*, recently received the Outstanding Dissertation Award from the AERA politics' section. Mehta is coauthor of *Rampage: The Social Roots of School Shootings* (Basic Books, 2004), which was a finalist for the C. Wright Mills Award. He is the author of the forthcoming book, *The Allure of Order: The Troubled Quest to Rationalize a Century of American Schooling* (Oxford University Press), which charts the growing "rationalization" of American schooling, asking what this shift means for the educational field, for the teaching profession, and for social justice. He is also working on a project, The Chastened Dream, about the limits and possibilities of using social science as a means of achieving social progress.

Robert B. Schwartz is the Francis Keppel Professor of Practice of Educational Policy and Administration at the Harvard Graduate School of Education. He held a wide variety of leadership positions in education and government before joining the HGSE faculty in 1996. He holds an MA from Brandeis University. From 1997 to 2002, Schwartz served as president of Achieve, Inc., an independent, bipartisan, nonprofit organization created by governors and corporate leaders to help states improve their schools. From 1990 to 1996, Schwartz directed the education grantmaking program of the Pew Charitable Trusts. In addition to his work at HGSE, Achieve, and the Pew Charitable Trusts, Schwartz has been a high school English teacher and principal, an education advisor to the mayor of Boston and the governor of Massachusetts, an assistant director of the National Institute of Education, a special assistant to the president of the University of Massachusetts, and executive director of the Boston Compact, a public-private partnership designed to improve access to higher education and employment for urban high school graduates.

Frederick M. Hess is an educator, political scientist, and author. He serves as executive editor of *Education Next*, as lead faculty member for the Rice Education Entrepreneurship Program, on the review board for the Broad Prize in Urban Education, and on the boards of directors for the National Association of Charter School Authorizers, 4.0 SCHOOLS, and the American Board for the Certification of Teaching Excellence. He holds a PhD in government from Harvard University. A former high school social studies teacher, Hess has taught at the University of Virginia, the University of Pennsylvania, Georgetown University, Rice University, and Harvard University. His recent books include *Carrots, Sticks, and the Bully Pulpit* (Harvard Education Press, 2012), *The Same Thing Over and Over* (Harvard University Press, 2010), *Education Unbound* (ASCD, 2010), *The Future of Educational Entrepreneurship* (Harvard Education Press, 2008), *Common Sense School Reform* (Palgrave Macmillan, 2004), *Revolution at the Margins* (Brookings Institution Press, 2002), and *Spinning Wheels* (Brookings Institution Press, 1998). He also pens the *Education Week* blog "Rick Hess Straight Up" (http://blogs.edweek.org/edweek/rick_hess_straight_up/).

ABOUT THE CONTRIBUTORS

Anthony S. Bryk is the ninth president of the Carnegie Foundation for the Advancement of Teaching. From 2004 until assuming Carnegie's presidency in September 2008, Bryk held the Spencer Chair in Organizational Studies in the School of Education and the Graduate School of Business at Stanford University. Prior to Stanford, he held the Marshall Field IV Professor of Urban Education post in the sociology department at the University of Chicago. He was founding director of the Center for Urban School Improvement, which supports reform efforts within the Chicago Public Schools and launched the University's professional development charter school in the North Kenwood/Oakland neighborhood. Bryk is also founding director of the Consortium on Chicago School Research. In 2003, he was awarded the Thomas B. Fordham Foundation Prize for Distinguished Contributions to Educational Scholarship and the Distinguished Career Contributions Award from the American Educational Research Association. His recent book is *Organizing Schools for Improvement* (University of Chicago Press, 2010).

Elizabeth A. City is the executive director of the Doctor of Education Leadership (EdLD) Program and lecturer on education at the Harvard Graduate School of Education. City has served as a teacher, instructional coach, principal, and consultant; in each role, she focused on helping all children, and the educators who work with them, realize their full potential. She holds a doctorate in administration, planning, and social policy from the Harvard Graduate School of Education. She recently authored or coauthored *Strategy in Action: How School Systems Can Support Powerful Learning and Teaching* (Harvard Education

Press, 2009), *Instructional Rounds in Education: A Network Approach to Improving Teaching and Learning* (Harvard Education Press, 2009), *Resourceful Leadership: Tradeoffs and Tough Decisions on the Road to School Improvement* (Harvard Education Press, 2008), *The Teacher's Guide to Leading Student-Centered Discussions: Talking About Texts in the Classroom* (Corwin Press, 2006), and *Data Wise: A Step-by-Step Guide to Using Assessment Results to Improve Teaching and Learning* (Harvard Education Press, 2005).

Richard F. Elmore is the Gregory R. Anrig professor of educational leadership at Harvard University. He joined the faculty of the Harvard Graduate School of Education in 1990, having previously taught at the College of Education, Michigan State University, and the Graduate School of Public Affairs, University of Washington. Elmore holds a bachelor's degree in political science from Whitman College, a master's degree in political science from the Claremont Graduate School, and a doctorate in educational policy from the Harvard Graduate School of Education. He is a member of the National Academy of Education, and a past president of the Association for Public Policy and Management. He has held positions in the federal government as a legislative liaison with the U.S. Congress on education policy issues. Elmore is currently director of the Doctor in Educational Leadership (EdLD) program at HGSE. His current research and clinical work focuses on building capacity for instructional improvement in low performing schools. He is coauthor of *Instructional Rounds in Education: A Network Approach to Improving Teaching and Learning* (Harvard Education Press, 2009), and author of *School Reform from the Inside Out: Policy, Practice, and Performance* (Harvard Education Press, 2004).

Adam Gamoran is the John D. MacArthur professor of sociology and educational policy studies and director of the Wisconsin Center for Education Research at the University of Wisconsin–Madison. Gamoran received his BA, MA, and PhD from the University of Chicago. His most recent books include *Tracking and Inequality* (in *The Routledge International Handbook of the Sociology of Education*, 2010), *Standards-Based Reform and the Poverty Gap: Lessons for No Child Left Behind* (Brookings Institution Press, 2007), and *Stratification in Higher Education: A Comparative Study* (Stanford University Press, 2007). His current studies include two large-scale randomized trials: the impact of professional development to improve teaching and learning in elementary science in the Los Angeles Unified School District, and the impact of a parent involvement program to promote family-school social capital and student success in school districts in San Antonio and Phoenix. Gamoran also chairs the congressionally mandated Independent Advisory Panel of the National Assessment of Career and Technical Education.

Louis M. Gomez is the John D. and Catherine T. MacArthur Foundation chair in digital media and learning at the Graduate School of Education & Information Studies at the University of California, Los Angeles, and is a senior fellow at the Carnegie Foundation for the Advancement of Teaching. Prior to his current post, he was the Helen S. Faison Chair in Urban Education at the University of Pittsburgh, director of the Center for Urban Education, and a senior scientist at the Learning Research and Development Center. From 2001 to 2008, he held a number of faculty appointments at Northwestern University, including the Aon Chair in the Learning Sciences at the School of Education and Social Policy. Gomez received his bachelor's degree in psychology from the State University of New York at Stony Brook in 1974 and a doctorate in cognitive psychology from the University of California, Berkeley, in 1979. His recent publications include *Education Reform in New York City: Ambitious Change in the Nation's Most Complex System* (Harvard Education Press, 2011), *Getting Ideas Into Action: Building Networked Improvement Communities in Education* (Springer, 2011), and *Complex Systems View of Educational Policy Research* (Science, 2010).

Jeffrey Henig is a professor of political science and education at Teachers College, and professor of political science at Columbia University. He earned his PhD in political science at Northwestern University in 1978. Among his books on education politics are *The Charter School Experiment* (Harvard Education Press, 2010), *Between Public and Private* (Harvard Education Press, 2010), *Spin Cycle* (Russell Sage Foundation/ Century Foundation, 2008), *Mayors in the Middle: Politics, Race, and Mayoral Control of Urban Schools* (Princeton University Press, 2004), *Building Civic Capacity: The Politics of Reforming Urban Schools* (Kansas, 2001), and *The Color of School Reform: Race, Politics and the Challenge of Urban Education* (Princeton, 1999). His scholarly work has appeared in *American Journal of Education, Educational Evaluation and Policy Analysis, Journal of Urban Affairs, Policy Sciences, Policy Studies Review, Political Research Quarterly, Political Science Quarterly, Social Science Quarterly,* and *Urban Affairs Review.*

Paul T. Hill is the John and Marguerite Corbally professor at the University of Washington Bothell and director of the Center on Reinventing Public Education. He is a nonresident senior fellow at the Brookings and Hoover Institutions and directed the National Working Commission on Choice in K–12 Education. He chairs the National Charter School Research Project and leads its Charter School Achievement Consensus Panel. Hill holds a PhD and MA from Ohio State University and a BA from Seattle University, all in political science. His books include *Learning as We Go: Why School Choice is Worth the Wait* (Hoover Institution Press, 2010), *Taking Measure of Charter Schools: Better Assessments, Better Policymaking, Better Schools* (Rowman & Littlefield, 2010), *Charter Schools Against the Odds* (Hoover Institution Press, 2006), *Making School Reform Work: New Partnerships for Real Change* (Brookings Institution Press, 2004), *Charter Schools and Accountability in Public Education* (Brookings Institution Press, 2002), *It Takes A City: Getting Serious About Urban School Reform* (Brookings Institution Press, 2000), and *Fixing Urban Schools* (Brookings Institution Press,1998). He is also the lead author (with Lawrence Pierce and James Guthrie) of *Reinventing Public Education: How Contracting Can Transform America's Schools* (University of Chicago Press, 1997).

Ben Levin is a professor and Canada Research Chair in education leadership and policy at the Ontario Institute for Studies in Education (OISE), University of Toronto. He has recently completed his post as deputy minister of education for the Province of Ontario. From 1999 until September 2002, he was deputy minister of advanced education and deputy minister of education, training, and youth for Manitoba, with responsibility for public policy in all areas of education and training. He holds a BA (Honors) from the University of Manitoba, an EdM from Harvard University and a PhD from OISE. His most recent books include *More High School Graduates* (Corwin, 2012), *Breaking Barriers* (Pearson Canada, 2012), *How to Change 5000 Schools* (Harvard Education Press, 2008), and *Governing Education* (University of Toronto Press, 2005). He is currently engaged in knowledge mobilization on how to increase connections among research, policy, and practice. He is also working with Michael Fullan on educational change focusing on leadership development and student impact in Alberta, Canada.

Doug Lynch is the former vice dean at the graduate school of education and an academic director for Wharton Executive Education at the University of Pennsylvania. Before Penn, Lynch worked at New York University (NYU), the College Board, and Arizona State University. He has done doctoral work in education evaluation (Arizona State University), economics and education (Columbia University), and political theory (New School), and has an MBA from NYU. At Penn, Lynch has launched several new endeavors, including the first joint doctoral program in work-based learning (with the Wharton School) and the executive master's for Teach for America corps members serving Philadelphia. His educational programs have won national awards, including the president's award for commercial innovation in exporting by the U.S. Department of Commerce, an APX award, and an HR Executive Top 10 award. He sits on six editorial boards; is the chair of the public policy council for the American Society for Training & Development and of the U.S. delegation to the International Standards Organization, setting standards for trade in continuing education; and sits on the board of visitors of the Central Intelligence Agency's university.

Helen Janc Malone is an advanced doctoral candidate at the Harvard Graduate School of Education and the project manager for the Futures of School Reform project. She holds an MA in education policy and leadership from the University of Maryland, College Park, and an EdM in education policy and management from Harvard University. She is currently an officer for AERA's Educational Change Special Interest Group (SIG) and the editor of an international series, *Lead the Change*. At AERA, she helped form two SIGs focused on youth development and school reform. She is currently on the editorial review board for a peer-reviewed journal, *Afterschool Matters,* and has recently served as an expert advisor on several projects at Harvard and Wellesley universities. She is a 2011 Phi Delta Kappa International Emerging Leader Award recipient. Her most recent publications include *Expanded Learning Time and Opportunities* (Jossey-Bass, 2011), *Year-Round Learning* (Harvard Family Research Project, 2011), and "Innovations in the U.S. Education Reform" (*Innovations in Teaching,* 2011).

Olivia Meeks is a research coordinator at District of Columbia Public Schools (DCPS), where she manages the value-added data for the IMPACT teacher evaluation system and serves on the district's research review board. Before working at DCPS, she served as a research assistant for Frederick M. Hess in the education policy studies department at the American Enterprise Institute (AEI). During her tenure at AEI, she coauthored several national reports on education reform, including "School Boards Circa 2010: Governance in the Accountability Era" for the National School Boards Association and "The Case for Being Bold:

A New Agenda for Business in Improving STEM Education" for the U.S. Chamber of Commerce. Her research focuses on collective bargaining, customized schooling, and education governance. She is an honors graduate of the University of Arkansas, where she was named an Economic Scholar for Undergraduate Research by the Federal Reserve Bank of Dallas in 2009 and a Harry S. Truman Scholar in 2008.

Terry M. Moe is the William Bennett Munro professor of political science at Stanford University and a senior fellow at the Hoover Institution. He holds a BA in economics from the University of California, San Diego, and a PhD in political science from the University of Minnesota. Moe has written extensively on public bureaucracy, the presidency, and political institutions more generally, and is considered a leading figure in these fields. His book (with John E. Chubb), *Politics, Markets, and America's Schools*, is among the most influential works on public education, and has been a major force in the movement for school choice in America and abroad. His recent books include *Special Interest: Teachers Unions and America's Public Schools* (Brookings Institution Press, 2011), *Liberating Learning: Technology, Politics, and the Future of American Education* (Jossey-Bass, 2009), *Schools, Vouchers, and the American Public* (Brookings Institution Press, 2001), and *A Primer on America's Schools* (editor; Hoover Institution Press, 2001).

Paul Reville is the Massachusetts secretary of education and a senior lecturer on education at the Harvard Graduate School of Education. He holds an EdM from Stanford University and several honorary doctorates. He is the former president of the Rennie Center for Education Research & Policy, the former chairman of the Massachusetts State Board of Education, and the former executive director of the Pew Forum on Standards-Based Reform. Secretary Reville was founding executive director of the Massachusetts Business Alliance for Education (MBAE), which provided key conceptual and political leadership for the Education Reform Act of 1993. He also served on the Massachusetts State

Board of Education, where he chaired the Massachusetts Commission on Time and Learning. From 1996 to 2003, Reville chaired the Massachusetts Education Reform Review Commission, and was founding executive director of the Alliance for Education. Reville began his educational career as a practitioner, first as a VISTA volunteer/youth worker and then as a teacher and principal in two urban, alternative high schools.

INDEX

AACTE. See American Association of
Colleges of Teacher Education
(AACTE)
Abecedarian project, 196
academic achievement
dynamics driving, 14
international common elements,
16–26
United States improvement, 13
academic performance, 195
accessibility to data, 135
accountability, 75–76
foot traffic data, 130
high-stakes, 179
outcome-based, 109
quantity and quality of services, 130
service providers, 134
shared, 134–138
versus standards, 129
state systems of, 127
top-down, 76
unbundling, 109–113
accountability era, learning what
works in, 129–132
accountability metrics, 116
accountability systems, 37
Achieve, 31
Achievement First, 188, 190
Achievement Reporting and
Innovation System (ARIS) data
warehouse, 113
action research, 41–44, 46
Addams, Jane, 196

Adler, Mortimer, 175–176
administrators not knowing what
schools need, 38
adoption theory, 156–157
affluent students and college
completion, 120
after action reviews, 165
afterschool programs, 131
agency, 170
AIR. See American Institutes for
Research (AIR)
Alliance for School Choice, 188
Amazon, 112
American Association of Colleges of
Teacher Education (AACTE)
Teacher Performance
Assessment, 31
American Association of Museums,
168
American Council on
Education's College Credit
Recommendation Service
(CREDIT) feedback, 167
American education
changing slowly, 63
institutional conservatism, 62
low-cognitive-demand, repetitive
tasks, 161
online learning, 92
reform stereotypes, 65
technology and, 72
American Institutes for Research
(AIR), 138

American Medical Association, 102
American National Standards Institute
    standards for certifying non-
    formal learning, 167
ARIS data warehouse. See
    Achievement Reporting and
    Innovation System (ARIS) data
    warehouse
Asian countries, consensual process to
    develop education policy, 26
assessment
    spillovers across policy sectors, 128
assessments
    linked to curriculum, 18–19
    multi-indicator approach, 129
    unbundling, 109–113
Atlantic, 194
Australia
    embracing a different kind of
        learning, 164–167
    federal states, 15
    high quality and high student
        performance, 164
    leadership development, 20
    population diversity, 15
    schools governed as unitary state
        system, 164
    schools needing additional support,
        19
    state of Victoria, 164–165
    Ultranet, 164–165
authoritative knowledge, 155
autonomy in schools, 89–90

Barnard, Henry, 97
beginning teachers, system for certify-
    ing, 31
Berger, Larry, 2
Bersin, Alan, 188
Berwick, Don, 44, 63
best practices approach, 3–4
Bidwell, Charles, 100–101

Blatt, Joseph, 168
blogosphere, 197
Boston teacher residency, 55
bottom-up political mobilization
    route, 147–148
Boy Scouts badges, 152, 166–167
British School Inspectorate, 111
Broad Foundation, 188
Bryk, Anthony, 2, 47, 51, 63
buggy whips, 172
bureaucratic Industrial Age structures,
    35
bureaucratic silos, moving beyond,
    134–138
bureaucratic systems, 182

C. S. Mott foundation, 124
CAEL portfolios. See Council for
    Adult and Experiential Learning
    (CAEL) portfolios
Campbell, Donald, 128
Canada
    federal states, 15
    leadership development, 20
    Ontario, Quebec, and Alberta
        provinces education
        improvement, 16
    population diversity, 15
    teacher education programs, 17
    teachers from top third of talent
        pool, 31, 40
Canada, Geoffrey, 121
careers, innovations in, 33
Carnegie Forum, 29
Carnegie Foundation for the
    Advancement of Teaching, 48,
    63
    coordination services to community
        colleges, 50
    networked improvement
        communities (NICs), 51–53
Caro-Bruce, Cathy, 43

Carter, James, 97
case-management services, 131
Catholic Church, 162–163
The Center for Education Reform, 188
challenges, simplifying nature of, 145
change
    first steps toward, 62–64
    lack of real, 178–181
    politics of significant, 208–210
chartering authorities, 70
charter schools, 16, 180
    devolving more authority to students, 191
    different culture of, 190
    education funds, 69–70
    ensuring quality, 191
    experimenting with new practices and ideas, 180
    human-capital-intensive, 191
    impact of, 190
    meeting parent and student demands, 189
    online learning, 73
    political objections to, 91
    popularity, 189
    regulations, 70–71
    scaling, 191
    teacher burnout, 191
    traditional organization, 80
    usable knowledge, 190
    virtual, 81
cherry-pick research, 145
Child and Youth Readiness Cabinet, 136
Children's Aid Society, 133
Childress, Stacey, 2
Christensen, Clayton, 104, 128, 157
Chubb, John, 105
Citizen Schools, 103–104
City, Elizabeth, 6, 157, 184, 198
City College of San Francisco, 136

City Connects, 126
classrooms
    Common School, 97
    gaps in skills and performance, 2, 5
    low levels of cognitive challenge, 2
    mixed model, 79–82
    student needs, 43
    unbundling, 104–106
    virtual, 80–81
CLC Partnership Networks, 133
CLCs. See Community Learning Centers (CLCs)
CLEP scores. See College-Level Examination Program (CLEP) scores
Coleman report, 195
collaboration
    barriers to, 132
    cross-sector, 132–134
    interagency, 132–134
    working with others, 169
collective bargaining
    free choice, 77
    mixed model, 77–78, 85
    restrictions, 85
    schools, 85
    states, 77
    teachers, 82–83
collective learning, 128
college graduates
    completion rate, 32
    interest in teaching, 103
College-Level Examination Program (CLEP) scores, 167
common concerns, lack of attention to, 194
Common Core State Standards, 31
common curriculum, 18–19
commonly understood problem space, 48–50
common market in education, 74–75
common protocols for inquiry, 50–51

Common School, problematic legacy, 97–99
common schooling theory, 204
common targets, 47–48
Communities Organizing Resources to Advance Learning (CORAL), 131
Community Action Agencies and Model Cities, 142
community colleges, 33
Community Learning Centers (CLCs), 133–134
Community Schools Act (1974), 124
comparable metrics, 117
compensation
one-size-fits-all approach, 108
performance-based, 108–109
step-and-lane pay scale, 108
complementarities, 201–203
compliance orientation, shifting to learning orientation, 173
comprehensive approach, 144
computers replacing routine tasks, 161
ConnCAN, 188
Connections Academy, 73
constraints limiting innovation, 162
consumer, shift in role of, 159
Consumer Reports, 111
content unbundling, 100
continuous quality improvement, 44–45
CORAL. See Communities Organizing Resources to Advance Learning (CORAL)
core knowledge, 205
Council for Adult and Experiential Learning (CAEL) portfolios, 167
Council of Chief State School Officers, 31, 209
countering reigning fatalism, 144–146

countries
academic achievement common elements, 15
educational outcomes improvement, 14
unitary systems, 15
court-focused approach to twenty-first-century education system, 146–147
creative destruction, 127–128
credentialing, 169
CREDIT feedback. See American Council on Education's College Credit Recommendation Service (CREDIT) feedback
cross-sector collaboration, 132–134
Crotonville, 174
crowd-sourced data reflecting user experience, 112
Cuban, Larry, 157, 161, 181
cultural norms around schooling, 138
curriculum
assessments linked to, 18–19
common, 18–19
developing new software and supporting materials for, 73
narrowing of, 130
customer satisfaction, 111
customizing education, 81

Darling-Hammond, Linda, 121
data
accessibility to, 135
aggregating from multiple providers, 112–113
DC Opportunity Scholarship investigators, 111
decentralized service options, 99
decision making, 90
defensive individualism norm, 39
Deming, W. Edwards, 44, 60

Democratic party, reformist ferment, 92
Denmark and career-oriented pathways, 23
Deschooling Society (Illich), 198
differentiation
theoretically and pragmatically developed ideas basis, 128
twenty-first-century education system, 138–139
digital badge systems, 166–167
disadvantaged students, 87–88
voucher programs for, 71
disadvantages of poverty
education system needed—not a school system, 122–123
good intentions and poor results, 119–122
why past is not prologue, 123–138
Disrupting Class: How Disruptive Innovation Will Change the Way the World Learns (Christensen, Horn, and Johnson), 104–105, 128
dissolving school system, 197–200
district-run schools
education funds, 70
governed from top down, 89
districts
accountability, 58, 75–76
authority given to schools, 76
autonomy, 78, 89
collective bargaining, 78
competition, 75–76
conforming to basic rules, 76
cost efficiencies, 116
facilitating and supporting better work in schools, 63
freeing up, 75–77
governance structures, 58
hold on America's children, 78–79

infrastructure, 58
institutional pasts, 67
network initiation and growth, 58
online learning, 73
operational decisions, 90
performing and earning clientele, 76
political control of, 59
politics against change, 91
portfolio model, 64, 76, 205
reform community practices, 191
reorganizing, 77
responsibilities, 98
running schools, 69
supporting growth of knowledge profession, 57–59
trustworthy data, 112
unresponsive, 76
Driscoll, Heather, 3
dropout rates, 49, 132
dropouts, 1–2
Duncan, Arne, 64

early-childhood programs, 131
eBay, 112
economy
complex communication and problem solving, 161
connecting secondary education to, 23–24
free market, 66
government-run, 66
education
achievement and socioeconomic status, 119
across state borders, 74–75
adoption versus use of, 156–158
choice and competition, 68–69
common market in, 74–75
common targets, 47–48
comprehensive approach to, 123–124

education (*continued*)
customization and flexibility, 132
customizing, 81
diversity in approach, 27
dropout problem, 49
equity, 30
experimenting society, 128–129
fads influence on, 29
first steps toward changed system, 62–64
government-run districts, 66–67
impacts of, 129
information technology revolution, 92
innovation, 27–29
institutional landscape of, 142
interagency and cross-sector collaboration, 132–134
interest groups, 93
leadership need, 149
learning as emergent phenomenon, 155
new infrastructure and institutions, 63
opening up to providers, 188
policies to fit local conditions, 14–15
politics, 93
positive approach to improvement, 25
readjusting existing roles, 63
reform impulse, 127–128
research, 27–29
resistance to change, 127
responsibility for, 143–144
segmentation, 117
silver bullet culture, 3
sound education as legally enforceable right, 147
subsystems of schooling enterprise, 49

technology benefits, 74
unions, 91
educational improvement research, 44–45
educational outcomes, 14–16
educational systems
comparative research on performance, 64
failure to sustain or scale up efforts, 124
high alignment at all levels, 26
integrated, 195
integrative vision, 200
stakeholders, 124
education funds, 69–70
education policy, 141
education providers, proliferation of, 92
education systems
broad network of partners, 122–123
choice and competition, 67
defined by sameness, 97
differentiating among students, 122–123
failing to professionalize, 185
healthy child development, 122
healthy platform for, 122–123
higher overall performance, 14
inability to realize goals, 181–184
instead of school system, 122–123
more equitable outcomes, 14
Progressive Era, 66, 181
responding to individual needs of students, 123
Education Unbound: The Promise and Practice of Greenfield Schooling (Hess), 3
educators, 116–117
slow to tap new pools of talent, 98
talented people as, 17–18

Elmore, Richard, 2, 6, 157, 184, 197, 198
employee learning and development, 165
employment, connecting secondary education to, 23–24
empowering students, 199
encyclopedias, 158–159
Engelbart, Douglas, 45–46, 51
environment, nurturing positive youth development, 131
equity, 170
  implications for, 61–62
  mixed model, 86–88
  out-of-school conditions, 195
  social advantage, 87–88
  technology advancement boosting, 88
  unbundling, 107–109
Europe
  apprenticeship systems, 23
  equipping young people with skills and credentials, 33
  mechanisms to discuss educational issues, 25–26
  social partnerships, 32
evidence, growing focus on, 143
excellence in professional and civic lives, 30
existing systems inability to realize goals, 181–184
exit governance, 204–205
expanding
  choice, 70–75
  school systems, 195–197
Expeditionary Learning, 191
Experience and Education (Dewey), 199
experienced teachers developing new knowledge, 61
experimenting society, 128–129

expert evaluation of services, 111
explanatory power, 42
external motivation, 199

Facilities Master Plan, 133
families
  academic performance, 195
  redirecting dollars spent on child, 116
  school choice, 79
federal standards-based reform, 3
federal states, 15
50 CAN, 188
Finland, 21–23
  developing education policy, 26
  diagnosing learning difficulties, 24
  early intervention and support, 21–22
  improvement in educational outcomes, 15–16
  joint components of preparation, 56
  periodic revision of curriculum, 19
  programs that prepare teachers, 17
  single comprehensive education system, 21
  special education programs, 21
  special teacher, 21, 24
  teachers as researchers, 56
  teachers from top third of talent pool, 31, 40
  untracked curriculum through lower secondary schools, 24
  within-school and between-school performance, 22
Flessner, Ryan, 43
Florida Virtual School, 105–106
formal learning, 163
foundations, 58
fragmentation, 194
framework of rules, 89–90
freeing up districts, 75–77

free market economy, 66
frontline practitioners, 39–40
Full-Service Community Schools
    Demonstration Project (2007),
    124
funding
    changes to, 140–141
    mixed model, 69–70
    online coursework, 73
    sustaining regime, 140–144
    unbundling, 115–116
    weighted student, 115
Futures of School Reform working
    group, 2–3
    ideas shared by, 4–7

Gamoran, Adam, 120
Gardner, Howard, 206
GE, 162
    advocating for improved education,
        174
general education, 159
Germany and career-oriented path-
    ways, 23
Getting Smart: How Digital Learning
    Is Changing the World (Vander
    Ark), 105
Girl Scouts badges, 152, 166–167
Glazer, Joshua, 42
goals for schools, 205–207
Goldstein, Michael, 2
Google, 197
Goren, Paul, 2
governance
    all-purpose, 114
    changes to, 140–141
    coordination and leadership, 141
    court-driven reform of, 147
    devolving essential decisions to
        schools, 89
    district-run schools, 89

exit, 204–205
    framework of rules, 89–90
    loyalty to, 204–205
    mixed model, 89–90
    redesigning, 115
    sustaining regime to, 140–144
    traditional approach, 89
    unbundling, 114–115
    voice in, 204–205
government
    declining trust in, 144, 186
    diminished expectations, 144
    disadvantaged children funds, 90
    online learning, 74–75
    power to induce state change, 148
    resolution to lack of trust in, 145
government-run economy, 66
governors, 148–149
grassroots efforts in twenty-first-
    century education system,
    147–148
Green Dot, 188
greenfield for social learning, 59–61
Gunn, Greg, 2, 183
Gutenberg, Johannes, 159

Harlem Children's Zone, 133, 210
Harvard Graduate School of
    Education, 2, 32, 168
Head Start, 196
health care quality improvement,
    44–45
Henderson, Kaya, 2
Henig, Jeffrey, 2, 144, 184, 195
Hess, Frederick, 2, 3, 161, 183,
    193–194
Hewlett Foundation, 209
Hiebert, James, 50
higher standards for students, 201
high expectations for students,
    20–22

high performing countries
  key topics in subjects and grade
    level, 18
  national curriculum, 18–19
high performing systems
  basing work on knowledge rather
    than ideology, 28
  career opportunities for teachers, 18
  early intervention and support for
    struggling schools, 24–25
  pathway leading to university or to
    career, 23–24
  prevention and early intervention,
    24–25
high-poverty students
  assumptions in education based on
    test scores, 132
  dropout rates, 132
  low college acceptance, 132
  replacing existing system for, 189
  success of schools for, 190
high-quality schools and disadvantaged students, 87–88
high school dropouts, 1–2
high-stakes accountability, 179
High Tech High, 55
High Tech High Graduate School of
  Education, 188
Hill, Paul, 2, 188, 189, 193
hiring teachers, 97–98
Hirschman, Albert, 204
home schooling
  community, 80
  growth of, 189
  students, 198–199
Horn, Michael, 104, 128, 157, 162
Hull House, 196
human being as interested learner, 198
human capital, 55–57
hybrid schools, 81, 84, 191–192
  varying in emphasis, 81–82

hybrid teaching, 102–103

IBM, 162
IHI. See Institute for Healthcare
  Improvement (IHI)
Illich, Ivan, 198
improvement, localized learning for,
  43
improvement science, 44
individual accountability, 6
ineffective teachers, 95
inequalities, 194
  failed public sector efforts to
    address, 144–145
informal learning, 162–163, 165
information
  changing definition of learning, 155
  filtering, 154
  growth outside of school, 155, 197
  increasing accessible, 153
  learning imputing meaning to, 153,
    155–156
  process of becoming knowledge,
    153
  schools, 152–156
Information Age and data, 152
information systems, multi-agency,
  134–135
information technology revolution,
  72, 92
innovations
  careers, 33
  careful assessment of impact, 29
  constraints limiting, 162
  crafting promising, 42
  education, 27–29
  effectiveness, 42
  essential to improvement, 29
  grounded in current knowledge, 29
  for innovation's sake, 203
  intentional and informed, 128

innovations (*continued*)
for its own sake, 127–129
mixed model, 86–88
reasonable theory of action, 29
scaling, 29, 42
stage-wide linear inquiry processes, 42
technical education, 33
United States, 27–29
input regulation, 109, 110
inquiry, common protocols for, 50–51
Institute for Healthcare Improvement (IHI), 45, 59
integrative institutions, 63
Institute of Education Sciences studies, 95–97
institutional inertia, 138
institutional silos, 142
institutions
controlling access to information, 153–154
learning as core part of mission, 168
instructional core, 6
integrated educational system, 195
integrative institutions, 63
Intel, 47
interagency collaboration, 132–134
interest groups influencing legislatures, 113–114
international academic achievement
building trust and commitment, 25–26
common elements, 16–26
connecting secondary education to economy and employment, 23–24
developing leaders, 19–20
engaging partners toward further improvement, 25–26
helping schools facing demographics challenges, 24–25

high expectations for students, 20–22
minimizing disparities in outcomes, 24–25
requiring and helping schools and educators improve, 18–19
talented people as educators, 17–18
what they do not do, 16
international examples of policy community, 186
International Standards Organization standards for certifying non-formal learning, 167
international studies for drawing more talented students into teaching, 186
intersections, 201–203
interventions, 42
intrinsic motivation, 199
isomorphism, 180

Japan
continuous learning and development of teachers, 18
examining teaching for improvement, 61
model of lesson study, 40
national participation in lesson study, 56
sharing teacher best practices, 19
teachers from top third of talent pool, 31
J.D. Power and Associates, 111
Jobs, Steve
death of, 156
impact on education, 157–158
John D. and Catherine T. MacArthur Foundation, 166
Johnson, Curtis, 104, 128, 157, 162
Johnston, Michael, 2

John W. Gardner Center for Youth and Their Communities, 135
Jupp, Brad, 2
Juran, Joseph, 44

K12, 73
Kaiser Family Foundation, 168
Kasarda, John, 101
K-12 education, unbundling, 99–101
Kellogg foundation, 124
Kentucky P-20 Data Collaborative, 133
Kerr, Steve, 174
King, John, 2
KIPP. See Knowledge Is Power Program (KIPP)
Klehr, Mary, 43
knowledge
    action research, 41–44
    authoritative, 154–155
    developing stock of, 55–56
    empowering people as creators, 197
    experienced teachers and, 56
    explosion of, 202
    generating for knowledge profession, 41–54
    how it is produced or used, 5–6
    information plus meaning, 153
    infrastructure creation, 186
    more about practice, 203
    more people's access to, 197
    networked improvement communities (NICs), 44–51, 55–56
    official, 154
    process of information becoming, 153
    schools, 152–156
    shift in authority, 158
    translational research, 41–44

knowledge base
    connected to practice, 40
    disciplined inquiry aimed at improving practice, 41–42
Knowledge Is Power Program (KIPP), 188, 190
knowledge mobilization, 28
knowledge profession
    building pipeline for, 55–57
    generating knowledge for, 41–54
    supporting growth of, 57–59
    system to support, 55–61
    training new teachers, 55–57
Korea
    connections between research centers, 28
    improvement in educational outcomes, 14–16
    policy-making apparatus in ministries of education, 28
    teacher education programs, 17
    teachers from top third of college, 40

lack of attention to common concerns, 194
leaders, attention to developing, 19–20
leadership and education, 149
leading PISA countries, 64
learners
    human being as interested, 198
    shift in role of, 159
learning
    adoption theory, 156
    changing, 174
    collaborate and work with others, 169
    collective enterprise, 175
    compliance to task-based shift, 173–174

learning (*continued*)
  conflict between old definition and
    new, 156
  customized experiences, 192
  design elements, 167
  displacing schooling, 168
  evolving into decentralized formal
    system, 172
  formal, 163
  future of, 163
  implications for, 61–62
  imputing meaning to information,
    155–156
  increasing exponentially, 158
  individual choices benefit society,
    171
  inequality of access, 172
  informal, 163, 165
  information becoming knowledge
    process, 153
  lifelong, 167–168
  lifewide, 167–168
  mastery, 166–167, 169
  migration of, 171
  military, 165
  networks of learners, 164–167
  on-the-job training, 165–166
  open-ended, 127–129
  outside of schools, 163, 172
  proficiency, 169
  redefining, 155
  remediation, 165
  responsibility of learner, 170
  schools, 152–156
  self-directed, 165
  self-organizing systems, 155
  skillful, 156
  socializing, 169
  social networks and, 154
  sorting students differently, 170
  spatial constraints, 154
    special characteristics and skills, 153
    structured, 165–166
    technology and, 157, 172
    transformation of, 171–176
    uncoupled from school, 156
    Web-based, 199
Learning Community project, 152,
    164
learning orientation shifting from
    compliance orientation, 173
legislatures and interest groups influ-
    encing, 113–114
letting teachers teach, 125–126
Levin, Ben, 2, 120, 193
Levitt, Theodore, 162, 172
Levy, Frank, 161
Liberating Learning: Technology,
    Politics, and the Future of
    American Education (Chubb
    and Moe), 105
lifelong learning, 166–168
lifewide learning, 167–168
  safe places, 170
Linux, 49–50
Loeb, Susanna, 2
low college acceptance, 132
low-income students
  college completion, 120
  consistent and significant gap,
    119–120
  importance of great teachers, 29
low performing schools, 87
  high performing systems, 24–25
loyalty to governance, 204–205
Lynch, Doug, 184, 198

Malone, Helen Janc, 184, 195
Mann, Horace, 97, 204
March, James, 29
market-based quality control, 109–
    110

markets, 194
American economy making use of,
65–66
Massachusetts as leading students
achievement state, 120
Mass Math and Science Initiative, 191
mastery, 166–167, 169
Match, 55
media and lifewide learning, 168
medical field specialization, 102
Meeks, Olivia, 183, 193
meritocratic selection, 186
meta-analysis, 51
methods, nonlinear, 43
Mexico, school systems embracing different kind of learning,
164–167
migration of learning, 171
military learning, 165
minority children and importance of
great teachers, 29
MIT, 197
Mitra, Sugata, 155, 169
mixed model, 67
accountability, 75–76
building blocks, 68–78
charter schools, 70–72
classrooms, 79–82
collective bargaining, 77–78,
85
equity, 86–88
expanding choice, 70–75
freeing up districts, 75–77
funding, 69–70
governance, 89–90
government and markets benefits,
93
innovation, 86–88
online learning, 72–75
opposition to, 68
performance, 86–88

politics of moving toward center,
90–93
problems and disappointments,
88
process of change, growth and
development, 79
public policy, 78
role of frameworks, 90
rules and dynamics, 88
schools, 79–82
teachers, 82–86
vested interests and, 91
what it would look like, 78–90
modern learning and improvement
organizations, 35
Moe, Terry, 2, 105, 188, 189, 193
money follows the child, 74
money to pay for coordination work,
60
Moore, Gordon, 47
Moore's Law, 47–48
motivation, 170, 199
multi-agency information systems,
134–135
multidimensional knowledge, 38–39
multiple providers, aggregating data
from, 112–113
Murnane, Richard, 161

NAEP. See National Assessment of
Educational Progress (NAEP)
National Academies reports, 28
National Assessment of Educational
Progress (NAEP), 2, 119
National Board for Professional
Teaching Standards (NBPTS),
30, 31, 209
National Center on Education and the
Economy, 63
National Commission on Teaching
and America's Future, 29

National Council for Accreditation of Teacher Education (NCATE) guidelines, 55
National Governors Association, 31, 209
National Park Service, 168
national policies and resources minimizing disparities in outcomes, 24–25
A Nation at Risk, 1, 178
A Nation Prepared report, 29
Naturalis Historia, 158
NBPTS. See National Board for Professional Teaching Standards (NBPTS)
NCATE guidelines. See National Council for Accreditation of Teacher Education (NCATE) guidelines
NCLB. See No Child Left Behind Act (NCLB (2001))
Netherlands and career-oriented pathways, 23
networked improvement communities (NICs), 44–51
    action research, 46
    bypassing schools, 162
    Carnegie Foundation for the Advancement of Teaching, 51–53
    commonly understood problem space, 48–50
    common protocols for inquiry, 50–51
    common targets, 47–48
    cross-organizational coordination, 45–46
    dropout problem, 49
    estimating initial targets, 48
    incremental and organic growth, 64

individual and collective routines, 54
    infrastructure, 57–58
    insight and innovations from practitioners, 46
    on-the-ground work improvement, 45
    operation of, 47–51
    practice of, 51–53
    professionalizing teaching, 53–54
    shared language, 48–50
    social science theories, 46
    strong professional control, 59
    successful organizations with characteristics of, 47–51
    translational research, 46
    trying different approaches, 59
    variation across context, 61
    working framework of practice improvement, 53
networks of learners, 164–167
New Hampshire Department of Education, 112
New Orleans, 67
The New Teacher Project, 188
new teachers and training, 55–57
new technology, 62
New Visions for Education, 57
New Visions for Public Schools, 191
New York City Department of Education, 112–113
NIC-generated knowledge, 55–56
NICs. See networked improvement communities (NICs)
No Child Left Behind Act (NCLB (2001)), 3, 127
    falling short of goal of proficiency, 145
    moving people to collective action, 47–48
    passage of, 130

public consequences for failing, 179
statutory right for meaningful education, 147
translational research, 42
no excuses charter schools, 190
around-the-clock commitment from teachers, 195–196
non-low-income students, 120
nonprofits, 58
nonreligious private schools, 71

Obama, Barack, 32, 208
Obama administration new investments in community colleges, 33
Occupational Safety and Health Administration, 173
OECD. See Organisation for Economic Co-operation and Development (OECD)
official knowledge, 154
one-size-fits-all model, 107–108
one-time short-run theory of change, 142
online learning, 73–74
American education, 92
disadvantaged kids, 88
efficiency, 84
new government policy framework for, 75
offering new options, 81
political objections to, 91
online teachers and hybrid schools, 84
Ontario, Canada, 24–26
improvement connected with research strategy, 28
primary reading instruction, 19
progress on interim indicators, 146
on-the-job training, 165–166

open-ended learning in place of innovation for its own sake, 127–129
Organisation for Economic Co-operation and Development (OECD), 40
report by, 20
organizations
learning as core part of mission, 168
reinventions, 162
outcomes, growing focus on, 143
outdated model of teaching, 96–97
out-of-school conditions and equality, 195
out-of-school needs, supporting, 202
outside social factors, 132
outside talent, 103–104

The Paideia Proposal (Adler), 175–176
parents and education, 117
Pathways to Prosperity: Meeting the Challenge of Preparing Young Americans for the 21st Century, 32
performance, 170
implications for, 61–62
mixed model, 86–88
teacher quality, 61–62
unbundling, 107–109
performance-based compensation, 108–109
performance pay, 179–180
Perkins Act (reauthorization (2006)), 23–24
Perry preschool, 196
Peurach, Donald, 42
Pew Forum on Education Reform, 2–3
philanthropic community schools, 124

PISA. See Program for International
  Student Assessment (PISA)
PISA leaders, 61
PISA leading nations, 210
Pliny the Elder, 158, 160
policies
  adapting to local conditions, 14–15
  effectiveness, 15
  greenfield for social learning, 59–61
  institutional silos or inducing
    cooperation, 142
  trade-offs and spillovers, 143–144
policing outcomes, 110
policy community, 186
policy learning, 128–129
policy makers
  external accountability systems, 37
  new pools of talent and, 98
political barriers, unbundling, 113–
  114
politicians building trust and public
  confidence, 63
politics
  bottom-up mobilization, 147–148
  changes to, 140–141
  education, 93
  of moving toward center, 90–93
  power and special interests, 91
  preserving existing system, 91,
    140–144, 199
  reform, 90–92
  of significant change, 208–210
population diversity, 15
portals
  controlling access to information,
    154–155
  increasingly restrictive, 154
  schools as, 152–156
portfolio districts, 64
post-secondary education, connecting
  secondary education to, 23–24

poverty
  addressing disadvantages, 119–149
  alleviating barriers to learning, 125
  concentrated, 182
  daily stressors, 125
  failed public sector efforts to
    address, 144–145
practice
  divorce of research from, 38
  questions for research grow directly
    out of, 61
practice-oriented continuous learning
  system, 131
Pressman, Jeffrey, 142
printing press, 162–163
private schools
  online learning, 73
  political objections to, 91
problem space, 48–50
process regulation, 109
professional development, 29–31
  practice and research, 56
professional development gurus,
  95–96
professionalizing strategy of reform,
  186
professional style of work organization, 39–40
professions, developing expertise, 37
proficiency, 169
Program for International Student
  Assessment (PISA), 2, 40, 186
  comparing performance of schools
    and students, 14
  findings (2009), 120
Progressive Era, 181
  coordinating services for children
    and youth in poverty, 123–
    124
  scientific management, 107
Promise Neighborhoods (2009), 124

public education
  defining features of, 101
  mixed model of, 67
  Progressive reformers, 66
public policy framework of rules, 78
Public/Private Ventures, 131
public schools, competition for, 71
purposes and schools, 205–207

quality
  continuous improvement, 44–45
  cost-effectiveness, 117
  new tools to gauge, 110–112
  student achievement, 117

race and gaps in student skills, 2, 5
RDDU sequences. See research, development, dissemination, and
  utilization (RDDU) sequences
Readiness Cabinet meetings, 136
reassembling school system, 192–194
Rebell, Michael, 147
recruitment, 29–31
reformers, 91
reformist ferment, 92
reforms
  American approach using
    unbundling, 193–194
  American strategies of, 186
  best practices approach, 3–4
  challenging assumptions, 5–6
  charter schools, 180
  differences between visions, 6
  diverse approaches, 128
  failures, 178–181, 182
  feeding through failed structure,
    185
  futures of, 4–7
  from outside in, 188–192
  performance pay, 179–180
  professionalizing strategy of, 186

standards-based, 3
standards movement, 178–179
through politics, 90–91
top-down, 36–37
traditional shortcomings, 161
twenty-first-century skills, 180–181
reform strategies
  limits of current, 177
  multiple, 1
  successful worldwide, 13–34
reigning fatalism, countering, 144–
    146
remediation, 165
replacing school systems, 188–192
research
  action, 41–44
  cherry-picking, 145
  countering source of underlying
    skepticism, 145
  criticalness of, 140
  divorce from practice, 38
  education, 27–29
  feedback and guidance to policy
    makers, 129
  organization to uncover promising
    ideas, 42
  question growing directly out of
    practice, 61
  translational, 41–44
  United States, 27–29
research, development, dissemination, and utilization (RDDU)
  sequences, 42
responsibility for education, 143–144
results changing significant part of
  structure, 200–201
Reville, Paul, 2, 6, 120, 136, 144,
    178, 184, 195
Rhee, Michelle, 5, 188
rigorous assessment, 128
roadmaps, 48–50

Rocketship Education, 106
Rocketship schools, 82
    teachers, 84
Rose, Joel, 173
Rotberg, Iris, 120
Rotherham, Andrew, 2
Rothstein, Richard, 121
rural schools, 30

safe place for children, 169–170
San Francisco Unified School District,
    136
Say Yes Foundation, 137
Say Yes to Education Syracuse, 136–
    138
scaling, 193
Scandinavian students in common,
    untracked curriculum, 24
Schliecher, Andreas, 40
school building, emphasis on, 98
school choice, 65, 194, 204–205
    autonomy, 77
    expansion of, 92
    families, 79
    New Orleans, 67
    unions inability to block, 92
school-community partnership model,
    126–127
school districts. See districts
schooling
    differences from schools, 100–101
    one-size-fits-all model, 107
    parents fundamentally conservative
        in notions of, 199
    process that students experience,
        101
    required to fit into time-bound
        blocks of instruction, 104
    technology delivering, 105–106
    as unifying American institution,
        204

School of One, 102–103, 105–106,
    173
schools
    academic achievement, 79–80
    access to learning, 199
    accountability, 16, 75–76
    apportioning instructional or
        administrative roles, 102–103
    asking too much from, 195
    autonomy, 89–90
    best practice reform, 3–4
    bureaucracy, 205
    bureaucratic Industrial Age
        structures, 35
    choice and competition, 16, 86, 111
    collective bargaining, 77–78, 85
    combining strategies, 210
    common approaches development,
        18–19
    common core standards, 206
    common culture, 194
    common movement, 97
    comparing performance, 14
    conservative in nature, 161
    consistency, 186
    cost efficiencies, 116
    credentialing, 169
    cultures of inquiry within, 40
    custodial function of, 169
    demographics challenges, 24–25
    developing curricula, 205
    developing leaders, 19–20
    differences from schooling, 100–
        101
    diverse student populations, 22
    doing what they are supposed to
        do, 143
    economically disadvantaged
        students, 121, 123
    effective organizational
        arrangements, 86

empowering students, 199
expectations of, 181
as extension of home, 208
faculty, 98
fading in importance, 6
failings of, 2, 5
felt needs, 43
formal learning inside, 163
frozen in time, 197
as general contractor, 192
geographically bounded, 74
getting more out of, 193
goals, 205–207
governance, 90, 114–115
governmental rules, 86–87
harnessing outside talents, 103
hierarchical and bureaucratic, 36
high performing and innovative, 87
high-poverty students, 190
hiring teachers, 97–98
hybrid, 81, 191–192
impervious to change, 160–161
improvement, 18–19
inequalities in society and, 22
informal learning outside, 163
information, 87, 152–156
innovation, 28–29
isolated from world, 184
knowledge, 152–156
learning, 152–156, 158
learning and improvement
    organizations, 35
learning equivalent of buggy whip,
    172
less traditional approach, 80
little real change or reform, 178–
    181
loosely coupled systems, 36
low performing, 87
major pillars of current system, 5
mastery, 166–167

mixed model, 79–82
multiple reform strategies, 1
new architecture or framework, 193
no longer ties to, 98–99
one-size-fits-all model, 107–108
operational decisions, 90
other services provided by, 168–171
outside forces and, 121, 199
payoffs, 143
perpetuating inequities, 170
philanthropy toward, 174
places where schooling takes place,
    101
as portals, 152–156
preparing students for college-level
    work, 182
public institutions, 209
purposes, 205–207
reform futures, 4–7
safe place for children, 169–170
shifting from compliance to task-
    based learning, 173–174
as single portal, 174–175
social problems, 126
sorting students, 181
student preparation, 206
substituting technology for labor,
    72
successful, 206
systematic improvement in, 33
top-down control, 182
transforming into full-service
    schools, 133
turning information into
    knowledge, 154
unbundling, 104–106
values, 205–207
voucher, 71–72
workplace relationship, 31–33
schools-only approach, limitations of,
    143

school systems
  changing structure, 200–201
  complementarities, 201–203
  cycling priorities, 183
  dissolving, 197–200
  distrust of, 186
  education system instead of, 122–
    123
  embracing different kind of
    learning, 164–167
  expanding, 195–197
  flexibility, 192
  future of, 184–200
  hierarchical form and social control
    orientation of, 38
  inability to adapt, 182
  inability to make changes, 198
  intersections, 201–203
  learning equivalent of buggy whip,
    172
  reassembling, 192–194
  reinventing themselves, 173
  replacing, 188–192
  reversing the tide, 196
  seeking new efficiencies, 116
  standardization, 183
  taken-for-granted tenet, 200
  tensions, 201–203
  transforming, 185
  twenty-first-century skills, 180–181
  unbundling, 192
  whether we already know what to
    do, 202
Schumpeter, Joseph, 127
Schwartz, Robert, 3, 6, 32, 120, 178
scientific evaluations, 111
Sears, Roebuck and Co. catalog, 114
secondary education, connecting to
    economy and employment,
    23–24
self-organizing systems, 155

semiconductor industry, 47–49
Service Integration Targets of
    Opportunity (1975), 124
service providers accountability, 134
services, expert evaluation of, 111
Sesame Street, 168
Shanker, Albert, 30
shared accountability, 134–138
shared language, 48–50
Shewhart, Walter, 44
Shulman, Lee, 38
silver bullet culture, 3
silver-bullet solutions, 145
Singapore, 28
  career opportunities for teachers, 18
  educational outcomes improvement,
    14–16
  school leaders identification and
    development, 20
  teacher education programs, 17
  teachers from top third of talent
    pool, 31, 40
skillful learning, 156
Smith, Frank, 112
Smith, Mike, 2
social advantage, 87–88
socializing, 169
social learning, 59–61
social network authority of knowledge,
    160
social partnerships, 32
social services and supports integra-
    tion, 136
social welfare institutions, 198
socioeconomic status and educational
    achievement, 119
special education system, 24
specialization, 102–103, 194
Spillane, James, 2
Spinning Wheels (Hess), 183
standardization, 36

standardized tests, 129
standards
  versus accountability, 129
  wring more out of existing system, 179
standards and accountability movement, 145
standards-based reform, 3, 145
  disappointing data, 146
standards movement, 6, 178–179
state laws and regulations, 73
states
  accountability systems, 116, 127
  adopting practices from reform community, 191
  barriers to trade, 74
  collective bargaining, 77
  education across borders, 74–75
  education regulations, 74
  escaping from institutional pasts, 67
  facilitating and supporting better work in schools, 63
  framework of rules, 89–90
  funds to save districts, 76–77
  growth of knowledge profession, 57–59
  infrastructure, 58
  infrastructure to support learning, 165
  redistribution and, 148
  responsibility for education, 148
step-and-lane pay scale, 108
stereotypes and American education reform, 65
Stewart, Thomas, 111
Stewart, Vivien, 20
strong education systems, 18
structural unbundling, 100
structured learning, 165–166
students
  achieving at high levels, 146
  additional support for, 21
  available knowledge and, 6
  behavior problems, 108
  comparing performance, 14
  core knowledge, 205
  educational performance, 120
  education funds, 69–70
  empowering, 199
  higher levels of success, 189
  higher standards for, 201
  high expectations for, 20–22
  home-schooled, 198–199
  intellectual challenge for, 201
  knowledge-based economy demands, 63–64
  learning difficulties, 108
  mastery demonstrations, 151–152
  nontraditional services and, 112
  out-of-school support, 196
  preventing failure, 24
  socioeconomic factors, 120
  support before starting school, 196
  supports necessary to help succeed, 170
  worldwide ranking, 2
successful schools, 206
successful systems, 24–25
summer learning loss, 131, 195
Superfine, Benjamin, 147
support services as unnecessary add-ons, 132
Switzerland
  career-oriented pathways, 23
  youth unemployment rates, 32
systems
  additional supports for students, 21
  supporting knowledge profession, 55–61

talented people as educators, 17–18
Teacher Performance Assessment, 31

teacher-quality debate, 95–96
  roots of quality shortage, 96–99
teachers
  administrative certification, 20
  advocates, 95
  around-the-clock commitment,
    195–196
  assessments linked to curriculum,
    18–19
  bureaucratic hierarchy and, 37
  burnout, 191
  career opportunities for, 18
  choice and competition, 85
  collective bargaining, 77–78, 82–83
  common approaches based on
    research and evidence, 18–19
  consistency, 186
  continuous learning and
    development, 17–18
  credentialing and evaluation, 114
  customizing what student learns,
    103
  defensive individualism norm, 39
  developing expertise, 19, 37,
    182–183
  developing leaders, 19–20
  differences from teaching, 100–101
  differentiated roles, 5
  diverse students, 98
  eliminating shortages, 31
  empowered by more capital, 85
  evaluation systems, 16
  fewer per student, 85
  finding appropriate services or
    helping students outside of
    school, 127
  functioning more like team, 83
  higher pay, 86
  hiring, 97–98
  identifying students in need of
    support, 126
  improvement of, 18–19
  ineffective, 95
  inherited notion of what they do,
    98
  inspiring students, 54
  interventions, 126
  as key school-service link, 125–127
  knowledge-based economy
    demands, 63–64
  letting them teach, 125–126
  mixed model, 82–86
  multidimensional knowledge,
    38–39
  overhauling schedules and student
    assignment, 108
  performance, 83
  performance-based compensation,
    108–109, 179–180
  professional development, 29–31
  professional expertise, 186, 202
  professional power, 186
  programs preparing, 17–18
  quality and performance, 61
  recruitment, 29–31
  remedies for, 96
  as researchers, 56
  rethinking job description, 101–107
  Rocketship schools, 84
  specialization, 192, 203
  standardized curriculum, 82
  tailoring instruction to different
    needs and interests, 107
  technology and, 84–85
  tiers of, 192
  top-down mandates resistance, 38
  traditional schools, 83
  training, 16
  useful input to schools, 85
  virtual schools, 83–84
teacher time, 60
Teacher U, 55, 188

Teach for America (TFA), 30, 31, 188, 209

teaching

assessments to measure standards, 30

attracting talented students into, 186

college graduates interest in, 103

Common School legacy, 97–99

complex, stimulating, and fulfilling, 203

differences from teachers, 100–101

difficulty of, 183

dispersion of, 92

diversification, 84–85

felt problems of practice, 44

field-based training, 186

geared to median students, 107

growth and professional development opportunities, 186

human capital, 55–57

hybrid, 102–103

lengthening time to tenure, 186

more variegated profession, 83

narrowing scope, 202

networked improvement communities (NICs), 53–54

organized around public theory, 53

outdated model of, 96–97

outside talent, 103–104

policy, 29–31

problems confronted by, 43–44

Progressive Era, 36

relationships with students, 54

reshaping professional identities, 54

rethinking parameters of, 98

rethinking talent pipeline, 56–57

rigorous professional practice, 44

rigorous standards for accomplished, 30

specialization, 102–103

teams, 102–103

traditional model, 38

unbundling, 96–107

what it means to, 203

team teaching, 102–103

technical education innovations, 33

technology

adoption theory, 156

advances boosting equity, 88

authority of knowledge shift, 158

benefits for education, 74

customizing education, 81

delivering schooling with, 105–106

disruptive force in education, 157

driving force of innovation, 73

from encyclopedia to Wikipedia, 158–160

facilitating unbundling and customization, 105

future of American education, 72

greater reliance on, 80

impact on learning, 157

means, not an end, 157

new paths to instructional delivery, 106

promise of new, 156–157

regulatory challenge, 74

substitution for labor, 92

supplemental providers and, 105

tasks where teachers can add limited value, 106

teachers and, 84–85

Teles, Steven, 188–192

tensions, 201–203

TFA. See Teach for America (TFA)

Thomas Edison State University, 167

TIMSS. See Trends in International Mathematics and Science Study (TIMSS)

Toll, Dacia, 2

top-down accountability, 76
top-down reforms, 36–37
top-down scenario, 148–149
top PISA nations, 57
Torvalds, Linus, 50
traditional reform, shortcomings of, 161
traditional schools
 in choice sector, 83
 geographically bounded, 74
 labor intensive, 80
 preference for, 80
 teachers, 83
training, on-the-job, 165–166
transformation of learning, 171–176
transforming school systems, 185
translational research, 41–44
 networked improvement
  communities (NICs), 46
Trends in International Mathematics
 and Science Study (TIMSS), 14
TripAdvisor, 112
Tucker, Marc, 40
Tutor.com and outside talent, 104
twenty-first-century education system
 achieving, 146–149
 benchmark indicators, 139
 bottom line and return on
  investment, 143
 bottom-up political mobilization,
  147–148
 combining reform with careful
  monitoring of near-term
  progress, 139
 comprehensive approach, 144
 constructing challenges, 138–146
 countering reigning fatalism,
  144–146
 court-focused approach to, 146–147
 critical spillovers, 143
 cultural norms, 138

differentiation, 138–139
grassroots efforts, 147–148
implementation and scaling, 138
indicators and benchmarks criteria,
 139
information technology and
 education-governance
 institutions, 143
interim benchmark indicators,
 146
measuring success, 139
metrics, 140
outcomes and evidence focus, 143
overcoming institutional inertia,
 138
research critical, 140
robust education system, 140
social interventions and outcomes,
 139
sustaining political and governance
 regime, 140–144
top-down scenario, 148–149
twenty-first-century skills, 180–181
Tyack, David, 161, 181

Ultranet, 164–165
unbundling
 accountability, 109–113
 American approach to school
  reform, 193–194
 assessments, 109–113
 choice, 194
 classrooms, 104–106
 content, 100
 controversial policies, 114
 difference between school and
  schooling, teachers and
  teaching, 100–101
 equity, 107–109
 funding, 115–116
 governance, 114–115

individual pacing and student
  preferences, 108
markets, 194
meeting kids where they are,
  107–108
new architecture or framework, 193
outside talent, 103–104
performance, 107–109
political barriers, 113–114
in practice, 101–113
reassembling parts of system, 200
reimagining how we organize work,
  193
schools, 104–106
school systems, 192
specialization, 194
structural, 100
subset of teachers, 203
teaching, 96–101, 101–107
weighted student funding, 115
unions, 91–92
responsibility for learning outcomes,
  62
unitary systems, 15
United States
academic achievement
  improvements, 13
assessments linked to curriculum,
  18–19
economy making use of markets,
  65–66
education variable by state and
  locality, 27
exporter of ideas and policies
  around the world, 15
feasible first steps for, 26–33
fractured educational systems, 26
high expectations for students, 21
inequality, 22–23
innovation, 27–29, 28–29
knowledge mobilization, 28

large gaps in performance, 5
learning from PISA models, 64
minimally training new teachers, 57
new approaches to improving
  education, 27
pluralism, 206–207
professional expertise skepticism,
  186
raising teaching status, 30
relationship between schools and
  workplace, 31–33
research, 27–29
socioeconomic status and academic
  achievement, 22, 120
student worldwide ranking, 2
teacher recruitment and
  development, 29–31
teachers and administrative
  certification, 20
upgrading teaching profession, 31
vocational education, 23–24
youth unemployment rates, 32
university-based teacher education
  programs, 57
urban schools, 30
U.S. Department of Education, 31, 64
U.S. Securities and Exchange
  Commission, 173
useful knowledge, 41

Vallas, Paul, 188
values and schools, 205–207
virtual charter schools, 81
virtual classrooms, 80–81
virtual schools, 81
homeschooling community, 80
teachers, 83–84
virtual classrooms, 80–81
vocational education in United States,
  23–24
voice in governance, 204–205

voucher schools, 71–72
  education funds, 69–70
  regulation, 72
  traditional organization, 80

Walton Foundation, 188
Web 2.0, 197
Web-based learning, 189, 199
weighted student funding, 115
Welch, Jack, 174
Wheeler, Lindsay, 196
why past is not prologue, 123–138
  agencies and organizations
    coordination, 132–134
  moving beyond bureaucratic silos,
    134–138
  open-ended learning in place of
    innovation for its own sake,
    127–129
  teachers as key school-service link,
    125–127

what has gone wrong in past,
    124
what works in accountability era,
    129–132
Wikipedia, 159–160, 197
Wildavsky, Aaron, 142
Wireless Generation, 2, 106
wisdom of practice, 38
Wolf, Patrick, 111
Woodrow Wilson National Fellowship
    Foundation, 103
workplace relationship with schools,
    31–33
World Book Encyclopedia, 158
writing interventions, 42

Youth Data Archive (YDA), 135–136,
    148
youth unemployment rates, 32

Zeichner, Kenneth, 43